THREE COMEDIES

THE BIRDS

THE CLOUDS

THE WASPS

Three Comedies by Aristophanes

The Birds

The Clouds

Translated by William Arrowsmith

The Wasps

Translated by Douglass Parker

Ann Arbor Paperbacks

The University of Michigan Press

First edition as an Ann Arbor Paperback 1969

ISBN 0-472-06153-4

Published in the United States of America by
The University of Michigan Press
Manufactured in the United States of America

1990 16

The Birds

Translated by William Arrowsmith

with sketches by Stuart Ross

CONTENTS

FOR JEAN

Introduction

The Play and Its Interpretation

Nobody denies that *The Birds* is a masterpiece, one of the greatest comedies ever written and probably Aristophanes' finest. Splendidly lyrical, shot through with gentle Utopian satire and touched by the sadness of the human condition, its ironic gaiety and power of invention never flag; in no other play is Aristophanes' comic vision so comprehensively or lovingly at odds with his world.

But if the play is by common consent a great one, there is little agreement about what it means. Thus it has, with great ingenuity and small cogency, been interpreted as a vast, detailed comic allegory of the Sicilian expedition: Pisthetairos stands for Alkibiades; Hoopoe is the general Lamachos; the Birds are Athenians, the gods Spartans, and so on. Alternatively, the play has been viewed as Aristophanes' passionate appeal for the reform and renewal of Athenian public life under the leadership of the noble Pisthetairos, a true Aristophanic champion cut from the same cloth as Dikaiopolis in *The Acharnians*. Again, probably in revenge for so much unlikely ingenuity, it has been claimed that *The Birds* is best understood as a fantastic escapist extravaganza created as a revealing antidote to the prevalent folly of Athenian political life. And, with the exception of the word "escapist," this last view seems to me essentially correct. But whatever else *The Birds* may be, it is not escapist.

Any translation worth the name necessarily involves an interpretation, and it is my hope that my version will make my interpretation clear and convincing. But because in some respects my view of the play is unorthodox and this is crucial to the interpretation, I offer the following points for the reader's consideration.

1) *The life of the Birds.* Like many Aristophanic comedies, *The Birds* takes its title from its chorus; but unlike, say, *Wasps*, which is

based upon a simple simile (jurors are waspish: they buzz, swarm, sting, etc.) *Birds* and *Clouds* are titles around which cluster a great many traditional associations, idioms, and ideas. Thus in *Clouds* the chorus symbolizes the Murky Muse, that inflated, shining, insubstantial, and ephemeral power which inspires sophists, dithyrambic poets, prophets, and other pompous frauds. Similarly, in *Birds* there is the same natural clustering of association and standard idiom, and the associations are crucial to the play's understanding. On the most natural level, of course, the life of the Birds symbolizes precisely what one would expect: the simple, uncomplicated rustic life of peace. But behind this natural symbolism, deepening it and particularizing it, lies the chronic and pervasive escape-symbolism of late fifth-century Athens. In play after play of Euripides, for instance, chorus and characters alike, when confronted by the anguish of tragic existence, cry out their longing to escape, to be a bird, a fact of which Aristophanes makes extensive use, shaping his play around the symptomatic mortal infatuation with the birds. It is for this reason, this pervasive hunger for escape from intolerable existence which haunts tragedy and society alike, that Aristophanes makes his Birds address his audience with words of tragic pathos:

O suffering mankind,
lives of twilight,
race feeble and fleeting,
like the leaves scattered!
Pale generations,
creatures of clay,
the wingless, the fading!
Unhappy mortals,
shadows in time,
flickering dreams!
Hear us now,
the ever-living Birds,
the undying,
the ageless ones,
scholars of eternity.

And these lines in their turn look forward to the ironic apotheosis of the mortal Pisthetairos with which the play closes. Mankind's crazy comic dream is a wish-fulfillment darkened by death. But the dream survives.

My point is this: far from writing an escapist extravaganza, Aristophanes dramatizes the ironic fulfillment in divinity of the Athenian man who wants to escape. What begins as hunger for the simple life ends—such is the character of Athenians and true men—in world-conquest and the defeat of the gods; or it would end there, if only it could. This is the *hybris* of enterprise and daring, the trait from which no Athenian can ever escape. Aristophanes' irony is, I think, loving.

2) *The Theme.* It is commonly said that *The Birds* is unlike other Aristophanic comedies in having no pointed central theme or particular concern (e.g., peace in *Acharnians* and *Peace;* demagoguery in *Knights,* sophistry in *Clouds,* etc.), and at first blush this seems to be true. But unless I am badly mistaken, the central concern of the play is less noticeable only because it is more comprehensive, including in itself most of the targets of the earlier plays. That concern is *polupragmosunē,* a concept which Athenians used as a general description of their most salient national characteristics. At its broadest *polupragmosunē* is that quality of spectacular restless energy that made the Athenians both the glory and the bane of the Hellenic world. On the positive side, it connotes energy, enterprise, daring, ingenuity, originality, and curiosity; negatively it means restless instability, discontent with one's lot, persistent and pointless busyness, meddling interference, and mischievous love of novelty. The Athenian Empire itself is a visible creation of political *polupragmosunē,* and so too are the peculiar liabilities to which empire made the Athenians subject: the love of litigation, the susceptibility to informers and demagogues, the violent changes in national policy and, most stunning example of all, the Sicilian expedition. In political terms, *polupragmosunē* is the very spirit of Athenian imperialism, its remorseless need to expand, the *hybris* of power and energy in a spirited people; in moral terms, it is a divine discontent and an impatience with necessity, a disease whose symptoms are disorder, corruption, and the hunger for change.

Athens with its *polupragmosunē* is unbearable for Pisthetairos and Euelpides, and so, rational escapists both, they set out to find among the Birds precisely what they miss in Athens: the quiet, leisurely, simple, uncomplicated peace-loving life of the Birds, which is called *apragmosunē.* Confronted by the hostility of the Birds to man, Pisthetairos ingeniously conceives the idea of Cloudcuckooland. And from this point on, totally forgetting his quest for *apragmosunē,* he becomes the open and skillful exponent of *polupragmosunē:* persuasive, ingenious, cunning, meddlesome, and imperialistic. The characterization could hardly be more explicit or the change more deliberate, as the peace-loving escapist, with ruthless policy and doubtful arguments, pushes ahead with his scheme for the New Athens of the Birds. It is both comic and ironic, and Aristophanes' point is that no Athenian can escape his origins. His character is *polupragmosunē,* and character is destiny, as Herakleitos said. Put an Athenian among the Birds, and he will be an imperialist with wings and fight with gods.

3) *Pisthetairos.* It is sometimes said—quite wrongly, I believe—that Aristophanes' characters move on a single plane, without depth or complexity. If I am right, Pisthetairos' character, like Dikaiopolis' and Strepsiades', displays itself in action, not in professions; its basic simplicity, the thrust for power, is not something given but something defined in action. Like Dikaiopolis and Strepsiades, he *realizes* his name; but whereas Dikaiopolis' purpose is good and his methods roguish, Pisthetairos has no purpose but power and his methods are the appropriate ones. He compels assent and even admiration, as politicians do, by sheer persuasiveness and virtuosity and energy, but the energy is the dither of power for its own sake, without a rational goal in sight, restless and unappeasable: sheer *polupragmosunē.* He is Aristophanes' example of a politician without a policy, or nearly without one, unless we count to his credit his success in protecting Cloudcuckooland from ravenous interlopers, gods, and other pests.

4) *Cloudcuckooland.* Like Pisthetairos, Cloudcuckooland itself is treated ironically. On the one hand it is a pipedream Utopia from which a few of the nuisances and spongers that infest cities are driven out by an enraged Pisthetairos; on the other it is, especially in the methods of its founding, a visible parody of the Athenian Empire. Historical parallels and allusions here can be overdone, but I wonder what Athenian could have failed to notice the way in which, point for point, the policies and strategies of imperial Athens toward the member-states of her empire are adapted to Cloudcuckooland's campaign against the gods. Pisthetairos specifically proposes to exterminate the gods by "Melian starvation," and the general proposals of boycott vividly recall the Megarian Decree. Also pertinent, I think, is the close resemblance between Pisthetairos and the Birds and Athens and her subject-cities, once her allies: slowly the Birds, like the allies, yield to the initiative of the stronger, putting their strength at the service of another intellect, thereby losing their freedom. It is Aristophanes' point that the Birds, like the allies, are stupid; Athens and Pisthetairos clever and unscrupulous. And significantly, I think, the play closes with a light irony as Pisthetairos and the gods prepare to celebrate their truce with

a dinner of—poultry; jailbirds, true, but birds for all that. It is, for the Birds, an ominous sign of things to come. All their campaign against the gods has brought them is a new tyrant, no less voracious than the old and just as treacherous.

But if Cloudcuckooland serves to parody the growth of Athenian power and imperialistic politics, it also serves as a convenient and satisfying appeal for Athens to renew herself by ridding the city of the informers, sponges, charlatans, sophists, bureaucracy, and abuses that have made it almost unliveable. Irony here crosses with irony, as Pisthetairos, the champion of *polupragmosunē,* beats out the rival champions. So too, in *Knights,* the improbable cause of Demos' resurgence is none other than the tripe-peddling demagogue who has out-Kleoned Kleon.

5) *The Apotheosis.* In Aristophanes' eyes the logical terminus of Athenian restlessness and aggressiveness is that man should become god, wear wings and rule the world. The blasphemy is prevented only by the impossibility of its realization. But the ambition survives and luxuriates in man's discontent with his condition, his mortal *hybris.* For Aristophanes that discontent was tragic and meant man's loss of his only possible happiness: peace lost in war, traditional dignity swallowed up in the restless greed for wealth and power, honor lost in the inhumanity of imperialism and political tyranny. But he also knew that such discontent was born of life and aggressive hunger for larger life.

Date and Circumstances

The Birds was first performed at the Great Dionysia in late March, 414 B.C. and was awarded the Second Prize. The First Prize was taken by Ameipsias with his *Komastai* ("The Revellers") and the Third Prize by Phrynichos with his *Monotropos* ("The Hermit"). The year preceding the play's performance, during its composition, must have been a grim and bitter time in Athens, especially for an exponent of peace and rational politics like Aristophanes. In May, 415, just as the Athenian fleet was about to sail for Sicily on its disastrous expedition, the entire city was thrown into a superstitious panic by the mutilation of the pillars of Hermes, the work either of drunken carousers or of a political faction bent on discrediting Alkibiades, the commander of the Sicilian expedition. As a result, the whole expedition seemed to hang under a heavy cloud; accusations were being made on all sides, and the general atmosphere of the city was one of suspicion, horror, and frenetic political activity. Finally, after the fleet had sailed, evidence was found which seemed to incriminate Alkibiades and a state galley was sent out with orders to bring him back to Athens to stand trial. It is unlikely that Alkibiades' escape and defection to Sparta were known at Athens at the time the play was performed.

The Translation

This translation is meant to provide a faithful, but not a literal, version of *The Birds.* Literalness in any case is out of the question: a literal Aristophanes would be both unreadable and unplayable, and therefore unfaithful. But fidelity is clearly a matter of degree and relation: *how* faithful and faithful to *what?*

It was my purpose to create a lively, contemporary acting version of the play, a translation which might also, I hoped, be read for pleasure or study, and which would be as loyal to Greek and Greek experience as I could make it without involving myself in disloyalty to English. Only by so doing, I thought, could I remain faithful to two languages and two cultures at the same time. For the same reason I have deliberately avoided wholly modernizing or "adapting" the play. If the diction of this version is essentially contemporary American English, its experience, I believe, is basically Athenian. Some modernization, of course, was not only inevitable but also desirable. But generally I have preferred to suggest the similarities between Athens and America without asserting, or forcing, an identity. If the language does its work, the experience should translate itself with only a little occasional help from the translator. Or so I thought.

For fidelity's sake, this is also a poetic version. A prose Aristophanes is to my mind as much a monstrosity as a limerick in prose paraphrase. And for much the same reasons. If Aristophanes is visibly obscene, farcical, and colloquial, he is also lyrical, elegant, fantastic, and witty. And a translation which, by flattening incongruities and tensions, reduces one dimension necessarily reduces the other. Bowdlerize Aristophanes and you sublimate him into something less vital and whole;

prose him and you cripple his wit, dilute his obscenity and slapstick, and weaken his classical sense of the wholeness of human life.

Translating comedy is necessarily very different from translating tragedy; not only is it more demanding, but its principles, because they are constantly being improvised or modified, are harder to state. Insofar as I can describe them or deduce them from my own practice, my general principles are these:

1) *Meter.* Aristophanes' basic dialogue line is a loose, colloquial iambic hexameter (*senarii*), and my English equivalent is a loose five-stress line. It was my opinion that the flexibility required by the Greek could best be achieved by a meter capable of modulating, without jarring or unnaturalness, back to the norm of English dramatic verse, the blank. At its most humdrum such a line is indistinguishable from prose, but worked up, patterned with regular stresses, it can readily be traditionalized as tragic parody or cant or realized as speakable poetry in its own right. The longer anapestic and trochaic lines I have rendered by a six-beat movement (except in the first section of the *parabasis,* where I have adapted William Carlos Williams' triplet-line to my own purposes). Because the convention of *stichomythia* seemed deadening when brought over into English and served no useful dramatic purpose, I have everywhere taken the liberty of breaking it down.

2) *Obscenity.* I have refused on principle to bowdlerize. Equally, I have tried to avoid the quicksands of archness or cuteness on the one hand and sledgehammer shock-tactics on the other. Where Aristophanes is blunt, I have left him blunt, but generally I have tried to realize his rhetorical obscenities with the elegance and neatness that might make them truly obscene.

3) *Stage Directions.* The Greek plays have come down to us almost entirely without stage directions. To some small degree they are supplied by the ancient scholiasts, but because this is an acting version of the play and because comedy constantly suggests and requires stage action, I have freely supplied stage directions. Wherever possible, I have relied on indications in the text, but when a direction was clearly required and the text offered no help, I have used my imagination.

4) *Improvisation.* There are occasions (e.g., a pun, an obscure reference, or a tangle of politics, pun and idiom) when the Greek is simply untranslatable. On such occasions it has been my practice to improvise (see, for instance, the note on p. 112. *Her lover*), on the grounds that literal translation would have slowed or obscured the dramatic situation, and this is fatal to comedy. Normally I have indicated when I have improvised and why. But I should also confess that there are a few passages in which I have improvised on my own, without warrant. My only excuse is the self-indulgent one that I thought they might be justified as compensation for losses elsewhere.

5) *Tragic and Poetic Parody.* Aristophanes constantly parodies tragedy and poetry, and these parodies were meant to be recognized. Since modern audiences cannot be expected to recognize them—especially since most of the originals are no longer extant—the translator is required to do the impossible and create the illusion of parody. This means in effect that the parodies must be so grotesque as to be instantly recognizable as parody, and to this end I have deliberately heightened fustian, archaism, and bombast. Thus the Poet in this play speaks a parody of Pindar that is sheer doggerel and utterly un-Pindaric. I can only plead that my purpose was not to slander Pindar but to make the Poet an obvious hack.

6) *Dialects and Nonsense.* Aristophanic comedy abounds with dialects—Skythian policemen, Spartan heralds, sham Persians, Boiotians, Megarians, and the pure jabberwocky god of *The Birds,* Triballos. Because these dialects seemed to me both comic and conventional, I have everywhere rendered them by an apposite contemporary comic dialect: mint-julep Southern, broad Brooklynese, Katzenjammerkids German, etc. Nothing, in my opinion, is less comic or more tiresome than dialectal realism; for comedy, a recognizable *comic* convention is required, whatever the cost in anachronism. In the case of Triballos, who speaks pure nonsense, I have preferred to invent some genuine English nonsense rather than transliterate his Greekish gibberish. Herakles, it should be noted, does *not* in the original speak a dialect at all, but his hungry lowbrow character seemed to me to require conventional treatment, and I accordingly arranged it.

7) *Rhetorical Conventions and Jargon.* What is true of dialects is also true of professional rhetoric and jargon: if they are to be comic,

they have to be translated into an apposite convention of English rhetoric or jargon. Invariably, this means that their language must be heightened and made even more ponderous than it is in the Greek. The astronomer Meton, for instance, is used by Aristophanes to parody the jargon and abstruse pomposity of sophistic science. But because Greek scientific jargon was a relatively immature growth (at least when compared with the jargons of modern science), his words, literally translated, sound to modern ears merely somewhat silly. In the circumstances I deliberately heightened his language, adding technical terms and jargonizing it further, in the belief that only by so doing could I create the effect of gobbledegook that Meton's demonstration was intended to have for Athenian ears.

8) *Personal and Topical Allusions.* Aristophanes' frequent allusions to persons and events present the translator with a ticklish problem. Some of them are so obscure as to be meaningless to anybody but a prosopographer; others exist because they offer happy opportunities for puns or gibes at topical personalities; still others are crucial to the play's meaning. In general, it has been my practice to simplify, suppressing totally obscure allusions (see, for instance, the note on p. 109, *this stinking, jabbering Magpie here*) altogether, and avoiding such cumbersome and evasive phrases as "you know who I mean" and the like. In the first case, it seemed important not to slow the action on a minor obscurity; in the second, no allusion at all seemed preferable to an unsatisfactory echo of one. But where names and events seemed essential to the meaning, I have retained them, wherever possible intruding a gloss which might minimize the difficulty even though it expanded the text. So far as I know, every suppressed allusion is mentioned and explained in the notes.

Text and Acknowledgments

The texts on which I have chiefly relied for this translation are those of R. Cantarella and Victor Coulon (Budé), supplemented by the Oxford text of Hall and Geldart. Like every modern English or American translator of Aristophanes, I have derived invaluable aid and comfort from the splendid text and commentary of Benjamin Bickley Rogers.

For suggestions, corrections, and *trouvailles* I owe thanks to colleagues and friends too many to mention. But my chief mentor has been my wife. It was she who endured with unflinching patience and even good humor the successive versions, and it is to her, as orniphile and critic, that this translation is dedicated.

Finally, I should like to thank both the Yaddo Corporation and the American Academy in Rome for grants of money and leisure which made this translation possible, and the Research Institute of the University of Texas for secretarial assistance.

Austin, Texas WILLIAM ARROWSMITH

Characters of the Play

EUELPIDES
(i.e., Hopeful), an Athenian
PISTHETAIROS
(i.e., Plausible), an Athenian
SANDPIPER,
servant of Epops the Hoopoe
EPOPS, or HOOPOE,
otherwise known as Tereus
CHORUS OF BIRDS
PRIEST
POET
PROPHET
METON
INSPECTOR
LEGISLATOR
FIRST MESSENGER
SENTRY
IRIS
HERALD
DELINQUENT
KINESIAS,
a dithyrambic poet
INFORMER
PROMETHEUS
POSEIDON
TRIBALLOS
HERAKLES
SECOND MESSENGER

SCENE: *A desolate wilderness.* In the background is a single tree and the sheer rock-face of a cliff. Enter, in the last stages of exhaustion, Euelpides and Pisthetairos. On his arm Euelpides carries a Magpie; Pisthetairos holds a Crow. They are followed by slaves with their luggage, consisting mostly of kitchen equipment, cauldrons, pots, spits, etc.*

EUELPIDES

To his Magpie.

Straight ahead, croaker? Over by that tree?

PISTHETAIROS

Damn this cracked Crow! He keeps cawing me backwards.

EUELPIDES

Look, halfwit, what's the point of hiking these hills?
If we don't stop this zigzagging pretty soon,
I'm through.

PISTHETAIROS

I must have been mad—trusting a Crow
to go trudging off on this hundred-mile hike.

EUELPIDES

You're mad?
Look at me, man—hitched to a Magpie
and my toenails worn away right down to the nub.

PISTHETAIROS

I'll be damned if I know where we are.

EUELPIDES

Say,
do you suppose we could find our way back home from here?

PISTHETAIROS

Friend, even Exekestides couldn't do *that*.*

EUELPIDES

Stumbling.

Hell.

PISTHETAIROS

That's just where we're headed now, old man.

EUELPIDES

You know,
that birdseller Philokrates who sold us these damn Birds
was a filthy fraud, that's what. Swearing up and down
that these two Birds here would lead us to the Hoopoe,

old Tereus* the Bird who used to be a man,
and swindling us with this stinking jabbering Magpie here*
for two bits and that cluckhead Crow of yours for six!
And what do they do but nip our fingers off?

To the Magpie.

Well, what are you gaping at, imbecile? Where?
Straight into the cliff? But there's no road there, idiot.

PISTHETAIROS

A *road*? Sweet gods, there isn't even a track!

EUELPIDES

Say, isn't your Crow croaking something about a road?

PISTHETAIROS

You know, now that you mention it, I think he *is* croaking
in a different key.

EUELPIDES

Something about a road, isn't it?

PISTHETAIROS

Naw, he's cawing he'll gnaw my fingers off.

EUELPIDES

It's a filthy shame, that's what. Think of it, man:
here we are dying to go tell it to the Birds,*
and then, by god, we can't even find the way.

To the Audience.

Yes, dear people, we confess we're completely mad.
But it's not like Sakas'* madness. Not a bit.
For he, poor dumb foreigner, wants in, while we,
born and bred Athenians both, true blue,
true citizens, not afraid of any man,
want out.
Yes, we've spread our little feet
and taken off. Not that we hate Athens—
heavens, no. And not that dear old Athens
isn't grand, that blessed land where men are free—
to pay their taxes.*

No, look to the locust
who, one month or two, drones and shrills
among the little thickets, while the men of Athens,
perched upon the thorny thickets of the law, sit
shrilling out their three score years and ten.
Because of legal locusts,* gentlemen, we have left,
lugging these baskets and pots and boughs of myrtle,
looking for some land of soft and lovely leisure*

where a man may loaf and play and settle down
for good. Tereus the Hoopoe is our journey's end.
From him we hope to learn if he has seen
in all his many travels such a place
on earth.

PISTHETAIROS

Pssst! Hey!

EUELPIDES

What's up?

PISTHETAIROS

Look at my Crow
staring up in the air.

EUELPIDES

And my Magpie's gaping too.
It looks as though he's pointing his beak at the sky.
I'll bet that means there's Birds somewhere hereabouts.
We'll find out soon enough if we make a ruckus.

PISTHETAIROS

I know. Try kicking the side of the cliff with your foot.*

EUELPIDES

Go bash it with your head. You'll make more noise.

PISTHETAIROS

Pick up a rock and pound.

EUELPIDES

Good idea. I'll try.

He picks up a rock and pounds on the cliff, shouting.

Boy! Hey, boy!

PISTHETAIROS

Don't call old Hoopoe "boy."
You'd better say, "Ho, Hoopoe!" or "Hey, Epops!"

EUELPIDES

Hey, Hoopoe!

No answer.

Hmmm. Shall I try him again?
Yoohoo, Hoopoe!

A concealed door in the cliff suddenly swings open and a Sandpiper with an enormous curved beak peers out, almost spitting Pisthetairos.

SANDPIPER

What are you whooping about?

EUELPIDES

Apollo help us! What a beak on the Bird!

In his fright he lets go of his Magpie who flaps off. Pisthetairos falls backward, losing his Crow, while the Sandpiper retreats in horror.

SANDPIPER

Halp!
Nest-robbers! Egg-stealers! Bird-catchers!
Halp!

EUELPIDES

You hear that? His bark is worse than his beak.

SANDPIPER

Mortals, you die!

EUELPIDES

But we're not men.

SANDPIPER

What are you?

EUELPIDES

Me? I'm *turdus turdus*. An African migrant.*

SANDPIPER

What nonsense.

EUELPIDES

Not nonsense, crap. Look at my feet.

SANDPIPER

Indicating Pisthetairos.

And that bird over there? What's his species?

PISTHETAIROS

Him?
Brown-tailed Smellyrump. Quail family.

EUELPIDES

To Sandpiper.

Say,
what about you, Birdie? What the hell are you?

SANDPIPER

I'm a Slavebird.*

EUELPIDES

I see. Some bantam thrash you
in a scrap?

SANDPIPER

No, but when the boss got himself changed
into a Hoopoe, I put in my application for feathers too
so I could stay in his service, doing odd jobs and buttling.

EUELPIDES

And since when have our Birds been having butlers?

SANDPIPER
He gets the habit, I think, from having once been human.
But suppose he wants some sardines. Up I jump,
dash down with a dish and catch him some fish.
If it's soup he wants, I grab a little ladle
and skitter to the kettle.

EUELPIDES
Quite the runner, eh?
Tell you what, runner-bird: just skitter inside
and fetch your master out.

SANDPIPER
But he's napping now.
He gorged himself silly on a mess of midges and myrtle.

EUELPIDES
His nap be damned. Go wake him.

SANDPIPER
I warn you:
He'll be grumpy. But just for a favor I'll do it.

Exit Sandpiper.

PISTHETAIROS
And then drop dead.

To Euelpides.

—Whoosh, I'm still shaking.

EUELPIDES
Me too. And guess what. My Magpie's gone,
got clear away.

PISTHETAIROS
Got away? Why you big baby,
were you so scared you dropped your load?

EUELPIDES
Well,
what about you? Where's your bird?

PISTHETAIROS
Where's my bird?
Right here in my hand.*

EUELPIDES
Right where?

PISTHETAIROS
Well, he *was* here.

EUELPIDES
And where were you? Holding on for dear life?

HOOPOE

From within.

CLEAR THE COPSE, I SAY, AND WHEEL ME OUT!

The eccyclema wheels out the Hoopoe, sitting on a pile of brush and peering out from a thicket. Except for his huge crest and beak and a few bedraggled feathers here and there, the Hoopoe is human.

EUELPIDES

Holy Herakles! That's no Bird, it's a freak.
Get a load of that plumage! What a tiara!

HOOPOE

Who *are* you?

EUELPIDES

Birdie, you looked bedraggled.
I'll bet the gods* gave you some nasty knocks.

HOOPOE

You dare sneer at my plumage? I, strangers,
was once a man.

EUELPIDES

Oh, we're not laughing at you.

HOOPOE

Then, what's so funny?

EUELPIDES

Your beak. It tickles me.

HOOPOE

I am dressed as the poet Sophokles disfigures me*
in that atrocious tragedy of his entitled *Tereus.*

EUELPIDES

Gee,
you're Tereus in person?
Are you Bird or Peacock?

HOOPOE

With ferocious dignity.

I am a Bird.

EUELPIDES

Then what happened to your feathers, Bird?

HOOPOE

They've fallen out.

EUELPIDES

Caught the mange, I suppose?

HOOPOE

I'll ignore that remark.
All Birds moult in winter,*

and then in Spring we grow fresh feathers back.
Now then, suppose you tell me who *you* are.

EUELPIDES

Mortals.

HOOPOE

Country?

EUELPIDES

Athens, land of lovely—warships.

HOOPOE

Then you must be jurymen.*

EUELPIDES

No, just the reverse:
we're non-jurymen.

HOOPOE

I thought that species had become extinct
in Athens.

EUELPIDES

You can still find a few growing wild—*
if you look hard enough.

HOOPOE

But what brings you here, gentlemen?

EUELPIDES

Your assistance and advice.

HOOPOE

My advice? About what?

EUELPIDES

You were mortal once as we are mortal now.
You once were plagued with creditors, and we're plagued now.
You welshed on your debts; we welsh on our debts now.
But though you were mortal once, you became a Bird
and flew the circuit of the spreading earth and sea;
yet both as Bird and Man you understand.
And so we come to you, to ask your help,
bearing our hope that you may know some land,
some country like a blanket, soft and snug,*
between whose folds two tired men might flop.

HOOPOE

And Athens won't do? You want something more . . . splendid?

EUELPIDES

It wasn't exactly splendor we had in mind. No,
we wanted a country that was made for just *us*.

HOOPOE

Ah, something more exclusive? An Aristocracy perhaps?

EUELPIDES

Ugh. Can't abide that Aristokrates.

HOOPOE

But my dear fellow,
what *do* you want?

EUELPIDES

Oh, the sort of country
where the worst trouble I could have would be
friends trooping to my door bright and early
in the morning to pester me with invitations to dinner:
"C'mon, old boy, I'm throwing a big celebration.
So fresh up, give your kiddies a bath,
and come on over. And don't go standing me up,
or I won't turn to you when I'm in trouble."

HOOPOE

Zeus, you like your troubles pleasant, don't you?

To Pisthetairos.

And you?

PISTHETAIROS

I like pleasant troubles too.

HOOPOE

For instance?

PISTHETAIROS

For instance, this. Some pretty little boy's old man
comes up, really peeved, giving me hell:
"Fine way you treat my son, you old stinker!
You met the boy coming home from the baths
and never fondled him, never even kissed him
or tickled his balls. And *you,* his daddy's pal!"

HOOPOE

Poor old bastard, you *are* in love with trouble.
Well, I've got just the place to please you both.
Now, down on the Red Sea—

EUELPIDES

Sweet gods, not the sea!
No, sir. I don't want any court-officials with summons*
and subpoenas showing up on ships at the crack of dawn.
Look here, don't you know of some city in Hellas?

HOOPOE

Well now, there's always Lepreus? How would that suit you?

EUELPIDES
Lepreus? Never heard of it. Offhand, I'd say no.
Smacks of old Melanthios. He's leprous.

HOOPOE
Hmmm.
Well, how about Opous then?

EUELPIDES
Count me out.
If Opountios comes from Opous,* then Opous
isn't for me. You couldn't pay me to live there.
But look here, what kind of life do you Birds lead?
You should know. You've lived here long enough.

HOOPOE
Life among the Birds? Not bad. And you don't need cash.

EUELPIDES
Well, that's the worst of life's big swindles disposed of.

HOOPOE
We scour the gardens for food, pecking mint,
scrabbling for poppyseed, sesame and myrtle-berries . . .

EUELPIDES
Gods alive, that's not life! That's a honeymoon!*

PISTHETAIROS

Suddenly illuminated.

WAIT!
WONDERFUL!
I'VE GOT IT!
WHAT A SCHEME!
If you Birds will just do what I say, we'll make it succeed.

HOOPOE
Do what?

PISTHETAIROS
First, take my advice. For instance,
stop flapping around with your beaks hanging open.
It looks undignified and people jeer at the Birds.
In Athens whenever we see some silly ass,
we ask, "Hey, who's that Bird?" and people say,*
"Oh, *him?* He's a real bat, dumb as a dodo,
booby, that's what, hasn't got the brains of a Bird."

HOOPOE
A palpable hit. And we deserve it too.
But what remedy do you suggest?

PISTHETAIROS

Found your own city.

HOOPOE

Found *our own city?* But who ever heard
of a City of Birds?

PISTHETAIROS

O Hebetude, thy name is Hoopoe!
Look down there.

HOOPOE

I'm looking.

PISTHETAIROS

Now look up there.

HOOPOE

I'm looking.

PISTHETAIROS

Way up. Crane your neck.

HOOPOE

By Zeus,
I'll be a helluva sight if I sprain my neck looking.

PISTHETAIROS

See anything?

HOOPOE

Nothing but clouds and a mess of sky.

PISTHETAIROS

Precisely. That mess of sky is the sphere of the Birds.

HOOPOE

Sphere? How do you mean?

PISTHETAIROS

Habitat, as it were.
The heavens, you see, revolve upon a kind of pole*
or axis, whence we call the sky a sphere.
Well then, you settle in your sphere, you build your walls,
and from this sphere of yours a city will appear.
And then, my friend, you'll be lords of all mankind
as once you were merely lords of locusts and bugs.
As for the gods, if they object or get in your way,
you can wipe them all out by starvation.*

HOOPOE

Wipe them out?
But *how?*

PISTHETAIROS

Your air is the boundary between earth and heaven.

Now just as we, when we make a trip to Delphi,
are required to secure a visa from the Theban government,
so you, when men propose a sacrifice to heaven,
impose a boycott, refusing your passport to these offerings
and forbidding any transit through your land,
until the gods agree to pay you tribute.

HOOPOE

By Earth!

Holy Snares! Sweet Springes and Nets!
A trickier gimmick I never heard of yet!
We'll put it to a vote. A referendum. We'll enlist your help
and build our city, provided the Birds agree.

PISTHETAIROS

But who will make the motion?

HOOPOE

You, of course.

Don't worry. They don't twitter nonsense any more.
They used to chirp, but now I've taught them Greek.

PISTHETAIROS

But can we muster a quorum?

HOOPOE

Nothing simpler.

I'll just step behind this little thicket here
and wake my sleeping wife, my lovely Nightingale.
We'll do a small duet and whistle them here.
They'll all come flocking in when they hear our song.

PISTHETAIROS

Hoopoe, old Bird, you're wonderful!

But hurry. Quick.

Go wake your sleeping Nightingale and sing your song.

The Hoopoe retires and begins to sing.

HOOPOE

Awake from sleep, my love!
Sing, O tawnythroat,
bird with honied tongue!
Awake and sing
your song and mine,
Itys, Itys!

From the thicket the flute begins its obbligato in imitation of the song of the Nightingale at her most melancholy.

Pure sound of sorrow!
Hear it rise,
a grief that goes,
Itys, Itys!
from the ivy's dark,
the tangled leaves,
and climbs and soars,
Itys, Itys!
till lord Apollo hears,
god with golden hair,
and sweeps his lovely lyre
in echo of your song,
Itys, Itys!
and throats that cannot die
sing the sorrow back,
Itys! Itys! Itys!

There is a short coda by the flute, accompanied now by the distant sweeping of the lyre.

EUELPIDES

Holy Zeus, just hear the little Birdie's song!
A sound like honey streaming through the woods . . .

PISTHETAIROS

Pssst.

Hush.

EUELPIDES

Hush? But why?

PISTHETAIROS

Shush.

EUELPIDES

But why?

PISTHETAIROS

The Hoopoe is preening to sing another song.

HOOPOE

Singing, with flute obbligato.

Epopopopopopopopoi!
Popopopopopopoi!
Io! Io! Io!
Hear ye ye ye ye ye ye ye!

Calling first to the landbirds.

O Birds of fellow feather come!
Come, you Birds who graze, who feed
over the farmers' fresh-sown fields!
Barley-eating tribes, in thousands come!

O peckers after seeds, hungry nations,
swift of wing! Come, O chirrupers!
All you who flitter in the furrows,
who throng, who flock the new-turned sod,
who sing your chirrup, chirrup-song,
tio tio tio tio tio tio tio!

All you who in the gardens nest,
who perch beneath the ivy's leaves!
O rangers on the mountain, come,
arbutus-stealers, olive-thieves!
Flock, fly to my call! Come, O come!
trio trio trio totobrix!

To the Birds of marsh and meadow.

O Birds of swamp and river, come!
You whose beaks snap up the whining gnats,
who splash in water where the earth is wet
or skim the meadows over Marathon!
O Birds of blazoned feather, come!

To the Seabirds.

Come, Birds who soar upon the sea
where the kingfisher swoops!
O Birds with delicate necks,
O taper-throated, come!
Come and see the world remade!
Come and see the Birds reborn!

Lo, a MAN has come, of skill and craft,
whose wit cuts like a knife,
and to the Birds he brings the Word
of more abundant life.

Hear ye, hear ye, hear ye!
Come to council, come!
Hither, hither, hither!

Toro toro toro tix
kikka bau, kikka bau
toro toro toro li
li lix!

PISTHETAIROS

Hey, seen any Birds yet?

EUELPIDES

Not a sign of one.
And my neck's damn near broken from looking too.

PISTHETAIROS

The way it looks to me, the Hoopoe hopped in
and whooped himself hoarse, and all for nothing.

HOOPOE

Toro tix! Toro tix!

As the Hoopoe's call ends, the first member of the Chorus enters. He is dressed as a Flamingo and is shortly followed by other members, each costumed in broad representation of some bird.

PISTHETAIROS

Pssst. Euelpides! Look over there! There's a Bird coming in!

EUELPIDES

By Zeus, it *is* a Bird! What do you suppose he is? A Peacock?

Enter Hoopoe.

PISTHETAIROS

The Hoopoe will tell us.
—Say, what sort of Bird is that?

HOOPOE

That, my friend, is a rare marshbird. Not the sort of Bird
you run into every day.

EUELPIDES

Golly, what a flaming red!

HOOPOE

Exactly. That Bird's a Flamingo.

EUELPIDES

Oooh. Look.

PISTHETAIROS

What is it?

EUELPIDES

That Bird.

Enter a second bird, dressed in gorgeous Persian costume, with a magnificent strut.

PISTHETAIROS

Say, he's exotic. Like something out of Aischylos.*
Prithee, sir,
how is yon strange and mountain-ranging mantic Bird yclept?

HOOPOE

We call him the Bedouin Bird.

PISTHETAIROS

You don't say? The Bedouin Bird!
But how could a Bedouin Bird get to Greece without a Camel Bird?

EUELPIDES

And look there! There comes another Bird with a whopping crest.

Enter a Hoopoe.

PISTHETAIROS

Say, that's odd. You mean you aren't the only Hoopoe going?
Is he a Hoopoe too?

HOOPOE

Yes indeed, he's a Hoopoe too.
But he's the son of the Hoopoe in Philokles' tragedy of *Tereus*.*
I'm his grandpa, and he's my namesake, Hoopoe Jr.—
You know the pattern, the way Kallias calls his son Hipponikos,
and then these Hipponikoses call all their sons Kalliases.

EUELPIDES

So this is the Kallias Hoopoe. Well, he sure looks plucked.

HOOPOE

He's quite the bird about town, so parasites strip him bare
and the chorus girls keep yanking his pretty feathers out.

Enter a dazzlingly brilliant bird with an enormous crest and a great protruding belly.

EUELPIDES

Sweet Poseidon! Look at that gorgeous Birdie strutting in!
What's he called?

HOOPOE

That one? He's the Crested Guzzleguzzle.

EUELPIDES

The Guzzleguzzle, eh? I thought that was our boy Kleonymos.*

PISTHETAIROS

No, this Bird has a crest. Our man is crestfallen now.
Don't you remember how he ditched his helmet and ran away?

EUELPIDES

Look, Hoopoe, what's the point of all this crestwork on the Birds?*
Dress parade?

HOOPOE

No. Partly self-defence, partly sanitation.
Some towns are built on crests of hills, others in the passes.
So some Birds sport their plumes on top, but others on their asses.

PISTHETAIROS

What an ungodly crowd of Birds! It gives me the jitters.

The rest of the Chorus, birds of every size and description, now stream into the orchestra.

Look, Birds everywhere!

EUELPIDES

Apollo, what a bevy of Birds!
Why, when they lift up their wings, they block out the entrance.

PISTHETAIROS

Look, there's the Partridge!

EUELPIDES

And here's the Hooded Ptarmigan!

PISTHETAIROS

And there's a Widgeon, I think.

EUELPIDES

Here comes a female Plover.
But who's that Bird on her tail?

PISTHETAIROS

Her lover. The Horny Pecker.*

EUELPIDES

What does her husband say?

PISTHETAIROS

He's a queer Bird and doesn't care.

HOOPOE

Here's the Owl.

PISTHETAIROS

Now there's a thought! Bringing Owls to Athens.*

HOOPOE

And Jay and Pigeon. Lark, Wren, Wheatear, and Turtledove.
Ringdove, Stockdove, Cuckoo, and Hawk. Firecrest and Wren,
Rail and Kestrel and Gull, Waxwing, Woodpecker, and Vulture . . .

In one last surge the remaining members of the Chorus stream into the orchestra, ruffling their feathers and chirping and hissing.

PISTHETAIROS

Birds, Birds, billions of Birds!

EUELPIDES

Indicating the Audience.

But most of them Cuckoos and Geese.

PISTHETAIROS

What a skittering and cackling!

EUELPIDES

Unless I'm much mistaken,
I detect a note of menace.*

PISTHETAIROS

They *do* seem somewhat peeved.
You know, I think they're glaring at *us*.

EUELPIDES

Damn right they are.

KORYPHAIOS

Who-oo-chee-who-chee-who-oo-oo-oo
who-oo-chee-oo-oo has summoned me?

HOOPOE

Me, that's who. Your old friend Hoopoe.

KORYPHAIOS

Spea-pea-pea-pea-speak, Hoopopopopopoi.

HOOPOE

Listen. Great news! Glorious news!
News of Profit, gravy for all!
Two brilliant men have come to call
on me.

KORYPHAIOS

On YOU?
But HOW?
And WHO?

HOOPOE

But I'm trying to tell you.
Two old men have come to call,
two old refugees who have renounced the human race for good
and who bring us a glorious scheme, a Plan of fantastic proportions,
gigantic, sublime, colossal—

KORYPHAIOS

Colossal's the word for your blunder.
Have you lost your mind?

HOOPOE

Wait, listen . . .

KORYPHAIOS

Explain. And fast.

HOOPOE

Listen. I welcomed two old men. Harmless ornithologists,
infatuated with the Birds. They want to live with their Feathered Friends.

KORYPHAIOS

What? You welcomed TWO MEN?

HOOPOE

What's more, I'd do it again.

KORYPHAIOS

You mean they're *here*? In our midst?

HOOPOE

As much as I. Look.

He raises his wings, revealing the two men cowering behind him.

CHORUS

—O Treachery!
O Treason!
—O!
BAD Hoopoe, to betray us so!
To think that you, the Birdies' friend,
could come to such a wicked end!
To think that I should one day see
the Bird who pecked the corn with me
dishonor and disgrace
the MAGNA CARTA of our race,
and sell us to our foe!
—O Treachery!
—O Treason!
—O!

KORYPHAIOS

All right, we'll settle accounts with this treacherous Hoopoe later.
As for these venerable old fools, we'll settle with them right now.
We'll shred them into tatters.

PISTHETAIROS

Gods, they're shredding us to tatters!

EUELPIDES

Well, it's all your fault. This whole damn trip was your idea.
Why in god's name did you lead me here?

PISTHETAIROS

To bring up my rear.

EUELPIDES

It's so hopeless I could cry.

PISTHETAIROS

Fat chance you'll have of crying.
Once those Birds are through with you, you won't have any eyes.

CHORUS

Advance the wings and charge the flanks!
The Rooster shrills ATTACK!
Aerial squadrons, take to the air!
Beat your enemy back.

These men are spies, their lives are lies,
so kill without regrets!
The skill to kill lies in your bills.
Your beaks are bayonets.

No cloud exists, no breaker is,
no fog on mountain peaks,
quite big or thick or black enough
to save them from our beaks!

KORYPHAIOS

Mount the attack!

Charge them, Birds! Bite them, tear them!
On the double!

Captain on the right! Advance your wing and charge!

The Chorus wheels in massed formation toward the stage. Euelpides in terror starts to run.

EUELPIDES

They're charging! Where can we run?

PISTHETAIROS

Run, man? Stand and fight!

EUELPIDES

And get torn to tatters?

PISTHETAIROS

What good's running? *They*'re flying.

EUELPIDES

But what should I do?

PISTHETAIROS

Listen to me and follow my orders.
First pick up that platter and use it as a shield. Now HOLD THAT LINE!

EUELPIDES

But what good's a platter?

PISTHETAIROS

Birds are skittish of platters.* They'll scatter.

EUELPIDES

Yeah? Well, what about that vulture there?

PISTHETAIROS

Snatch up a skewer.
Now stick it out front like a spear.

EUELPIDES

But what about my eyes?

PISTHETAIROS

Jam a jug on your head. Now cover your eyes with saucers.

EUELPIDES

What a kitchen tactician! What crockery-strategy! Gee,
old Nikias is tricky, but he can't compare with you.

KORYPHAIOS

FORWARD!

Spit them with your beaks! At 'em, Birds!

CHARGE!

Rip 'em, scratch 'em, flay 'em, bite! BUT BREAK THAT POT!

HOOPOE

Intervening.

Truce, truce.

No more of this bitterness. You Birds should be ashamed.

Why should you kill these men? What harm have they done to you?

Somewhat more to the point, they're both closely related to my wife.*

KORYPHAIOS

Why spare these men any more than wolves? What worse enemy
than men do we Birds have?

HOOPOE

Enemies by nature, I admit.

But these men are exceptions to the rule. They come to you as friends.

Moreover, they bring a scheme from which we Birds stand to profit.

KORYPHAIOS

Are you suggesting that Birds should take advice from men?
What can *we* learn from men?

HOOPOE

If wise men learn from their enemies,

then why not you?

Remember the advantage of keeping an open mind.

Preparedness, after all, is not a lesson taught us by our friends
but by our enemies. It is our enemies, not our friends, who teach us to survive.

I might cite the case of cities: was it from their friends or their foes
that mankind first learned to build walls and ships in self-defence?
But that one lesson still preserves us all and all we have.

KORYPHAIOS

There's something in what you say.

Perhaps we'd better hear them.

PISTHETAIROS

To Euelpides.

They're beginning to show signs of reason. Don't say a word.

HOOPOE

To the Chorus.

That's better, friends. You're doing right, and you'll thank me for it later.

KORYPHAIOS

We've never disobeyed your advice before.

PISTHETAIROS

They seem more peaceful now.
So you can ground the pan
and put the platter down.
But stand your ground
and keep that spit on hand,
while I look round
our little camp of crocks
and see how matters stand
by peeking over pots.

EUELPIDES

Chief, suppose we die
in combat?

PISTHETAIROS

Then we'll lie
in Athens at public cost.*
They'll give us hero's honors
and bury us like gods
when we say our lives were lost
fighting foreign soldiers
at very heavy odds.
In fact, I'll use those very words
(omitting, for effect, of course
any reference to Birds.)*

KORYPHAIOS

All right, you Birds, FALL IN!
The war's over.
AT EASE!
You there, quiet!
QUIET, PLEASE!

The Chorus returns to its normal position in the orchestra. Much whispering, nodding, and shuffling. Then silence.

Now we have to inquire
who these strangers are
and why they've come.
Look here, Hoopoe.

HOOPOE

Um?

KORYPHAIOS

Who are these fellows?

HOOPOE

Two humans from Hellas
where genius grows greener than grass.

KORYPHAIOS

But why have they come?
What do they hope to get from the Birds?

HOOPOE

Their motive is Love.
Love is the burden of all their words.
Love of your life
and Love of you,
to live with you
in Love always.

KORYPHAIOS

Is *that* what they say?
But what is the gist of their scheme?

HOOPOE

They envisage a vision of glory,
a dream so fantastic
it staggers the sensible mind.

KORYPHAIOS

Well, it doesn't stagger mine.
What's in it for them?
Who are they trying to stick?

HOOPOE

No one.
This is no trick.
What this means is bliss.
Believe me, utter bliss. Sheer
and absolute.

Viz.
all shall be yours,
whatever is,
here or there,
far or near,
all, everywhere.
And this they swear.

KORYPHAIOS

Crackpots, eh?

HOOPOE

Right as rain.
Foxes, not men.
Boxes of slyness,
brimming with brain.

KORYPHAIOS

Then let them talk! We're all in a twitter to hear.

HOOPOE

So be it, then.
—Men, take these weapons inside
the house and hang them up beside the blazing hearth
where the god of fire presides. They'll bring us luck.

Servants pick up the pots and plates and skewers and carry them inside. The Hoopoe turns to Pisthetairos.

Pisthetairos, you have the floor. Proceed with your case.
Explain your proposal.

PISTHETAIROS

By Apollo, only on condition
that you Birds agree to swear a solemn truce with me
like the truce which that armor-making baboon—you know who I mean—*
signed with his wife: no biting, scratching, or cutting,
no hauling around by the balls, no shoving things—

EUELPIDES

Bending over.

—Up there?

PISTHETAIROS

In my eyes, I was going to say.

KORYPHAIOS

We accept your terms.

PISTHETAIROS

First you have to swear to them.

KORYPHAIOS

We swear it then, but on this one condition only:
that you guarantee that this comedy of ours will win First Prize
by completely unanimous vote of the Judges.

PISTHETAIROS

Agreed.

KORYPHAIOS

Splendid. If, however, we Birds should break the truce,
we agree to forfeit, say, forty-nine per cent
of the votes.

HOOPOE

To the Chorus.

Fall out!
Pick up your weapons, men
and return at once to your quarters. On the double!
Company Assignments will be posted on the bulletin boards.

CHORUS

—Man by nature is a liar made.
He plays a double game.
—Dishonesty's his stock-in-trade.
Deception is his name.
—We say no more.
—But it may be
your canny mortal brain may see
what our poor feeble wits cannot—
—some gift of noble intellect
we once possessed and then forgot
as our race declined;
—some genius of the will
or wisdom of the mind,
—grown rusty with neglect,
but fusting in us still.
—It seems to us fantastic.
—But still, it *could* be true.
—And, of course, we'd split the profits—
—if any such accrue.

KORYPHAIOS

Pisthetairos, proceed. You may say whatever you wish. With impunity.
We pledge you our words as Birds: we won't renege on the truce.

PISTHETAIROS

By god, I'm wild to begin!

The dough of my vision has risen,

and there's nothing now but the kneading.

—Boy, bring me a wreath.

Someone fetch water for my hands.*

EUELPIDES

Hey, we going to a feast?

PISTHETAIROS

A dinner of words, a fat and succulent haunch of speech,
a meal to shiver the soul.

—Unhappy Birds, I grieve for you,

you who once were kings—

KORYPHAIOS

—Kings? Of what?

PISTHETAIROS

Kings of everything.

Kings of creation. My kings. This man's kings. Kings of king Zeus.
More ancient than Kronos. Older than Titans. Older than Earth.

KORYPHAIOS

Older than Earth?

PISTHETAIROS

Older than Earth.

KORYPHAIOS

And to think I never suspected!

PISTHETAIROS

Because you're a lazy Bird* and you haven't reread your Aesop.
For Aesop states that the Lark is the oldest thing in the world,
older than Earth. So ancient, in fact, that when her father died,
she couldn't find him a grave, for the Earth hadn't yet been made,
and therefore couldn't be dug. So what on earth could she do?
Well, the little Lark was stumped. Then suddenly she had it!
She laid her daddy out and buried him under her tail.

EUELPIDES

She did for a fact.

And that's how Asbury* got its name.

PISTHETAIROS

Hence my argument stands thus: if the Birds are older than Earth,
and therefore older than gods, then the Birds are the heirs of the
world.
For the oldest always inherits.

EUELPIDES

It stands to reason, friends.
So pack some bone in your bills and hone them down to a point.
Old Zeus won't rush to resign and let the Woodpeckers reign.*

PISTHETAIROS

Think of it, the springtime of the world!
The Age of the Birds!
Primal lords of Creation! Absolute masters of man!
But the gods are mere upstarts and usurpers of very recent date.
And proof abounds.
Let me adduce, for instance, the case of the Rooster.
Aeons and aeons ago, ages before the age of Darius,
the kingdom of Persia lay prostrate beneath the sway of the Rooster
And the Rooster, ever since, has been called the Persian Red.

EUELPIDES

And that's why, even now, he swaggers and struts like a king
and keeps a harem of hens. And, unique among the Birds,
he wears the royal red tiara of the ancient Persian kings.

PISTHETAIROS

And talk of power!
Why, even now its memory remains,
enshrined in habit. For when the Cock his matins crows,
mankind goes meekly off to work—bakers, smiths, and potters,
tanners and merchants and musical-instrument makers.
And when he crows at dusk, the night-shift goes.

EUELPIDES

I'll vouch for that.
It was thanks to his night-shift crowing that I lost my warmest coat.
I'd gone downtown to dinner, see, in honor of a birth.
Well, after a while I'd had five or six and passed out cold,
when that blasted Rooster started to crow. Needless to say,
I thought it was dawn, jumped into my clothes and tore off to work.
But just outside the gate, somebody conked me with a club
and I passed out cold again. And when I came to, no coat!

PISTHETAIROS

What's more, once upon a time the Kites were the kings of Hellas.

KORYPHAIOS

The *kings* of Hellas?

PISTHETAIROS

Right. The Kites were the kings of Hellas.
And it was during their reign that the custom began in Greece

of falling flat on your face whenever you saw a Kite.*

EUELPIDES

You know, I once spotted a Kite and went down on the ground—
so damn hard I swallowed my money* and two of my teeth.
I damn near starved.

PISTHETAIROS

And once the Cuckoo was king of Egypt.
And when the call of the Cuckoo was heard in the land, every Egyptian
grabbed his scythe and ran to the fields to reap.

EUELPIDES

That's a fact.
And that's why, even today, we still call the Egyptians cuckoo.*

PISTHETAIROS

Why, so great was the power of the Birds that even the greatest kings—
Agamemnon and Menelaos, to name only two of the greatest—
had their sceptres tipped with Birds, and the Birds got a cut in the take.

EUELPIDES

So *that's* it. That explains all that funny business in the plays
I never understood before—where Priam, for instance, walks in,
and there on his sceptre, large as life, some Bird is perching.
I used to think he was there to keep an eye peeled down below
on the rows where the politicians sit,* to see where our money goes.

PISTHETAIROS

But the crowning proof is this: the present incumbent, Zeus,
wears an Eagle upon his helmet as the symbol of royal power.
Athena uses the Owl, and Apollo, as aide to Zeus, a Hawk.

EUELPIDES

By Demeter, they do! But why do the gods use these Birds as emblems?

PISTHETAIROS

An unconscious admission of the Birds' ancient power and supremacy.
That's why when men sacrifice to the gods, the Birds swoop down and snatch the food,
thereby beating out the gods, and so asserting their old priority.
Again, no one ever swore by the gods, but always by the Birds.

EUELPIDES

Doctors still swear by the Duck.* That's why we call them quacks.

PISTHETAIROS
But these were the honors you held in the days of your greatness.

Whereas now you've been downgraded.
You're the slaves, not lords, of men.
They call you brainless or crazy.
They kill you whenever they can.

The temples are no protection:
the hunters are lying in wait
with traps and nooses and nets
and little limed twigs and bait.

And when you're taken, they sell you
as tiny *hors d'oeuvres* for a lunch.
And you're not even sold alone,
but lumped and bought by the bunch.

And buyers come crowding around
and pinch your breast and your rump,
to see if your fleshes are firm
and your little bodies are plump.

Then, as if this weren't enough,
they refuse to roast you whole,
but dump you down in a dish
and call you a *casserôle*.

They grind up cheese and spices
with some oil and other goo,
and they take this slimy gravy
and they pour it over you!

Yes, they pour it over you!

It's like a disinfectant,
and they pour it piping hot,
as though your meat were putrid,
to sterilize the rot!

Yes, to sterilize the rot!

As Pisthetairos finishes, a long low susurrus of grief runs through the Chorus and the Birds sigh, weep, and beat their breasts with their wings.

CHORUS

Stranger, forgive us if we cry,
  reliving in your words
those years of cowardice that brought
  disaster to the Birds:—
  that tragic blunder
  and our fathers' crime,
  complacency whose cost
  was greatness and our name,
  as dignity went under
  in a chicken-hearted time,
  and all was lost.

But now, by luck,
or heaven-sent,
a Man has come
to pluck us from disgrace.

Hail, Pisthetairos!
Hail, Savior of the Birds,
Redeemer of our Race!
To you we now commit:
    ourselves,
    our nests,
    our chicks,
      et cet.

KORYPHAIOS

Sir, you have the floor once more. Proceed with your explanation.
Until our power is restored, life means less than nothing
to the Birds.

PISTHETAIROS

My Plan, in gist, is this—a city of the Birds,
whose walls and ramparts shall include the atmosphere of the world
within their circuit. But make the walls of brick, like Babylon.

EUELPIDES

A Babylon of the Birds!* What a whopping, jumbo-size city!

PISTHETAIROS

The instant your walls are built, reclaim your sceptre from Zeus.
If he shilly-shallies or fobs you off with a lot of excuses,
proclaim a Holy War, a Great Crusade against the gods.
Then slap embargoes on their lust, forbidding any gods
in manifest state of erection to travel through your sky

on amatory errands down to Earth to lay their women—
their Semeles, Alkmenes, and so forth. Then, if they attempt to ignore
your warning, place their offending peckers under bond
as contraband and seal them shut. That will stop their fun,
I think.
Second, appoint some Bird as your official ambassador
to men, and serve them formal notice that the Birds demand priority
in all their sacrifices. The leftovers, of course, will go to the gods.
But for the future, even when they offer sacrifices to the gods,
each Bird must be paired with a god*—whichever one seems most apt.
Thus, if Aphrodite is offered a cake, the Wagtail will get one too.
When Poseidon gets his sheep, the Seagull must have his wheat.
Greedy Herakles shall eat—when the glutton Jay is fed.
And as for Zeus, why, Zeus must wait his turn until the Kinglet,
lord of all the Birds, receives his sacrificial gnat.

EUELPIDES

I *like* that gnat. Old has-been Zeus can rumble with rage!

KORYPHAIOS

But why should men believe we're gods and not just shabby Birds?
These wings are a giveaway.

PISTHETAIROS

Rubbish. Hermes is a god, isn't he?
But he goes flapping around on wings. And so do loads of gods.
There's Victory on "gildered wings," and don't forget the god of Love.
And Homer says that Iris looks like a dove with the jitters.

EUELPIDES

And lightning too, that's got wings. Hey, what if lightning fell on us?

KORYPHAIOS

And what if men are blind and go on truckling to Olympos
and refuse to worship the Birds?

PISTHETAIROS

Then swarms of starving Sparrows
shall descend on their fields in millions and gobble up their seeds.
They'll damn well go hungry. We'll see then if Demeter will feed them.

EUELPIDES

If I know that Demeter, she'll have plenty of excuses ready.

PISTHETAIROS

Then we'll muster the Crows and Ravens and send them down in droves
to peck out the eyes of the oxen and make the sheep go blind.
Dr. Apollo can cure them—but I'd hate to pay the fee.

EUELPIDES

Give me the nod when you're ready. I want to unload my ox.

PISTHETAIROS

If, on the other hand, mankind accepts you as their gods,
their manifest Poseidon, their Earth, their Principle of Life,
all their wishes shall come true.

KORYPHAIOS

All their wishes? For instance?

PISTHETAIROS

Why, enormous plagues of locusts will not infest their vines:
a single regiment of our Owls will wipe the locusts out.
And the gallfly and the mite will no longer blight their figs
since we'll send down troops of Thrushes to annihilate the bugs.

KORYPHAIOS

But what about money? Money's Man's dominant passion.

PISTHETAIROS

Duck soup for you. Your oracles will tell them what they want—
the whereabouts of the richest mines, when the market is right
to make a killing, and so forth. And no more shipwrecks either.

KORYPHAIOS

No more shipwrecks?

PISTHETAIROS

No shipwrecks. You take your omens, you see,
and some Bird pipes up, "Bad weather brewing" or "Forecast: fair."

EUELPIDES

To hell with the Birds! A ship for me! I'm off to sea!

PISTHETAIROS

You'll show them buried treasure; you'll tell them where to find gold.
For Birds know all the answers, or so the saying goes—
"A little Bird told me." People are always saying that.

EUELPIDES

The hell with the sea! A shovel for me! I'm off to dig for gold!

KORYPHAIOS

But how will we give them health? That lies in the hands of the gods.

PISTHETAIROS

Give them wealth, you give them health. They're really much the same.

EUELPIDES

And that's a fact. The man who's sick is always doing badly.

KORYPHAIOS

But longevity and old age also lie in the hands of the gods.
How will a man grow old if the gods refuse him Old Age?
Will he die in childhood?

PISTHETAIROS

Die? The Birds will add to his life
three centuries at least.

KORYPHAIOS

But how?

PISTHETAIROS

From their own lives, of course.
What doth the poet say?
"Five lives of men the cawing Crow
outliveth."*

EUELPIDES

Long live the Birds! Down with Zeus!

PISTHETAIROS

I'm with you there,
and think of the money we'll save!

For Birds won't want any shrines;
marble just leaves them cold.
They don't give a hoot for temples
with doors of beaten gold.

They'll live in woodses and copses—
that's plenty of shrine for them.
And the social-register swells
can strut on an olive limb.*

And we'll go no more to Delphi!
To hell with Ammon's seat!
We'll amble out under the olives
and toss them bits of wheat,

and hold up our paws to heaven
  and make the Birds a prayer,
and the Birds will grant all our wishes
  for cutting them a share.

And we won't be out of pocket.
  No, the only dough we'll need
is a little loaf of barley
  and a tiny pinch of seed.

KORYPHAIOS

The Birds' best friend! And to think how we misjudged you once, most generous of men!

Ask us what you will. It shall be done.

CHORUS

Amen, we say.

And now, presuming you concur,
  we Birds propose an oath
of mutual assistance, sir,
  and binding on us both.

Arm to wing, we'll soar to war!
  Our cause needs no excuse.
We'll storm up Mt. Olympos, friend,
  and make a pulp of Zeus!

KORYPHAIOS

We await your orders, sir. Tasks that need mere brawn and muscle
we Birds can do. The complicated mental stuff we leave to you.

HOOPOE

Action, dammit, action! That's what we need.
Strike while the iron's hot. No dawdling around
like slowpoke Nikias.

—Dear me, I nearly forgot.
You two gentlemen must see my little nest,
my trash of sticks and straw and kickshaw stuff.
And good heavens! We haven't been formally introduced.

PISTHETAIROS

Pisthetairos here.

HOOPOE

Ah. And this gentleman?

EUELPIDES

Euelpides.

From Athens.

HOOPOE

Enchanted, I'm sure.

PISTHETAIROS

The pleasure's ours.

HOOPOE

Please come in.

PISTHETAIROS

No, after you.

HOOPOE

This way, gentlemen.

The Hoopoe begins to flap his wings to flutter into his nest.

PISTHETAIROS

Hey, you!
Damn it, stop! Back water, blast you!
Look here, what sort of partnership is this supposed to be
if you start taking off when we can't even fly?

HOOPOE

Does it matter?

PISTHETAIROS

Remember what old Aesop tells us*
in his fable of the Eagle and the Fox in business
who couldn't get along? The Fox got swindled by the Eagle.

HOOPOE

Don't be nervous. I know of a wonderful magic root.
Merely nibble on it and you'll sprout a set of wings.

PISTHETAIROS

Splendid. Then let's go in.
—You there, Xanthias.
Hey, Manodorus! Bring our luggage inside the house.

KORYPHAIOS

One moment, please. Hoopoe, when you go inside . . .

HOOPOE

Yes?

KORYPHAIOS

By all means take your human guests and feast them well.
But first do one little favor for the Chorus, please.
Bring out your wife, your lovely Nightingale,
the bird with honeyed tongue, the Muses' love,
and let the Chorus play with her a little while.

PISTHETAIROS
I add my entreaty to theirs. In the name of heaven,
bring her out from the bed of rushes where she hides.

EUELPIDES
Please, please do. Bring the pretty Birdie out.
I've never met a Nightingale before.

HOOPOE
With all my heart.
I'd be delighted, gentlemen.

Calling inside.

Oh Prokne! Prokne.
Please come out, my dear, and meet our visitors.

A lovely well-rounded young flutegirl shyly appears. She is dressed in the rich gold-encrusted robes of a young Athenian matron of high birth. On her head she wears the mask of the Nightingale.

PISTHETAIROS
Almighty Zeus! Gosh, what a baby of a Birdie!
What curves! What grace! What a looker!

EUELPIDES
Gee! By god,
I'd like to bounce between her thighs right now!

PISTHETAIROS
And what a shimmer of gold! Just like a bride.

EUELPIDES
By god, I've got half a mind to kiss her!

PISTHETAIROS
Look out,
you old lecher, her beak's a pair of skewers.

EUELPIDES
Very well.
Then I'll treat her like an egg and peel her shell.
I'll lift her little mask and kiss her—so.

HOOPOE
Harrumph. This way.

PISTHETAIROS
And may good fortune go with us.

Exeunt Pisthetairos, Euelpides, and Hoopoe, followed by the slaves with the luggage.

CHORUS

O love,
tawnythroat!
Sweet nightingale,
musician of the Birds
Come and sing,
honey-throated one!
Come, O love,
flutist of the Spring,
accompany our song.

The Chorus turns sharply and faces the audience, while the flutegirl begins the song of the nightingale at its most mournful. The flute obbligato accompanies the Chorus throughout.*

O suffering mankind,
lives of twilight,
race feeble and fleeting,
like the leaves scattered!
Pale generations,
creatures of clay,
the wingless, the fading!
Unhappy mortals,
shadows in time,
flickering dreams!
Hear us now,
the ever-living Birds,
the undying,
the ageless ones,
scholars of eternity.
Hear and learn from us
the truth
of all there is to know—
what we are,
and how the gods began,
of Chaos and Dark.
(And when you know
tell Prodikos to go
hang:* he's had it!)
There was Chaos at first
and Night and Space
and Tartaros.
There was no Earth.
No Heaven was.

But sable-wingèd Night
laid her wind-egg there*
in the boundless lap
of infinite Dark.
And from that egg,
in the seasons' revolving,
Love was born,
the graceful, the golden,
the whirlwind Love
on gleaming wings.
And there in the waste
of Tartaros,
Love with Chaos lay
and hatched the Birds.
We come from Love.
Love brought us to the
light.
There were no gods
till Love had married
all the world in love.
Then the world was made.
Blue Heaven stirred,
and Ocean,
the Earth and ageless gods,
the blessèd ones
who do not die.
But we came first.
We Birds were born
the first-born sons of Love,
in proof whereof
we wear Love's wings,
we help his lovers.
How many pretty boys,
their prime not past,
abjuring Love,
have opened up their thighs
and yielded,
overborne by us,
bribed by a Bird,
a Coot, a Goose,
a little Persian Cock!
Think of the services
we Birds perform
for all mankind.

We mark your seasons off,
summer, spring,
winter, fall.
When for Africa
the screaming Crane departs,
you sow your fields.
And then the sailor
takes his ease
and hangs his rudder up,
and thief Orestes
weaves himself a cloak
and robs no man.
And then the Kite appears,
whose coming says
the Spring is here,
the time has come
to shear the sheep.
And so the Swallow
brings his summer,
when mankind lays
its winter weeds away.
And we are Ammon
and Dodona.
We are your Apollo,
that prophetic voice
to whom you turn
in everything you do—
practical affairs,
commerce and trade,
and marriage too.
Birds are your signs,
and all your omens
are governed by Birds:
words are omens
sent by the Birds.
And the same for sneezes,
meetings, asses, voices:
all are omens,
and omens are Birds.
Who are we then
if we are not
your prophetic Apollo?

The obbligato of the flute ceases as the Chorus now shifts to a lighter vein and a quicker tempo.

So elect us as your gods
and we, in turn, shall be
your weathervane and Muse,
your priests of prophecy,
foretelling all,
winter, summer, spring, and fall.

Furthermore, we promise we'll
give mankind an honest deal.
Unlike our smug opponent, Zeus,
we'll stop corruption and abuse.
NO ABSENTEE ADMINISTRATION!
NO PERMANENT VACATION
IN THE CLOUDS!
And we promise
to be scrupulously honest.

Last of all, we guarantee
to every single soul on earth,
his sons and their posterity:
HEALTH
WEALTH
HAPPINESS
YOUTH
LONG LIFE
LAUGHTER
PEACE
DANCING
and
LOTS TO EAT!
We'll mince no words.
Your lives shall be
the milk of the Birds!
We guarantee
you'll all be
revoltingly
RICH!

O woodland Muse
with lovely throat,
tio tio tio tinx!

who with me sing
whenas in glade or mountain, I,
perched upon the ashtree cry,
tio tio tio tinx!
my tawny-throated song of praise,
to call the Mother to the dance,
a song of joy for blessed Pan,
totototototototinx!
whence, like a bee,
the poet stole his honied song,*
my ravished cry,
tio tio tio tinx!

Do *you* suffer pangs of conscience?
Nervous?
Jumpy?
Scared?
Need a hideout from the law? Some cozy place to pass the time?
Well, step right up, friend!
We'll get you a berth with the Birds.
We do things differently up here.
What your laws condemn,
the things that you think shady or immoral are compulsory with us.
Consider the case, for instance, of a boy who beats up his dad.
Admit it: you're shocked. The idea! But *we* call it courage
when some bantam twirps, "C'mon, old Bird, put up your spurs and fight!"
Or suppose you've deserted. You're a runaway, branded with shame.
Hell, come and live with us! We'll call you a Yellow Chicken.
Or perhaps you happen to come from some foppish hole in Asia?
Come on up, you fairy fop, and be an Asiatic Finch.
Or suppose you're a slave from Krete, like our friend Exekestides—
We'll call you little Cuckoo and pawn you off as our own.
Was Peisias your father?
Are you a future traitor too?
Hell, make like a partridge then. That's what your Daddy did.
And who are we Birds to fuss at shamming hurt and partridge tricks?

And so the swans
their clamor cry,
tio tio tio tinx!
and beating wings
and bursting throats
lord Apollo sing,
tio tio tio tinx!
by Hebros' waters, swarming, crying,
tio tio tio tinx!
And every living thing is still.
On bird, on beast, the hush of awe.
The windless sea lies stunned when—
totototototototinx!
All Olympos rings,
and wonder breaks upon the gods,
and echoing, the Graces sing,
and lovely Muses raise the cry,
tio tio tio tinx!

Friends, you haven't really lived till you've tried a set of FEATHERS!
Think, spectators.
Imagine yourselves with a pair of wings!
The sheer joy of it! Not having to sit those tragedies out!
No getting bored. You merely flap your little wings and fly off home.
You have a snack, then make it back to catch the COMIC play.
Or again, suppose you're overtaken by a sudden need to crap.
Do you do it in your pants?
Not a bit.
You just zoom off,
fart and shit to your heart's content and whizz right back.
Or perhaps you're having an affair—I won't name any names.
You spot the lady's husband attending some meeting or other.
Up you soar, flap your wings, through the window and into bed!
You make it a quickie, of course, then flutter back to your seat.
So what do you say?
Aren't wings just the most *wonderful* things?
Look at Dieitrephes, our vulgar Ikaros of trade,*
who started life on wicker wings but rose to captain's rank,
and now, still riding high, is colonel of a wing of horse.
From horse's ass to Pegasos! But *that's* what wings can do!

The Chorus now turns and faces the stage as Pisthetairos and Euelpides return. Both of them now sport tiny wings, a few feathers, and outsize beaks.

PISTHETAIROS

Well, here we are.

EUELPIDES

Sweet gods, in all my days,
I've never seen a sillier sight than you!

PISTHETAIROS

Yeah,
what's so damn funny?

EUELPIDES

You and those baby wings.
They tickle me. You know what you look like, don't you?

PISTHETAIROS

You look like an abstraction of a Goose.

EUELPIDES

Yeah?
Well, if you're supposed to be a Blackbird, boy,
somebody botched the job. You're more bare than Bird.

PISTHETAIROS

We made the choice that gave these barbs their bite.
Remember the poor Birds in that Aischylos play*—
"Shot down by shafts of their own feathers made?"

EUELPIDES

What's the next move?

PISTHETAIROS

First, we'll give our city
some highfalutin' name. Then a special sacrifice
to our new gods.

EUELPIDES

A special sacrifice? Yummy.

KORYPHAIOS

To work, men. How do you propose to name our city?

PISTHETAIROS

How about Sparta? That's a grand old name
with a fine pretentious ring.

EUELPIDES

Great Herakles,
call my city Sparta? I wouldn't even insult
my mattress by giving it a name like Sparta.*

PISTHETAIROS

Well,

what do you suggest instead?

EUELPIDES

Something big, smacking

of the clouds. A pinch of fluff and rare air.
A swollen sound.

PISTHETAIROS

I've got it! Listen—
CLOUDCUCKOOLAND!

KORYPHAIOS

That's it! The perfect name. And it's a *big* word too.

EUELPIDES

CLOUDCUCKOOLAND!
Imagination's happy home,
where Theogenes builds castles in the air, and Aischines
becomes a millionaire.

PISTHETAIROS

Better yet, here we have
the plain of Phlegra, that windy battlefield of blah and bluff,
where the gabbling gods outbragged the wordy giants.

KORYPHAIOS

A suave and splendid city.
—But which of the gods
should we designate as patron and protector?

EUELPIDES

Why not Athena?

PISTHETAIROS

But it's bound to seem a bit odd, isn't it? I mean,
a female goddess protecting our walls with a spear
while men like Kleisthenes sit home with their knitting?

KORYPHAIOS

And, come to think of it, who will guard our Storkade?*

PISTHETAIROS

A Bird.

KORYPHAIOS

One of us, you mean?

PISTHETAIROS

Why not the Rooster?
They're terrible scrappers and famous fighting Birds.
Little chicks of Ares.

EUELPIDES

Little Corporal Cock!
He's the perfect Bird for protecting our rock.

PISTHETAIROS

To Euelpides.

Hop it, man!*
Quick, up the rigging of the air!
Hurry! Done? Now supervise the workers on the wall.
Run the rubble up!
Quick, mix the mortar, man!
Up the ladder with your hod—and then fall down!
Don't stop!
Post the sentries!
Bank the furnace!
Now the watchman's round.
All right, catch two winks.
Rise and shine!
Now send your heralds off,
one to the gods above, one to the mortals below.
Then scurry back.

EUELPIDES

As for you, just stay right here—
and I hope you choke.

PISTHETAIROS

Obey your orders, friend.
Unless you do your share, we shan't get done.

Exit Euelpides.

Now, let me see.
First, a priest to supervise
our sacrifice.
—Boy!

An Acolyte appears.

Boy, go fetch me a priest.
And when you're finished, bring me a basket and a laver.

Exit Acolyte.

CHORUS

The Birds agree
most heartily.
You're absolutely right.

Hymns and laud
are dear to god,
but dinner's their delight.

Yes, gratitude
is shown with food,
so rise and offer up,

in witness of
our shrunken love,
one miserable lamb chop!

KORYPHAIOS

Flutist, come in.*
Now let our sacrifice begin.

Enter the Flutist, a Raven whose beak is an enormous flute which is strapped to his mouth by means of a leather harness. After strenuous huffing, he manages to produce what are unmistakably caws.

PISTHETAIROS

Stop that raucous Rook!
In the name of god,
what are you anyway?
I've seen some weird sights,
but this is the first time in my life I ever saw
a Blackbird propping his beak with a leather belt.*

Exit Flutist. Enter Priest, followed by the Acolyte with the paraphernalia of the sacrifice.

At last.
—Eminence, you may begin the inaugural sacrifice.

PRIEST

Your humble servant, sir.
—But where's my acolyte?

*The Acolyte steps forward. The Priest raises his hands and begins the Bidding Prayer of the Birds.**

Now let us pray—
PRAY TO THE HESTIA OF NESTS,
TO THE HOUSEHOLDING HARRIER HAWK,
TO ALL THE OLYMPIAN COCKS AND COQUETTES,
TO THE SWOOPING STORK OF THE SEA—

PISTHETAIROS

ALL HAIL, THE STORK! HAIL, POSEIDON OF PINIONS!

PRIEST

TO THE SWEETSINGER OF DELOS,
THE APOLLONIAN SWAN,
TO LETO THE QUEEN OF THE QUAIL,
TO ARTEMIS THE PHOEBE—

PISTHETAIROS

HAIL TO THE PHOEBE, VIRGIN SISTER OF PHOIBOS!

PRIEST

PRAY TO WOODPECKER PAN,
TO DOWITCHER KYBELE,
MOTHER OF MORTALS AND GODS—

PISTHETAIROS

HAIL, DOWAGER QUEEN, GREAT MOTHER OF BUSTARDS!

PRIEST

PRAY THAT THEY GRANT US
HEALTH AND LENGTH OF LIFE,
PRAY THAT THEY PROTECT US,
pray for the Chians too*—

PISTHETAIROS

You know, I like the way he tacks those Chians on.

PRIEST

COME, ALL HERO BIRDS,
ALL HEROINE HENS AND PULLETS!
COME, O GALLINULE!
BRING DICKYBIRD AND DUNNOCK,
COME, CROSSBILL AND BUNTING!
ON DIPPER, ON DIVER,
ON WHIMBREL AND FINCH!
COME CURLEW AND CREEPER,
ON PIPIT, ON PARROT,
COME VULTURE, COME TIT—

PISTHETAIROS

Stop it, you fool! Stop that rollcall of the Birds!
Are you utterly daft, man, inviting Vultures and Eagles
and suchlike to our feast? Or weren't you aware
one single beak could tuck it all away?
Clear out, and take your blasted ribands with you.
So help me, I'll finish this sacrifice myself.

Exit Priest.

CHORUS

Again we raise
the hymn of praise
   and pour the sacred wine.

With solemn rite
we now invite
   the blessèd gods to dine.

But don't *all* come—
perhaps just one,
   and maybe then again,

there's not enough
(besides, it's tough),
   so stay away. Amen.

PISTHETAIROS

Let us pray to the pinion'd gods—

Enter a hungry, ragged Poet, chanting.

POET

In all thy songs, O Muse,
      let one city
      praisèd be—
CLOUDCUCKOOLAND THE LOVELY!

PISTHETAIROS

Who spawned this spook?
      —Look here, who are you?

POET

One of the tribe of dulcet tongue and tripping speech—
"the slave of Poesy,
whose ardent soul
the Muses hold in thrall,"
as Homer hath it.*

PISTHETAIROS

Judging from your clothes, friend, your Muses must be bankrupt.
Tell me, bard, what ill wind plopped you here?

POET

I've been composing poems in honor of your new city—
oodles of little odes, some dedication-anthems,
songs for soprano voice, a lyric or two
à la Simonides—

PISTHETAIROS

How long has your little poetic mill
been grinding out this chaff?

POET

Why, simply ages.
Long, long since my Muse commenced to sing
Cloudcuckooland in all her orisons.

PISTHETAIROS

Long ago?
But that's impossible. This city's still a baby.
I just now gave birth. I just baptised her.

POET

Ah, but swift are the mouths of the Muses,
more swift than steeds the galloping news
of the Muses!

He turns to the altar and with outstretched hands invokes it in Pindaric parody.

O Father,
Founder of Etna,*
of thy bounty give,
O Hiero, O Homonym,
Great Hero of the Fire,
just one slender sliv-
-er to my desire,
some tidbit to savor,
some token of favor—

PISTHETAIROS

You know, I think we'd better bribe this beggar bard
to leave before we die of doggerel.

To the Acolyte.

—You there,
strip and let the beggar poet have your overcoat.

He hands the coat to the Poet.

Dress.
Why, you poor poet, you're shivering with cold.

POET

My Muse accepts with thanks
this modest donation.

But first, before I leave,
one brief quotation,
a snatch of Pindar
you might ponder—

PISTHETAIROS

Gods above, will this poor man's Pindar never leave?

POET

*Undressed amidst the nomad Skyths,**
the Frozen Poet fareth,
as Beastly Cold as Bard may be,
who Next-to-Nothing weareth.

Genius, ah, hath deck'd his Song,
but oh, th' Ingratitude!
Whilst other Blokes be warm as Toast,
the Poet's damn near Nude.

You catch my drift?

PISTHETAIROS

Yes, I catch your drift.
You want some underwear.

To the Acolyte.

All right, off with it, lad.
We can't allow our delicate poets to freeze to death.
And now clear out, will you?

POET

I go, I go,
but first my final valediction to this little village—

Singing.

O Muse on golden throne,
Muse with chattering teeth
sing this capitol of cold,
this frigorifical city!

I have been where the glebe is frozen with frore.
I have traipsed where the furrows are sown with snow.
Alalai!
Alalai!
G'bye.

Exit Poet.

PISTHETAIROS

Well, how do you like that? Griping about the cold
after making off with an entire new winter outfit!
And how in the name of heaven did that poetic plague
discover us so fast?

To the naked and shivering Acolyte.

—You there, to work again.
Take up your laver and circle the altar, boy,

and we'll resume our inaugural sacrifice once again.
Quiet now, everyone.

As Pisthetairos approaches the altar with the sacrificial knife, an itinerant Prophet with a great open tome of oracles makes his appearance.

PROPHET

HALT! Forbear, I say!
Let no one touch the victim.

PISTHETAIROS

Who the hell are you,
may I ask?

PROPHET

I am a Prophet, sir, in person.

PISTHETAIROS

Then beat it.

PROPHET

Ah, the naughty wee scamp.
But we mustn't scoff.
Friend, I have brought you an oracle of the prophet Bakis,
transparently alluding to the city of Cloudcuckooland.

PISTHETAIROS

Why did you wait till after I founded my city
before disgorging this revelation of yours?

PROPHET

Alas,
I could not come. The Inner Voice said No.

PISTHETAIROS

I suppose we'll have to hear you expound your oracle.

PROPHET

Listen—
LO, IN THAT DAY WHEN THE WOLF AND THE CROW
DO FOREGATHER AND COMPANION,
AND DOMICILE IN THE AIR, AT THAT POINT
WHERE KORINTH KISSETH SIKYON*—

PISTHETAIROS

Look here, what has Korinth got to do with me?

PROPHET

Why,
it's ambiguous, of course. Korinth signifies "air."

Resuming.

PRESENT, I SAY, A WHITE SHEEP TO PANDORA,
BUT TO THE SEER WHO BRINGS MY BEHEST:
IN PRIMIS, A WARM WINTER COAT
PLUS A PAIR OF SANDALS (THE BEST)—

PISTHETAIROS
The *best* sandals, eh?

PROPHET
Yup. Look in the book.

Resuming.

ITEM, A GOBLET OF WINE,
ITEM, A GIBLET OF GOAT—

PISTHETAIROS
Giblet? It says giblet?

PROPHET
Yup. Look in the book.

Resuming.

IF, O BLESSÈD YOUTH, THOU DOST AS I ENJOIN,
REGAL EAGLE WINGS THIS VERY DAY ARE THINE.*
NOT SO MUCH AS PIGEON FLUFF, IF THOU DECLINE.

PISTHETAIROS
It really says that?

PROPHET
Yup. Look in the book.

PISTHETAIROS
Drawing out a huge tome from under his cloak.
You know, your oracles somehow don't mesh with mine,
and I got these from Apollo's mouth.
Listen—

LO, IF IT CHANCE THAT SOME FAKER INTRUDE,
TROUBLING THY WORSHIP AND SCROUNGING FOR FOOD,
LET HIS RIBS BE BASHED
AND HIS TESTICLES MASHED—

PROPHET
I suspect you're bluffing.

PISTHETAIROS
Nope. Look in the book.

Resuming.

SMITE ON, I SAY, IF ANY PROPHET SHOULD COME,
YEA, THOUGH HE SOARETH LIKE THE SWALLOW.
FOR THE GREATER THE FAKER,* THE HARDER HIS BUM
SHOULD BE BATTERED.

GOOD LUCK.

Signed,

APOLLO.

PROPHET

Honest? It says that?

PISTHETAIROS

Yup. Look in the book.

Suddenly throwing his tome at him and beating him.

Take that!

And that!

And that!

PROPHET

Ouch. Help!

PISTHETAIROS

Scat. Go hawk your prophecies somewhere else.

Exit Prophet. From the other side enters the geometrician and surveyor Meton, his arms loaded with surveying instruments.*

METON

The occasion that hath hied me hither—

PISTHETAIROS

Not another!

State your business, stranger. What's your racket?
What tragic error brings you here?

METON

My purpose here
is a geodetic survey of the atmosphere of Cloudcuckooland
and the immediate allocation of all this aerial area
into cubic acres.

PISTHETAIROS

Who are *you*?

METON

Who am *I*?

Why, Meton, of course. Who else could *I* be?
Geometer to Hellas by special appointment.
Also Kolonos.

PISTHETAIROS

And those tools?

METON

Celestial rules,

of course.

Now attend, sir.

Taken *in extenso,*

our welkin resembles a cosmical charcoal oven*
or potbellied stove worked by the convection principle,
though vaster. Now then, with the flue as my base,
and twirling the calipers thus, I obtain the azimuth,
whence, by calibrating the arc or radial sine—
you follow me, friend?

PISTHETAIROS

No, I don't follow you.

METON

No matter. Now then, by training the theodolite here
on the vectored zenith tangent to the Apex A,
I deftly square the circle, whose conflux, or C,
I designate as the center or axial hub of Cloudcuckooland,
whence, like global spokes or astral radii,
broad boulevards diverge centrifugally, forming,
as it were—

PISTHETAIROS

Why, this man's a regular Thales!

Whispering confidentially.

Pssst. Meton.

METON

Sir?

PISTHETAIROS

I've taken quite a shine to you.
Take my advice, friend, and decamp while there's still time.

METON

You anticipate danger, you mean?

PISTHETAIROS

The kind of danger
one meets in Sparta. You know, nasty little riots,
a few foreigners beaten up or murdered, knifings,
fighting in the streets and so on.

METON

Dear me, you mean
there might actually be revolution?

PISTHETAIROS

I certainly hope not.

METON

Then what *is* the trouble?

PISTHETAIROS

The new law. You see,
attempted fraud is now punishable by thrashing.

METON

Er, perhaps I'd best be going.

PISTHETAIROS

I'm half afraid
you're just a bit too late.
Yes!
Look out!
Here comes your thrashing!

He batters Meton with a surveying rod.

METON

HALP! MURDER!

PISTHETAIROS

I warned you. Go survey some other place, will you?

Exit Meton. From the other side enters an Inspector, dressed in a magnificent military uniform and swaggering imperiously.*

INSPECTOR

Fetch me the Mayor, yokel.

PISTHETAIROS

Who's this popinjay?

INSPECTOR

Inspector-general of Cloudcuckooland County, sir,
invested, I might add, with plenary powers—

PISTHETAIROS

Invested?
On whose authority?

INSPECTOR

Why, the powers vested in me
by virtue of this piddling piece of paper here
signed by one Teleas of Athens.

PISTHETAIROS

Look. Let me propose
a little deal, friend. I'll pay you off right now,
provided you leave the city.

INSPECTOR

A capital suggestion.
As it so happens, my presence is urgently required
at home. They're having one of their Great Debates.
The Persian crisis, you know.*

PISTHETAIROS

Really? Splendid.
I'll pay you off right now.

Violently beating the Inspector.

Take that!
And that!

INSPECTOR

What does this outrage mean?

PISTHETAIROS

The payoff. Round One
of the Great Debate.

INSPECTOR

But this is mutiny! Insubordination!

To the Chorus.

Gentlemen, I call on you Birds to bear me witness
that this man wilfully assaulted an Inspector.

PISTHETAIROS

Shoo, fellow,
and take your ballot-boxes with you* when you go.

Exit Inspector.

What confounded gall! Sending us one of their Inspectors
before we've even finished the Inaugural Service.

Enter an itinerant Legislator reading from a huge volume of laws.*

LEGISLATOR

BE IT HEREBY PROVIDED THAT IF ANY CLOUD-CUCKOOLANDER SHALL WILFULLY INJURE OR WRONG ANY CITIZEN OF ATHENS—

PISTHETAIROS

Gods, what now? Not *another* bore with a book?

LEGISLATOR

A seller of laws and statutes, sir, at your service.
Fresh shipment of by-laws on special sale
for only—

PISTHETAIROS

Perhaps you'd better demonstrate your wares.

LEGISLATOR

Reading.

BE IT HEREBY PROVIDED BY LAW THAT FROM THE DATE SPECIFIED BELOW
THE WEIGHTS AND MEASURES OF THE CLOUD-CUCKOOLANDERS ARE TO BE ADJUSTED
TO THOSE IN EFFECT AMONG THE OLOPHYXIANS—

PISTHETAIROS

Pummelling him.

By god, I'll Olo-phyx you!

LEGISLATOR

Hey, mister, stop!

PISTHETAIROS

Get lost, you and your laws, or I'll carve mine
on the skin of your tail.

Exit Legislator. Enter Inspector.

INSPECTOR

I summon the defendant Pisthetairos
to stand trial in court on charges of assault and battery
not later than April.

PISTHETAIROS

Good gods, are *you* back too?

He thrashes Inspector who runs off. Re-enter Legislator.

LEGISLATOR

IF ANY MAN, EITHER BY WORD OR ACTION, DO IMPEDE OR RESIST
A MAGISTRATE IN THE PROSECUTION OF HIS OFFICIAL DUTIES, OR REFUSE
TO WELCOME HIM WITH THE COURTESY PRESCRIBED BY LAW—

PISTHETAIROS

Great thundery Zeus, are *you* back here too?

He drives the Legislator away. Re-enter Inspector.

INSPECTOR

I'll have you sacked. What's more, I'm suing you
for a fat two thousand.

PISTHETAIROS

By Zeus, I'll fix you
and your blasted ballot boxes once and for all!

Exit Inspector under a barrage of blows. Re-enter Legislator.

LEGISLATOR

Remember that evening when you crapped in court?

PISTHETAIROS

Dammit.

Someone arrest that pest!

Exit Legislator.

And this time stay away!

But enough's enough.

We'll take our goat inside

and finish this sacrifice in peace and privacy.

Exit Pisthetairos into house, followed by Acolyte with basket and slaves with the sacrifice.

CHORUS*

Wheeling sharply and facing the audience.

Praise Ye the Birds, O Mankind!
Our sway is over all.
The eyes of the Birds observe you:
we see if any fall.

We watch and guard all growing green,
protecting underwing
this lavish lovely life of earth,
its birth and harvesting.

We smite the mite, we slay the pest,
all ravagers that seize
the good that burgeons in your buds
or ripens on your trees.

Whatever makes contagion come,
whatever blights or seeks
to raven in this green shall die,
devoured by our beaks.

KORYPHAIOS

You know, gentlemen, that proclamation that's posted everywhere in town—

WANTED, DEAD OR ALIVE! DIAGORAS OF MELOS.

ONE TALENT'S REWARD FOR ANY MAN WHO KILLS THE TYRANT!

Well, we Birds have published our own public proclamation:—

"HEAR YE!

WANTED DEAD OR ALIVE!

PHILOKRATES

THE BIRDSELLER!

DEAD, 1 TALENT'S REWARD. 4 TALENTS IF TAKEN ALIVE,

BUT PROCEED WITH CAUTION. THIS MAN IS DANGEROUS.

WANTED FOR MURDER AND CRUELTY TO BIRDS ON THE FOLLOWING COUNTS:—

For the Spitting of Finches, seven to a skewer;
item, for Disfiguring Thrushes by means of inflation;
item, for Insertion of Feathers in Blackbirds' nostrils;
item, for Unlawful Detention of Pigeons in Cages;
item, for Felonious Snaring of Innocent Pigeons;
item, for Flagrant Misuse of Traps and Decoy-devices."

So much for Philokrates.
But as for you, dear spectators,
we give you solemn warning.
If any boy in this audience
has as his hobby the keeping of Birds in captivity or cages,
we urgently suggest that you let your pets go free. Disobey,
and we'll catch *you* and lock you up in a wicker cage
or stake you out to a snare as a little decoyboy!

CHORUS

How blessèd is our breed of Bird,
dressed in fluff and feather,
that, when hard winter holds the world,
wears no clothes whatever.

And blazoned summer hurts no Bird,
for when the sun leaps high,
and, priestly in that hellish light,
the chaunting crickets cry,

the Birds keep cool among the leaves
or fan themselves with flight;
while winter days we're snug in caves
and nest with nymphs at night.

But Spring is joy, when myrtle blooms
and Graces dance in trio,
and quiring Birds cantatas sing
vivace e con brio.

KORYPHAIOS

Finally, gentlemen, a few brief words about the First Prize
and the striking advantages of casting your vote for *THE BIRDS*
of Aristophanes—
advantages compared to which that noble prince,
poor Paris of Troy, was very shabbily bribed
indeed.
First on our list of gifts comes a little item
that every judge's greedy heart must be panting to possess.
I refer, of course, to those lovely little owls of Laurium,
sometimes called the coin of the realm.
Yes, gentlemen,
these lovely owls, we promise, will flock to you by the thousand,
settle down in your wallets for good and hatch you a brood
of nice little nest eggs.
Secondly, gentlemen, we promise
to redesign your houses.
See, the sordid tenements vanish,
while in their place rise splendid shrines whose dizzy heights,*
like Eagle-eyries, hang in heaven.
Are you perhaps
a politician faced with the vexing problem of insufficient plunder?
Friend, your problems are over. Accept as our gift to you
a pair of Buzzard claws designed with special hooks
for more efficient grafting.
As for heavy eaters,
those suffering from biliousness, heartburn, acid indigestion
or other stomach ailments and upsets, we proudly present them
with special lifetime Bird-crops, guaranteed to be virtually
indestructible.
If, however, gentlemen, you withhold your vote,
you'd better do as the statues do and wear a metal lid
against our falling guano.
I repeat.
Vote against *THE BIRDS,*
and every Bird in town will cover you with—vituperation!

The Chorus turns and faces the stage. Enter Pisthetairos.

PISTHETAIROS

Birds, the omens are favorable. Our sacrifice has been auspicious.
But I wonder where in the world our messenger is
with news about our wall.

A sound of furious panting offstage.

Aha. There he is now.
I'd recognize that awful huffing and puffing anywhere.
Those are the true Olympic pants and puffs I hear.

Enter Messenger, panting.

MESSENGER
Where anh where hoo where uh where can he be?
Where is Pisthetairos hanh?

PISTHETAIROS
Here hunh here.

MESSENGER
Whew, the wall's all up! The wall's done!

PISTHETAIROS
Splendid.

MESSENGER
What a wonderful, whopping, well-built wall! Whew!
Why, that wall's so wide that if you hitched up
four Trojan Horses to two huge chariots
with those braggarts Proxenides in one and Theogenes in the other,
they could pass head-on. *That's* the width of your wall!

PISTHETAIROS
Wow, what a width!

MESSENGER
And what a height! Measured it myself.
Six hundred feet high!

PISTHETAIROS
Poseidon, what a height!
Who in the world could have built a wall like that?

MESSENGER
The Birds.
Nobody but Birds.
Not one Egyptian.
No bricklayers. No carpenters. Or masons.
Only the birds. I couldn't credit my eyes.
What a sight it was:
Thirty thousand Cranes
whose crops were all loaded with boulders and stones,*
while the Rails with their beaks blocked out the rocks
and thousands of Storks came bringing up bricks
and Plovers and Terns and seabirds by billions
transported the water right up to the sky!

PISTHETAIROS

Heavens!

But which Birds hauled the mortar up?

MESSENGER

Herons,

in hods.

PISTHETAIROS

But how was the mortar heaped in the hods?

MESSENGER

Gods, now *that* was a triumph of engineering skill!
Geese burrowed their feet like shovels beneath
and heaved it over their heads to the hods.

PISTHETAIROS

They did?

Ah Feet! Ah, Feet! O incredible feat!*
What can compete with a pair of feet?

MESSENGER

And, sir,

you should have seen the Ducks with their aprons on
go hauling the bricks! And how the Swallows came
swooping, dangling their trowels behind them like boys,
and darting and dipping with mouthfuls of mortar!

PISTHETAIROS

Why,

if this is true, then human labor is obsolete.
But what happened next? Who finished off the job?
Who did the woodwork on the wall?

MESSENGER

Mastercraftsmen birds.

It was Pelicans, like carpenters, with handy hatchet-beaks
who hewed the gates, and what with the racket and hubbub
of all that hacking and chopping and hewing and banging,
sir, you'd have sworn it was a shipyard down at the docks.
Or so it sounded to me.

But the gates are done,

the bolts shot home, watchbirds make their rounds
with clanging bells, the guards patrol their beats
and every tower along the circuit of the wall
blazes with its watchfire. And in three words, sir,
all is well.

But I must go and wash my face.

My job is done. The rest is up to you.

Exit Messenger.

KORYPHAIOS

Well,
wasn't it a wonder the way that wall of ours shot up?

PISTHETAIROS

A damn sight too wonderful. If you're asking me,
I think it's all a lie.

—But look what's coming:
another messenger, and a sentry judging by his looks.

*Enter Sentry, whirling on stage in the wild steps of a military dance.**

—What are you, fellow? A soldier or a ballerina?

SENTRY

ALAS! ALACKADAY!

OCHONE!

WOE IS ME!

PISTHETAIROS

Well, what's troubling *you?*

SENTRY

Sir, we are diddled
and undone.

Some god has given us the slip,
I wot not which. Carommed through the gates
out into territorial air. The Daws on guard
never spotted him.

PISTHETAIROS

Gad. A national scandal.
Which god?

SENTRY

We couldn't tell. But he was wearing wings,
that much we know.

PISTHETAIROS

Were Pursuitbirds sent up
to intercept him?

SENTRY

Everything we had took off, sir.
The Sparrowhawk Reserve, thirty thousand Falcons,
every claw-carrying Harrier we could throw
in the sky:—Kestrels, Buzzards, Owls, Eagles,
Vultures, you name it.

Why, the whole atmosphere
is throbbing and buzzing with the whirr of beating wings
as they comb the clouds for that sneaky little god.
if you're asking me, he's not so far away either.
He's hereabouts. I'm sure.

Exit Sentry.

PISTHETAIROS

Where's my bow?
Bring me my sling!
Archerbirds, fall in!
Now shoot to kill.
Dammit, where's my sling?

CHORUS

Now words are weak
and ACTIONS speak
ineffably of War.

Let every Bird
for battle gird:
the gods are at our door!

Rise up, defend
your native land!
Go mobilize the Air!

Immortal spies
now prowl our skies.
And saboteurs. Take care.

KORYPHAIOS

Quiet.
I hear the whirr of beating wings.
Listen. Some god comes whizzing through our air.

With a loud whoosh and a burst of baroque movement and color, Iris descends in the machine. She is a young girl with golden wings and billowing rainbow-colored robes. From her dress and hair, in gracious and extravagant loops of color, pennants and ribbons and streamers trail out behind.

PISTHETAIROS

Ship ahoy!
Belay!
Where are you cruising?
Down anchors!
And stop luffing those wings.
Now who are you? Home Port? Purpose of voyage?

IRIS

I am Iris the fleet.

PISTHETAIROS

Clippership or sloop?

IRIS

What does this mean?

PISTHETAIROS

Some Buzzard flap up
and arrest that bitch.

IRIS

You dare arrest *me*?
What sort of joke is this?

PISTHETAIROS

You'll see, sister.

IRIS

But I must be dreaming. This can't be real.

PISTHETAIROS

What gate did you enter by? Answer, you slut.

IRIS

Gates? What would a goddess know about gates?

PISTHETAIROS

A glib little piece. Just listen to those lies.
—Well, did you report to the Daw on duty at the gate?
Mum, eh?
Where's your Storkpass?

IRIS

I must be mad.

PISTHETAIROS

What? You never even applied?

IRIS

You must be mad.

PISTHETAIROS

Was your form filled out by Colonel Cock
and properly punched?

IRIS

Just let him try!
Why, the very idea!

PISTHETAIROS

So that's your game, is it?
To sneak in here, infiltrate our territorial air,
spy on our city—

IRIS

But where can a poor god go?

PISTHETAIROS

How should I know? But not here, by god!
You're trespassing. What's more, it would serve you right
if I ordered you put to death this very instant.
If ever a god deserved to die, that god is you.

IRIS

But I *can't* die.

PISTHETAIROS

Well, you damn well should.
A pretty pickle it would be if the whole world
obeyed the Birds while you gods got uppity
and defied your betters.
Now then, you aerial yacht,
state your business here.

IRIS

My business? Why,
I am bearing the following message from my father Zeus
to mankind:
"LET HOLOCAUSTS MAKE GLAD THY GODS
AND MUTTON BARBECUES ON BEEFY ALTARS TOAST,
YEA, TILL EVERY STREET DOTH REEK WITH ROAST
AMBROSIALLY."

PISTHETAIROS

Hmm. I think he wants a sacrifice.
But to which gods?

IRIS

To *which* gods? To *us,* of course.
Who else could he mean?

PISTHETAIROS

But that's quite absurd.
You, gods? I mean, really!

IRIS

Name me any other gods.

PISTHETAIROS

Why, the Birds, madam. Birds are now the gods.
Men worship Birds, not gods. Good gods, no!

IRIS

*In the high tragic manner.**

Then beware, O Mole, lest thou court the choler
of the gallèd gods, and Justice with the angry pick
of peevèd Zeus prise up thy pedestals
and topple all thy people, leaving not a smitch;
yea, and forkèd levin sear thee to a crisp,
lambasted low amongst thy mortal porticoes
by lightnings blunderbuss'd, yea—

PISTHETAIROS

Listen, lady,
stow that tragic guff. You're starting to slobber.

And kindly stop twitching.

What do you think I am?

Some poor Lydian or Phrygian slave* you can browbeat with that bogey-talk?

Go back and tell your Zeus

if he messes around with me, I'll fry him to a cinder!
What doth the poet say?*

Aye, with eagles belching levin,
I shall scorch the halls of heav'n,
till Zeus doth frizzle in his juice
and Amphion, e'en Amphion—

—But what am I saying?

How does Amphion fit in here?

Well, no matter.

But you tell your Zeus that if he crosses me, by god,
I'll send six hundred Porphyrions up against him,
and every Bird-Jack of the lot tricked out as a panther.
I'd like to see his face. I remember the time
when one poor piddling little Porphyrion
was one too many for Zeus.

But as for *you,*

Miss Messenger Iris, sail my way once more
and I'll lay my course right up your lovely legs,
and board you at the top.

Mark my words:

you'll be one flabbergasted little goddess
when you feel the triple ram on this old hulk.

IRIS

What a disgusting way to talk.

PISTHETAIROS

Skedaddle, slut.

IRIS

Just you wait till my Father hears about this.

PISTHETAIROS

Heaven defend me from this flying flirt. Beat it!
Go singe some youngster with your lechery, will you?

Exit Iris in the machine.

CHORUS

The gods' attack
has been rolled back,
rebuffed by our Blockade.

Let god and man
now heed our ban:
NO TRANSETHEREAL TRADE!

No more, no more
do victuals soar;
no savory ascends;

and chops and stew
are now taboo:
the party's over, friends!

PISTHETAIROS

You know, it's rather odd about that other messenger
we despatched to earth. He should be back by now.

Enter Messenger in great haste. He throws himself to the ground at Pisthetairos' feet and salaams profoundly.

MESSENGER

O Pisthetairos! O Paragon! O Pink!
Thou Apogee of Genius! Sweet Flower of Finesse!
O Phoenix of Fame! Flimflam's Non-Pareil!
O of every noble attribute the Plus!
O Happy Happy Chap! O Blest! O Most!
O Best!—

oh, balls.

PISTHETAIROS

You were about to say, my friend,
when you so rudely interrupted yourself?

MESSENGER

Rising and crowning Pisthetairos.

Deign, my lord, to accept this crown of solid gold,
proffered in honor of your glorious wisdom and chicane
by an adoring world.

PISTHETAIROS

I am deeply honored sir.
But why should man's election fall on me?

MESSENGER

O fabulous founder of great Cloudcuckooland,
how can you ask such a question? Have you not heard
that Pisthetairos has become the darling of the mortal world,
a name to conjure with? That all mankind
has gone Cloudcuckoolandophile,
madly, utterly?

And yet, only yesterday,
before your dispensation in the skies became a fact,
the Spartan craze had swept the faddish world.
Why, men went mad with mimicry of Sokrates,*
affected long hair, indifferent food,
rustic walking sticks, total bathlessness,
and led, in short, what I can only call
a Spartan existence.
But then suddenly, overnight,
the Birds became the vogue, the *dernier cri*
of human fashion.* And men immediately began
to feather their own nests; to cluck and brood;
play ducks and drakes; grub for chickenfeed;
hatch deals, and being rooked or gulled,
to have their little gooses cooked. But if they grouse,
they still are game.
In sum, the same old life,
but feathered over with the faddish thrills of being
chic.
But the latest word in Birds is names.
The gimpy peddler is tagged Old Partridge now;
Menippos is called Cuckoo; Opountios, Stool Pigeon;
Philokles is the Lark; Theogenes, the Pseudo-Goose;
Lykourgos, Lame Duck; Chairephon is Bats;
Syrakosios, of course, is called the Jaybird,
and as for Meidias, why, he's the Sitting Duck—
and judging from that ugly clobbered beak of his,
no man ever missed.
And that's not all.
Mankind has gone so utterly batty over Birds
that all the latest songs are filled with them—
Swallows, Pigeons, Ducks, Geese, you name it.
Any tune with feathers in it or a pinch or fluff
becomes a hit.
And that's how matters stand
below.
But one last point before I leave.
Vast swarms and coveys of men are on the move,
all migrating here to Cloudcuckooland in quest of wings
and the Feathered Way of Life. Somehow, sir,
you'll have to wing these mortal immigrants.

Exit Messenger.

PISTHETAIROS

Gad!

We'd best get busy.

To a Slave.

—You there.

Run inside.

Stuff every hamper you can find with sets of wings
and tell Manes to bring them out. I'll stay here
to give my greeting to these wingless refugees in person.

Exit Slave.

CHORUS

Upon thy head, Cloudcuckooland,
the crown of praise we set:
O Beautiful for Swarming Skies—

PISTHETAIROS

—Don't count your chickens yet.

CHORUS

This feather'd isle, this pinion'd place,
where martyr-Birds have bled,
where men aspire on wings of fluff—

Enter Manes, slowly and empty-handed.

PISTHETAIROS

—Their legs are made of lead.

Exit Manes.

CHORUS

What greater bliss can men require?
Here the lovely Graces go,
and Wisdom strolls with sweet Desire,
and Peace comes tripping slow.

Enter Manes carrying two wings.

PISTHETAIROS

She's miles ahead of Manes.

—Dammit, blockhead, move!

CHORUS

To work, dull clod! Heave-ho the wings!

Exit Manes.

To Pisthetairos.

Now show him you're the master.
Flog him, thrash him—

Enter Manes with two more wings.

PISTHETAIROS

—What's the use?
A mule could manage faster.

Exit Manes.

CHORUS

Now sort the wings in pinion-piles
by order of professions:
Seabird's wings for nautical types,
Warblers' for musicians—

Enter Manes with three wings.

PISTHETAIROS

—So help me, Kestrels, if I don't bash your head
to a pulp, you lazy, stupid, bungling ass!

Beats him. Manes scurries off, instantly reappearing with crates and hampers of wings which he quickly dumps and sorts into the appropriate piles. Suddenly from offstage is heard the tenor voice of Delinquent, singing:

*If I had the wings of an Eagle,**
o'er this barren blue brine I would fly . . .

PISTHETAIROS

That messenger of ours was telling the truth, by god.
Here comes someone crooning Eagle-ballads.

Enter Delinquent, a strapping boy in his teens.*

DELINQUENT

Some kicks!
There's nothin' on earth like flyin'! Whee!
Chee,
Cloudcuckooland's the roost for me! Hey, man,
I'm bats about the Birds! I'm with it chum!
I wanna be a Bird! I want your way of life!

PISTHETAIROS

Which way? We Birds have bushels of ways.

DELINQUENT

If it's strictly for the Birds, then it's for me, man.
But best of all I like that splendid custom you've got
that permits a little Bird to choke his daddy dead.

PISTHETAIROS

True. We think it very manly of a young Bird
if he walks up and takes a poke at his old man.

DELINQUENT

That's it, Dad.
Exactly why I'm here. I want to throttle
the old man and inherit his jack.

PISTHETAIROS

One moment.

We Birds observe another custom older still.
You'll find it preserved in the Scrolls of the Storks. I quote:
"ONCE THE AGÈD STORK HATH REARED HIS BROOD
AND HIS CHICKS HAVE MADE THEIR MAIDEN FLIGHT ALONE,
THEY MUST IN TURN SUPPORT THEIR FATHER IN HIS AGE."

DELINQUENT

A fat lot of good I've got from coming here, chum,
if I have to go back home and support the old man.

PISTHETAIROS

I tell you what. You seem a decent lad,
and I'll adopt you as our city's official Mascot-Bird.
But first some good advice I received as a toddler
at my mother's knee:
Don't drub your dad.
Take this wing instead.
With your other hand,
accept this spur. Here, your helmet is this crest.
Now march off, rookie. Drill, stand your guard,
live on your pay and let your father be.
You look aggressive: flutter off to Thrace.
There's fighting there.

DELINQUENT

By god, I think you're right.
What's more, I'm game.

PISTHETAIROS

You damn well better be.

Exit Delinquent. From the other side enters the dithyrambic poet Kinesias. His splay-footed galumphing entrance is in sharp contrast to his aerial pretensions.

KINESIAS

*On gossamer I go,**
delicately wending,
up, up, up the airy stairs
of Poesy ascending—

PISTHETAIROS

By god, we'll need a boatload of wings at least
to get this limping poet off the ground!

KINESIAS

—forth through the Vast Unknown,
original, alone—

PISTHETAIROS
Welcome, Kinesias, bard of balsa-wood!
What made you whirl your splay-foot hither, bard?

KINESIAS
I yearn, I burn, thou know'st it well,
to be a lilting Philomel.

PISTHETAIROS
A little less lilt, please. Could you stoop to prose?

KINESIAS
Wings, dull wight, wings!
Vouchsafe me wings
to percolate amidst the churning scud and rack
of yon conceited clouds from which I'll pluck and cull
tornado similes of blizzard speech.

PISTHETAIROS
You mean you plagiarize the clouds?

KINESIAS
Ah, my dear sir,
but our poet's craft depends completely on the clouds.*
Why, the most resplendent poem is but the insubstantial shimmer
refracted from that blue and bubbled murk of froth,
that featherfillip'd air.
Judge for yourself.

PISTHETAIROS
I won't.

KINESIAS
Ah, but you shall, dear boy, you shall.
I'll do my Aerial Aria, and just for you.
Ready?

Singing.

Now wingèd wraiths
of the hovering Plover
over yon Ether rove—

PISTHETAIROS
GALE WARNINGS POSTED! STAND BY, ALL SHIPS AT SEA!

KINESIAS
—over the billows pillow'd aloft,
in the buffeting gust of the gathered gale—

PISTHETAIROS
By god, I'll give you some buffets you won't like!

He snatches a pair of large wings from a pile and beats Kinesias who runs about, still spouting.

KINESIAS

—now north, now south,
and where they fare, fare I,
cutting my wake
on the harborless lake
of the featherfillip'd sky.

Get that, old boy? A catchy figure, what?

PISTHETAIROS

Lashing him again.

Get that? What? No taste for featherfillips, poet?

KINESIAS

What a beastly way to welcome a poetic genius
for whose services the entire civilized world competes!

PISTHETAIROS

Then stay with us. You can train an All-Bird
Chorus. Leotrophides will conduct his own compositions.
He likes the delicate stuff.

KINESIAS

Durst despise me, sir?
Know then, I ne'er shall cease from Poesy
until with wings I waltz upon Cloudcuckooland.
Farewell.

Exit Kinesias. Enter an Informer in a tattered coat, singing.

INFORMER

*What suspicious Birds are these**
that own no clothes and house in trees?
O Cuckoo, Cuckoo, tell me true!

PISTHETAIROS

We've passed the nuisance stage. This is crisis.
Here comes a warbler humming treason-trills.

INFORMER

Ho!
Again I cry:
O Cuckoo, Cuckoo, tell me true!

PISTHETAIROS

I think it must be an epigram on his tattered coat.
He's so cold he's calling the Cuckoo to bring the Spring.*
Poets are always talking out loud to Cuckoos in April.

INFORMER

You there. Where's the guy who's handing out the wings?

PISTHETAIROS
You're looking at him now. What do *you* want, friend?

INFORMER
Wings, fellow, wings! Got it?

PISTHETAIROS
I get it:
to hide the holes in your coat.*

INFORMER
Listen, Buster:
my business is the indictment of islands for subversive activities.*
You see in me a professional informer.

PISTHETAIROS
A splendid calling.

INFORMER
Also an *agent provocateur* of lawsuits and investigations.
That's why I want the wings. They'd come in handy
for whizzing around the islands delivering my indictments
and handing out subpoenas in person.

PISTHETAIROS
I see. And these wings
would increase your efficiency?

INFORMER
Increase my efficiency? Impossible.
But they'd help me dodge the pirates I meet en route.
Then, coming home, I'd load the crops of the Cranes
with writs and suits for ballast.

PISTHETAIROS
And *that's* your trade?
A husky lad like yourself earning his livelihood
by indicting foreigners?

INFORMER
But what am I supposed to do?
I don't know how to dig.

PISTHETAIROS
Great Zeus Almighty,
Aren't there enough honest means of earning a living
without this dirty little dodge of hatching suits?

INFORMER
Listen, mister: it's wings I want, not words.

PISTHETAIROS
But my words *are* wings.

INFORMER

Your words are *wings?*

PISTHETAIROS

But of course. How else do you think mankind won its wings
if not from words?

INFORMER

From words?

PISTHETAIROS

Wings from words.
You know the old men, how they loll around at the barbershop*
grousing and bitching about the younger generation?—
"Thanks to that damned Dieitrephes* and his damned advice,"
growls one, "my boy has flown the family nest
to take a flier on the horses."
"Hell,"
pipes another, "you should see that kid of mine:
he's gone so damn batty over those tragic plays,
he flies into fits of ecstacy and gets goosebumps
all over."

INFORMER

And *that's* how words give wings?

PISTHETAIROS

Right.
Through dialectic the mind of man takes wing and soars;
he is morally and spiritually uplifted. And so I hoped
with words of good advice to wing you on your way
toward some honest trade.

INFORMER

It just won't work.

PISTHETAIROS

But why won't it?

INFORMER

I can't disgrace the family name.
We've been informers now for several generations,
you see.
So give me wings—Hawk's or Kestrel's
will suit me fine, but anything's all right by me
provided they're fast and light. I'll slip them on,
dart out to the islands with stacks of subpoenas and summons,
whizz back home to defend the case in court,
then zip right back to the islands again.

PISTHETAIROS

I get it.

When they arrive, they find their case is lost by default;
they've been condemned *in absentia.*

INFORMER

You've got it.

PISTHETAIROS

And while they're coming here, you're going there
to confiscate their property? Right?

INFORMER

You've got it.

I'll whirr around like a top.

PISTHETAIROS

Right. I've got it:

you're a top. And guess what I've got here for you:
a lovely little set of Korkyrean wings.

He pulls out a whip.

INFORMER

Hey, that's a whip!

PISTHETAIROS

Not a whip, it's wings

to make your little top go round.

He lashes Informer with the whip.

Got it?

INFORMER

Ouch! Owwooooo!

PISTHETAIROS

Flap your wings, Birdie!

That's it, old top, wobble on your way!

By god,

I'll make this legal whirligig go round!

Exit Informer under the lash. Pisthetairos signals to his slaves to pick up the piles of wings.

—Hey,

you there. Gather up the wings and bring them inside.

Exeunt Pisthetairos and Attendants with the hampers of wings.

CHORUS*

Many the marvels I have seen,
 the wonders on land and sea;
but the strangest sight I ever saw
 was the weird KLEONYMOS-tree.

It grows in faraway places;
   its lumber looks quite stout,
but the wood is good for nothing,
   for the heart is rotten out.

In Spring it grows gigantic
   with sycophantic green,
and bitter buds of slander
   on every bough are seen.

But when, like war, cold winter comes,
   this strange KLEONYMOS yields,
instead of leaves like other trees,
   a crop of coward's shields.

And far away (but not so far),
   we saw a second wonder,
a place of awful, dismal dark—
   when the sun goes under.

And there by day dead heroes come
   and talk with living men,
and while it's light no ghost will hurt,
   but when it's dark again,

then thieves and ghosts take common shape,
   and who knows which is which?
So wise men dodge that dive at night—
   but most of all the rich.

For any man who ventures in
   may meet ORESTES there,
the ghost who paralyzes men,
   the thief who strips them bare.

Enter Prometheus, so muffled in blankets as to be completely unrecognizable. His every motion is furtive, but his furtiveness is hampered by an immense umbrella which he carries underneath his blankets. He speaks in a whisper.*

PROMETHEUS

Easy does it. I hope old Zeus can't see me.

To a Bird.

Psst. Where's Pisthetairos?

PISTHETAIROS

What in the world is *this?*
—Who are you, blanket?

PROMETHEUS

Shh. Are there any gods
on my trail?

PISTHETAIROS

Gods? No, not a god in sight.
Who *are* you?

PROMETHEUS

What's the time? Is it dark yet?

PISTHETAIROS

You want the time? It's still early afternoon.
Look, who the hell *are* you?

PROMETHEUS

Is it milking-time, or later?

PISTHETAIROS

Look, you stinking bore—

PROMETHEUS

What's the weather doing?
How's the visibility? Clear skies? Low ceiling?

PISTHETAIROS

Raising his stick.

By god,
if you won't talk—

PROMETHEUS

Dark, eh? Good. I'm coming out.

Uncovers.

PISTHETAIROS

Hullo: it's Prometheus!

PROMETHEUS

Shh. Don't make a sound.

PISTHETAIROS

What's the matter?

PROMETHEUS

Shh. Don't even whisper my name.
If Zeus spots me here, he'll cook my goose but good.
Now then, if you want to learn the lay of the land
in heaven, kindly open up this umbrella here
and hold it over my head while I'm talking.
Then the gods won't see me.

Pisthetairos takes the umbrella, opens it up, and holds it over Prometheus.

PISTHETAIROS

Say, that's clever.
Prometheus all over.*
—All right. Pop underneath
and give us your news.

PROMETHEUS

Brace yourself.

PISTHETAIROS

Shoot.

PROMETHEUS

Zeus has had it.

PISTHETAIROS

Since when?

PROMETHEUS

Since the moment
you founded the city of Cloudcuckooland. Since that day
not a single sacrifice, not even a whiff of smoke,
no savories, no roast, nothing at all
has floated up to heaven. In consequence, my friend,
Olympos is starving to death. And that's not the worst of it.
All the Stone Age gods* from the hill country
have gone wild with hunger, screaming and gibbering away
like a lot of savages. And what's more, they've threatened war
unless Zeus succeeds in getting your Bird-embargo lifted
and the tidbit shipments back on the move once more.

PISTHETAIROS

You mean to say there are *other* gods in Heaven?
Stone Age gods?

PROMETHEUS

Stone Age gods for Stone Age people.
Exekestides must have something to worship.

PISTHETAIROS

Heavens,
they *must* be savages. But what do you call them?

PROMETHEUS

We call them Triballoi.

PISTHETAIROS

Triballoi? From the same root
as our word "trouble," I suppose.

PROMETHEUS

Very probably, I think.

But give me your attention. At present these Triballoi gods
have joined with Zeus to send an official embassy
to sue for peace. Now here's the policy you must follow:
flatly reject any offers of peace they make you
until Zeus agrees to restore his sceptre to the Birds
and consents to give you Miss Universe* as your wife.

PISTHETAIROS

But who's Miss Universe?

PROMETHEUS

A sort of Beauty Queen,
the sign of Empire and the symbol of divine supremacy.
It's she who keeps the keys to Zeus' thunderbolts
and all his other treasures—Divine Wisdom,
Good Government, Common Sense, Naval Bases,
Slander, Libel, Political Graft, Sops to the Voters—

PISTHETAIROS

And *she* keeps the keys?

PROMETHEUS

Take it from me, friend.
Marry Miss Universe and the world is yours.
—You understand
why I had to tell you this? As Prometheus, after all,
my philanthropy is proverbial.

PISTHETAIROS

Yes, we worship you
as the inventor of the barbecue.*

PROMETHEUS

Besides, I loathe the gods.

PISTHETAIROS

The loathing's mutual, I know.

PROMETHEUS

Just call me Timon:
I'm a misanthrope of gods.
—But I must be running along.
Give me my parasol. If Zeus spots me now,
he'll think I'm an ordinary one-god procession. I'll pretend
to be the girl behind the boy behind the basket.

PISTHETAIROS

Here—take this stool and watch yourself march by.

Exit Prometheus in solemn procession, draped in his blanket, the umbrella in one hand, the stool in the other. Pisthetairos and the Attendants retire.

CHORUS*

There lies a marsh in Webfoot Land,
   the Swamp of Dismal Dread,
and there we saw foul SOKRATES
   come calling up the dead.

And there that cur PEISANDROS came
   to see if he could see
the soul he'd lost while still alive
   by dying cowardly.

He brought a special sacrifice,
   a little camel lamb;
then, like Odysseus, slit its throat—
   he slit its throat and ran!

And then a phantom shape flew down,
   a specter cold and wan,
and on the camel's blood he pounced—
   the vampire CHAIREPHON!

Enter the Peace Delegation from Olympos: first, Poseidon, a god of immense and avuncular dignity, carrying a trident; then Herakles with lion skin and club, a god with the character and build of a wrestler and an appetite to match; and finally Triballos, hopelessly tangled up in the unfamiliar robes of Olympian civilization.

POSEIDON

Here we are. And there before us, ambassadors,
lies Cloudcuckooland.

Triballos, by now hopelessly snarled up in his robes, trips and falls flat on his face.

—Damn you! Back on your feet,
you hulking oaf. Look, you've got your robes
all twisted up.
No. Screw them around to the right.
This way. Where's your dignity, you heavenly hick?
O Democracy, I fear your days are numbered
if Heaven's diplomatic corps is recruited like this!
Dammit, stop twitching! Gods, I've never seen
a gawkier god than you!
—Look here, Herakles,
how should we proceed in your opinion?

HERAKLES

You hoid me,
Poseidon. If I had my way, I'd throttle the guy,
any guy, what dared blockade the gods.

POSEIDON

My dear nephew,
have you forgotten that the purpose of our mission here
is to treat for peace?

HERAKLES

I'd throttle him all the more.

Enter Pisthetairos, followed by Attendants with cooking utensils. He pointedly ignores the presence of the Divine Delegation.

PISTHETAIROS

To Attendants.

Hand me the cheese grater. Vinegar, please. All right,
now the cheese. Poke up that fire, somebody.

POSEIDON

Mortal, three immortal gods give you greeting.

Dead Silence.

Mortal, three immortal—

PISTHETAIROS

Shush: I'm slicing pickles.

HERAKLES

Hey, what kind of meat is dat?

PISTHETAIROS

Those are jailbirds
sentenced to death on the charge of High Treason
against the Sovereign Birds.

HERAKLES

And dat luscious gravy
gets poured on foist?

PISTHETAIROS

Looking up for the first time.

Why hullo there: it's Herakles!
What do you want?

POSEIDON

Mortal, as the official spokesman
for the Divine Delegation, I venture to suggest that—

PISTHETAIROS

Holding up an empty bottle.

Drat it. We're out of oil.

HERAKLES

Out of oil?
Say, dat's a shame. Boids should be basted good.

POSEIDON

—As I was on the point of saying, official Olympos
regards the present hostilities as utterly pointless.
Further, I venture to observe that you Birds
have a great deal to gain from a kindlier Olympos.
I might mention, for instance, a supply of clean rainwater
for your Birdbaths and a perpetual run, say,
of halcyon days. On some such terms as these
we are formally empowered by Zeus to sign the articles
of peace.

PISTHETAIROS

Poseidon, you forget: it was not the Birds
who began this war. Moreover, peace is our desire
as much as yours. And if you gods stand prepared
to treat in good faith, I see no obstacle to peace.
None whatsoever. Our sole demand is this:
Zeus must restore his royal sceptre to the Birds.
If this one trifling concession seems agreeable to you,
I invite you all to dinner.

HERAKLES

Youse has said enough.
I vote Yes.

POSEIDON

You contemptible, idiotic glutton!
Would you dethrone your own Father?

PISTHETAIROS

I object, Poseidon.
Look at it in this light.
Can you gods be unaware
that you actually stand to increase, not diminish your power,
by yielding your present supremacy to the Birds? Why,
as things stand now, men go skulking around
under cover of the clouds, with impunity committing perjury
and in your name too. But conclude alliance with the Birds,
gentlemen, and your problems are over forever. How?
Suppose, for instance, some man swears a solemn oath
by Zeus and the Raven and then breaks his word. Suddenly
down swoops a Raven when he's least suspecting it
and pecks out his eyes!

POSEIDON

Holy Poseidon! You know,
I think you've got something there.

HERAKLES

Youse is so right.

POSEIDON

To Triballos.

What do you say?

TRIBALLOS

Fapple gleep.

HERAKLES

Dat's Stone Age for Yeah.*

PISTHETAIROS

And that's not all.
Suppose some fellow vows to make a sacrifice to the gods
and then later changes his mind or tries to procrastinate,
thinking, *The mills of the gods grind slow;*
well, so do mine.
We Birds, I can promise you,
will put a stop to sophistry like that.

POSEIDON

Stop it? But how?

PISTHETAIROS

Someday our man will be busily counting up his cash
or lolling around in the tub, singing away,
and a Kite will dive down like a bolt from the blue,
snatch up two of his sheep or a wad of cash
and whizz back up to the gods with the loot.

HERAKLES

Friend,
youse is right. Zeus should give dat sceptre
back to the Boids.

POSEIDON

What do *you* think, Triballos?

HERAKLES

Threatening him with his club.

Vote Yes, bub, or I'll drub youse.

TRIBALLOS

Schporckl nu?
Momp gapa birdschmoz kluk.

HERAKLES

See? He votes wid me.

POSEIDON

If you both see eye to eye, I'll have to go along.

HERAKLES
Dat does it. Hey, youse. The sceptre's yours.

PISTHETAIROS
Dear me, I nearly forgot one trifling condition.
We Birds willingly waive any claim we might have to Hera:
Zeus can have her. We don't object in the slightest.
But I must have Miss Universe as my wife. On that demand
I stand absolutely firm.

POSEIDON
Then you won't have peace.
Good afternoon.

The Delegation prepares to leave, Herakles with great reluctance.

PISTHETAIROS
It's all the same to me.
—Oh chef:
make the gravy thick.

HERAKLES
God alive, Poseidon, where in the world
is youse going? Are we going to war for the sake of a dame?

POSEIDON
What alternative would you suggest?

HERAKLES
Peace, peace!

POSEIDON
You poor fool, don't you realize that you're being tricked?
What's more, you're only hurting yourself.
Listen here:
if Zeus should abdicate his throne in favor of the Birds
and then die, you'd be left a pauper. Whereas now
you're the legal heir of Zeus. Heir, in fact,
to everything he owns.

PISTHETAIROS
Watch your step, Herakles.
You're being hoodwinked.

Taking Herakles by the arm and withdrawing a little.

—Now, just step aside with me.
I have something to tell you.
Look, you poor chump,
your uncle's pulling a fast one. Not one cent
of Zeus' enormous estate will ever come to you.
You see, my friend, you're a bastard.

HERAKLES

What's dat, fella?
I'm a bastard?

PISTHETAIROS

Of course you're a bastard—by Zeus.
Your mother, you see, was an ordinary mortal woman,
not a goddess. In other words, she comes
of foreign stock. Which makes you legally a bastard,*
pure and simple.
Moreover, Pallas Athene*
is normally referred to as The Heiress. That's her title.
But how in the name of Zeus could Athene be an heiress
if Zeus had any legitimate sons?

HERAKLES

Maybe.
Youse could be right. But what if the Old Man
swears I'm his son?

PISTHETAIROS

The law still says No.
In any case, Poseidon here, who's been egging you on,
would be the first person to challenge the will in court.
As your father's brother, he's the next-of-kin, and hence
the legal heir.
Let me read you the provisions of the law.

He draws a lawbook from his robes.

In the words of Solon himself:
SO LONG AS LEGITIMATE ISSUE SHALL SURVIVE THE DECEASED, NO BASTARD SHALL INHERIT. IN THE CASE THAT NO LEGITIMATE ISSUE SURVIVES, THE ESTATE SHALL PASS TO THE NEXT OF KIN.

HERAKLES

Youse mean to say I won't inherit a damn thing
from the Old Man?

PISTHETAIROS

Not a smitch. By the way,
has your Father ever had your birth legally recorded
or had you registered in court as his official heir?

HERAKLES

No, never. I always thought there was something fishy.

PISTHETAIROS

Come, my boy, chin up. Don't pout at heaven
with that sullen glare. Join us. Come in with the Birds.

We'll set you on a throne and you can guzzle pigeon's milk
the rest of your endless days.

HERAKLES

You know, fella,
I been thinking about that dame you want so bad.
Well, I vote youse can have her.

PISTHETAIROS

Splendid.
What do you say, Poseidon?

POSEIDON

No. A resounding No.

PISTHETAIROS

Then it rests with Triballos.
—What's your verdict, my friend?

TRIBALLOS

Gleep? Schnoozer skirt wotta twatch snock!
Birdniks pockle. Ugh.

HERAKLES

He said she's for the Boids.
I hoid him.

POSEIDON

And I distinctly heard him say the opposite:
A firm No—with a few choice obscenities added.

HERAKLES

The poor dumb sap never said a doity word.
All he said was: *Give 'er to the Boids.*

POSEIDON

I yield.
You two can come to terms together as you please.
Since you seem to be agreed on everything, I'll just abstain.

HERAKLES

To Pisthetairos.

Man, youse is getting everything youse wants.
Fly up to Heaven wid us, and get your missus
and anything else your little heart desires.

PISTHETAIROS

And we're in luck. This feast of poultry I've prepared
will grace our wedding supper.

HERAKLES

Youse guys push along.
I'll stay here and watch the barbecue.

POSEIDON

Not on your life.
You'd guzzle grill and all. You'd better come along
with us, my boy.

HERAKLES

Aw, Unc, but it woulda tasted so good.

PISTHETAIROS

To Attendants.

—You there, servants.
Bring my wedding clothes along.

Exeunt Pisthetairos, the gods and Attendants.

CHORUS*

Beneath the clock in a courtroom,
down in the Land of Gab,
We saw a weird race of people,
earning their bread by blab.

Their name is the Claptraptummies.
Their only tool is talk.
They sow and reap and shake the figs
by dexterous yakkity-yak.

Their tongues and twaddle mark them off,
barbarians every one;
but the worst of all are in the firm
of GORGIAS & SON.*

But from this bellyblabbing tribe,
one custom's come to stay:
in Athens, when men sacrifice,
they cut the tongue away.

Enter a Messenger.

MESSENGER

O blessèd, blessèd, blessèd breed of Bird,
more happy than human tongue can tell:
welcome your lord and King as he ascends to heaven!
Attend him now!
Praise him, whose glory glisters
more brightly than the rising stars at dusk
flare their loveliness upon the golden evening air,
purer than the blazoned sun!
He comes, he comes,

and with him comes the splendid glory of a bride
whose beauty has no peer. In his hand he shakes
the wingèd thunderbolt at Zeus, the flash of lightning.
Unspeakably sweet, a fragrance ascends to heaven
and curls of incense trace their lovely spirals
on the drinking air.
He comes!
Greet your King with song!
Raise the wedding song the lovely Muses sing!

Re-enter Pisthetairos, gorgeously attired, his long golden train carried by the three gods. Beside him, dressed in the magnificent golden robes of a bride, walks the veiled figure of Miss Universe.*

KORYPHAIOS

Make way! Make way!
Fall back for the dancers!
Welcome your King with beating wings!
Dance, dance!
Praise this happy Prince!
Sing the praise of handsome youth,
sing the loveliness of brides!
Weave with circling feet, weave and dance
in honor of the King, in honor of his bride!
Now let the Golden Age of Birds begin
by lovely marriage ushered in,
Hymen Hymenaios O!

CHORUS

To such a song as this,
the weaving Fates once led
the universal King,
Zeus, the lord of all,
to lovely Hera's bed.
O Hymen! Hymenaios O!

And blooming Love was there,
Love with shimmering wings,
Love the charioteer!
Love once held the reins,
Love drove the happy pair!
O Hymen! Hymenaios O!

PISTHETAIROS

I thank you for your songs and dance. Thank you, thank you, one and all.

KORYPHAIOS

Now praise the lightnings of your King!
Sing his thunders crashing on the world!
Sing the blazing bolts of Zeus, praise the man
who hurls them!
Sing the flare of lightning;
praise, praise the crashing of its awful fire!

CHORUS

O Lightning, flash of livid fire,
O javelin of Zeus,
everliving light!

A great low roll of thunder is heard.

O thunders breaking on this lovely world,
rumble majestic that runs before the rain!
O Lightning and Thunders,
bow low, bow down,
bow before this man, bow to the lord of all!

Another great crack of thunder.

He wields the thunder as his very own.
Lightnings flare at the touch of his hand,
winning, achieving
the Bride of Heaven and the Crown of God!
O Hymen! Hymenaios O!

PISTHETAIROS

Now follow our bridal party, one and all.
Soar on high, you happy breed of Birds,
to the halls of Zeus, to the bed of love!

He extends his hand to his bride and together they dance toward the waiting machine.

Reach me your hand, dear bride.
Now take me by my wings,
oh my lovely,
my sweet,
and let me lift you up,
and soar beside you
through the buoyant air!

Pisthetairos and his bride dance toward the waiting machine. With slowly beating wings they rise gradually heavenward. The gods and Attendants bow down in homage, the Chorus divides and flocks triumphantly toward the exits, chanting as they go.

CHORUS

Alalalai!
Io!
Paion!
O greatest of the gods!
Tenella Kallinikos O!

Notes

page 13. *A desolate wilderness:* The locale of the Hoopoe's nest belongs, of course, to the same fabulous geography as Cloudcuckooland itself. Since in mythology Tereus was the king of the Daulians, a Thracian people, the scene may be laid "somewhere in Thrace"—an extremely imprecise designation.

13. *even Exekestides couldn't do that:* Cf. Glossary, EXEKESTIDES. From the frequent allusions in the play to men who, technically ineligible, had somehow managed to get themselves enrolled as Athenian citizens, it is tempting to believe that proposals to revise the citizenship lists were in the air or had recently been carried out. The climax of these allusions comes in the final scene of the play, in which Pisthetairos attempts to prove that Herakles is technically a bastard (and hence cannot inherit Zeus' estate) because his mother was an ordinary mortal, i.e., of foreign stock.

14. *Epops Tereus who used to be a man:* Cf. Glossary, TEREUS. "Epops" is nothing more than the Greek name for the Hoopoe, a name probably based on the Hoopoe's characteristic cry.

Despite the violent story which tells how Tereus became the Hoopoe, Prokne the Nightingale, and Philomela the Swallow, Aristophanes' Tereus and Prokne live happily together in marital bliss.

14. *this stinking, jabbering Magpie here:* In the Greek, the Magpie is actually called "son of Tharraleides." According to the Scholiast, Tharraleides' son was Asopodoros, a diminutive man commonly ridiculed as a runt. There may also be a pun on the word θαρραλέος, loquacious or impudent.

14. *dying to go tell it to the Birds:* Literally, the Greek says "dying to go to the crows," a common Athenian imprecation, and roughly equivalent to "go to perdition" or "go to hell" in English. Pisthetairos and Euelpides propose merely to follow the imprecation in its literal meaning —only to get lost en route.

14. Cf. Glossary, SAKAS and the note on *even Exekestides,* above.

14. *to pay their taxes:* A slight modernization of the Greek which says: "to pay fines."

14. *because of legal locusts:* Aristophanes' favorite complaint against

Athens, and one to which the entire *Wasps* is devoted. But although Aristophanes here develops Athens' love of litigation as the major source of dissatisfaction, elsewhere throughout the play the other grievances emerge: the restless (and mischievous) Athenian character (called πολυπραγμοσύνη); the plague of informers; the victimization of the Allies; the ambition for power, an ambition which knows no limits and whose only goal is World Mastery (βασιλεία).

page 14. *soft and lovely leisure:* Pisthetairos and Euelpides are looking, that is, for a place that offers them what Athens does not: release from the tortured, nervous, frenetic restlessness of Athenian life.

In Greek this quality of Athenian national restlessness was called πολυπραγμοσύνη, and its lexical meanings include "officiousness," "meddling," and "the activities of the busybody." Translated to social and political life, the word connotes those national characteristics which made the Athenians at once the wonder and the bane of the Greek world: national enterprise and energy vs. a spirit of unsatisfied restlessness; adventurous daring of action and intellect as against a spirit that seemed destructive of tradition and the life of rural peace; hunger for innovation and change undercut by the inability to temporize or be still. The word, in short, expresses precisely those qualities—daring, energy, ingenuity, strain, dynamic action, restlessness, ambition for acquisition and conquest, glory in change—that typify the Athens of the fifth century. It was these qualities that had made Athens great; they also made Athens imperial and thereby propagated themselves; they were responsible for the senseless protraction of the Peloponnesian War and they would, Aristophanes believed, eventually destroy Athens as they had already destroyed the countryside of Attika and the virtue it fostered: ἀπραγμοσύνη, the contented leisure of traditional order and the rural conservatism of peaceful life.

The word is, of course, crucial to the play. For if Aristophanes shows us in Pisthetairos here an Athenian exhausted by years of national restlessness and in search of ἀπραγμοσύνη among the Birds, it is precisely his point that no Athenian can escape his origin. And once arrived among the Birds, Pisthetairos promptly exhibits the national quality from which he is trying to escape. He is daring, acquisitive, ruthlessly energetic, inventive, and a thorough-paced imperialist. And finally, in the apotheosis that closes the play, he arrives at his logical destination—divinity. For πολυπραγμοσύνη, as Aristophanes ironically observed, is moved by nothing less than man's divine discontent with his condition, and the hunger of the Athenians to be supreme, and therefore god.

15. *Try kicking the side of the cliff with your foot:* As the Scholiast explains it, this line is an echo of a children's jingle: "Kick the rock with your foot, and the birds will fall down."

16. *I'm turdus turdus. An African migrant:* I have taken a liberty here in an attempt to make English of the Greek which literally says: "I'm a

Scaredstifflet. A Libyan species." *Turdus turdus* (the scientific name of the thrush) seemed to introduce the right scientific note, as well as to accommodate the obscenity which follows.

page 16. *I'm a Slavebird:* Cock-fighting cant. Greeks called the loser in a cock-fight the "slave" of the winner.

17. *Right here in my hand:* If, as I suspect—contrary to the belief of most scholars—the phallus was worn in Aristophanic comedy, these words have a point that is otherwise lacking. Pisthetairos, having let his bird escape, finds himself holding his own phallus in terror. It is good fun based on good observation.

18. *I'll bet the gods:* The Greek introduces the official *Twelve* Gods here, probably for emphasis. I have omitted them for clarity's sake.

18. *as the poet Sophokles disfigures me:* Sophokles had produced a tragedy called *Tereus* (lost) in which he may have described Tereus' metamorphosis into a Hoopoe. In the Aristophanic play, Tereus is obviously only slightly—and rather shabbily—metamorphosed, and he ascribes his shabbiness to his Sophoklean origins.

    In appearance the European Hoopoe is a stunning and unusual bird, with brilliant black and white wing pattern and pink plumage and splendid black-tipped erectile crest.

18. *All Birds moult in winter:* With this statement the Hoopoe realistically accounts for his bedraggled plumage in March, when the play was performed.

19. *Then you must be jurymen:* The familiar taunt: everybody in Athens is on a jury.

19. *Yau can still find a few growing wild:* Aristophanes means that the only Athenians still untouched by the national disease of litigation were countrymen. The countryside breeds ἀπραγμοσύνη; the city, πολυπραγμούνη which finds expression in the suits brought by informers, etc.

19. *some country like a blanket, soft and snug:* ἀπραγμοσύνη again.

20. *court-officials with summons:* Euelpides is terrified by the thought of officials with summonses who may show up *anywhere* near the sea, even the Red Sea. The Greek mentions the "Salaminia," the galley used in Athens for official business, and the very vessel which had, a few months earlier, been despatched to Sicily with orders for the recall of Alkibiades to Athens to stand trial.

21. *If Opountios comes from Opous:* The pun here is untranslatable. Opountios was a one-eyed Athenian informer; Opous was a town in Lokris, and the word Oupountios designates an inhabitant of Opous as well as the Athenian informer.

21. *That's a honeymoon!:* Poppyseed was used in making wedding cakes, and myrtle berries were used for wedding wreaths.

21. *And people say:* In the manuscript it is Teleas—and not people—who sneers at the Birds. Teleas was evidently an extremely flighty and silly

Athenian official and Aristophanes' point is the obvious one: it takes a Bird to recognize a Bird.

page 22. *The heavens, you see, revolve upon a kind of pole:* This line and the three that follow it involve a series of untranslatable puns and some difficult scientific jargon. The Greek for "the vault of the heavens" is πόλος, which leads naturally to πολεῖται (revolves), which resembles πολῖται (citizens), which in turn yields πόλις (city). The argument is a fine specimen of sophistic doubletalk.

22. *wipe them all out by starvation:* The manuscript says literally, "wipe them out with a Melian famine." The year before the performance of *The Birds,* the small neutral island of Melos had been blockaded by an Athenian fleet and reduced by slow starvation. When finally captured, the entire male population was put to the sword and the women and children enslaved.

It is, of course, a deliberate part of Aristophanes' general ironic design that the tactics used by Pisthetairos against the gods are, in fact, the brutal military tactics of Athenian imperialism. However fantastic the play may seem, its purpose is the relentless satirical equation of Athens and Cloudcuckooland.

27. *like something out of Aischylos:* The line which follows is a quotation from the (lost) *Edonoi* of Aischylos.

28. *the son of the Hoopoe in Philokles' tragedy of Tereus:* The passage is a complicated one. But its basis seems to be an elaborate comparison between three generations of Hoopoes and three generations of the family of Kallias, and its point is surely (1) a charge of plagiarism against the tragedian Philokles and (2) the charge of profligacy against the younger Kallias.

There are three *Hoopoes*: (1) Hoopoe *grandpère* (the Hoopoe who married Prokne and the hero of Sophokles' *Tereus*); (2) Hoopoe *père* (the Hoopoe of Philokles' *Tereus,* a plagiarism of—and therefore descended from—Sophokles' play); and (3) Hoopoe *fils,* the dissolute and bedraggled Hoopoe of the Chorus. To these correspond: (1) Kallias *grandpère,* a distinguished Athenian; (2) Hipponikos, son of Kallias (1), and also distinguished; and (3) Kallias *fils,* the unworthy and profligate scion of a distinguished line. (The family was evidently addicted to alternating names with each generation: Kallias, Hipponikos, Kallias, Hipponikos, etc.)

28. *our boy Kleonymos:* Kleonymos was a notorious glutton and an equally notorious coward. Since cowards have lost their crests (by throwing away their helmets on the battlefield), the Crested Guzzleguzzle should not be confused with Kleonymos.

28. *this crestwork on the Birds:* This joke depends upon a pun on the word λόφος, which means: (1) the crest of a bird, (2) the summit—or crest—of a hill.

29. *Her lover. The Horny Pecker:* This is Arrowsmith, not Aristophanes,

and so too is the following line. But the lines seemed to me utterly untranslatable since they involved an impossible pun on the word κειρύλος (which means both "kingfisher" and "barber") and an obscure barber by the name of Sporgilos. In the circumstances it seemed better to betray the letter than the spirit.

page 29. *Bringing Owls to Athens:* The Athenian equivalent of "bringing coals to Newcastle."

29. *I detect a note of menace:* The effect of the entire following scene depends upon our understanding of the *natural* hostility between Birds and Man (cf. 1. 369 ff.). In a country policed by the bird-loving vigilantes of the Audubon Society, Aristophanes' Birds might seem unreasonably hostile and suspicious of human motives. But anyone who has ever seen a Mediterranean bird-market or been offered pickled thrushes or *uccellini con polenta* will understand. Those who do not are advised to read closely the second Parabasis (1058 ff.) and to ponder Pisthetairos' little poem at 523 ff. Seen in the light of this total hostility, Pisthetairos' persuasion of the Birds is an extraordinary feat, designed, I believe, in order to exhibit his characteristic Athenian resourcefulness and eloquence and cunning.

32. *Birds are skittish of platters:* In the Greek it is owls who are said to be skittish of platters. The reason for this skittishness is not known; it may be because owls are sacred to Athena and Athena was supposed to have invented the art of pottery. I preferred in the circumstances to emphasize the Birds' terror of becoming a meal.

33. *closely related to my wife:* Tereus' wife Prokne was Athenian and all Athenians regarded themselves as related by virtue of the very kinship-structure of the city.

34. *in Athens at public cost:* Soldiers who fell on the battlefield for Athens were buried at public expense in the Kerameikos outside the city.

34. *any reference to Birds:* Literally, the Greek says, "we will say that we died fighting the enemy at Orneai." "At Orneai" in the Greek is a pun on ὄρνις (bird), i.e., "at Birdland," and the town of Orneai which lay between Korinth and Sikyon and which, in 416, underwent a bloodless one-day siege.

36. *you know who I mean:* "The armor-making baboon" seems to have been a certain knife-maker called Panaitios who was married to an extremely promiscuous shrew. They managed to arrive at a marital *modus vivendi* only by making a formal compact of truce.

38. *Someone fetch water for my hands:* An orator put on a crown of myrtle before beginning his speech, but the wreath and the washing of hands are the customary preparations for a feast; hence Euelpides' question.

38. *Because you're a lazy Bird:* In the Greek κοὐ πολυπράγμων, uninquisitive, not on one's toes, sluggish, without curiosity. The Birds' fallen estate and decadence is directly traceable to their lack of πολυπραγμοσύνη,

Pisthetairos' most outstanding trait. Cf. note on p. 110, *soft and lovely leisure.*

page 38. *And that's how Asbury got its name:* A complicated bit of foolery crowned by Euelpides' elaborate pun, which I have freely altered for the effect. Pisthetairos actually says that, according to "Aesop," the Lark buried her father in her own head. The word for "head" in Greek is κεφαλή, which is also the name of an Athenian deme. Hence Euelpides' crack: the father of the Lark is buried at κεφαλή.

39. *and let the woodpeckers reign:* Since the oak tree was sacred to Zeus and the woodpeckers attacked the oaks, Zeus would be particularly unwilling to yield his sceptre to the Woodpecker.

40. *falling flat on your face whenever you saw a Kite:* The Kite was a harbinger of Spring, according to the Scholiast, and one which was evidently welcomed with almost religious joy.

40. *I swallowed my money:* It was common in antiquity for people to carry their coins in their mouth, probably as a precaution against theft.

40. *we still call the Egyptians cuckoo:* The cuckoo's call was in Egypt a call to reap, as Pisthetairos explains. To this Euelpides replies with a proverbial expression whose meaning is obscure—though almost certainly obscene. Since I could not translate what I could not understand, I have tried to make Euelpides' reply consistent with his zaniness elsewhere.

40. *on the rows where the politicians sit:* Literally, the Greek says that the birds on sceptres were keeping an eye on Lysikrates, to see whether he was bribed. Lysikrates was an Athenian general of a dishonest and corrupt character.

40. *Doctors still swear by the Duck:* A deliberate improvisation of my own to circumvent the complexity of the Greek. Literally, the line reads: "Lampon swears by the Goose when he's trying to cheat you." Lampon was a notorious soothsayer, but evidently superstitious enough that he tried to mitigate his perjury when fleecing a victim: instead of swearing an oath by Zeus (Ζῆνα), he swore by the Goose (Χῆνα).

42. *A Babylon of the Birds:* Cf. Glossary, BABYLON.

43. *each Bird must be paired with a god:* These pairs depend upon similarity in character or upon puns, and I have altered several of them accordingly. Thus in the manuscript Aphrodite is paired with the phalarope (which is suggested by *phallos*); Poseidon, god of the sea, is matched by a seabird; the glutton Herakles by the cormorant; and Zeus, king of the gods, by the wren, king of the birds.

45. *"Five lives of men the cawing Crow outliveth":* A garbled echo of Hesiod, frag. 50.

45. *can strut on an olive limb:* The olive was sacred to Athena and hence should be acceptable even to aristocratic birds.

47. *Remember what old Aesop tells us:* According to the Scholiast, the fable should be ascribed to Archilochos rather than Aesop. But the gist of the fable seems to be as follows. The Fox and the Eagle swore

lasting friendship and built their homes close together: the Eagle up in the tree, the Fox at the foot. During the Fox's absence one day, the Eagle swooped down, carried off the Fox's cubs, and proceeded to make a meal of them. The Fox, unable to climb the tree, could not take vengeance.

page 50. *The CHORUS turns sharply and faces the audience:* The Parabasis, (or Digression), that part of an Aristophanic comedy in which the Chorus steps forth and addresses the audience directly, usually on behalf of the poet. In this play the Parabasis is linked with unusual coherence to the action, whereas in most comedies the Chorus employs the Parabasis to expound the topical social and political views of the comedian.

The opening anapestic section of the Parabasis is devoted to what might be called an Avine Cosmogony, a splendid and eloquent exposition of the origins of the world and the creation of the Birds and the gods. This defense of the antiquity of the Birds then passes into an overtly humorous bid for support, as though the Birds were campaigning for the votes which will make them gods. This is followed by a lovely lyric strophe ("O woodland Muse") which is succeeded by the *epirrhema* in a more topical and satirical vein; then the lyric antistrophe ("And so the swans") and the farcical *antepirrhema* ("You haven't really lived till you've tried a set of FEATHERS!").

The relevance of the opening cosmogony to the theme of the play has been questioned, but unreasonably I think. If Cloudcuckooland is an Athenian Utopia, the meaning of Utopia is scored when Pisthetairos achieves his apotheosis in the finale. He has built Utopia by becoming god, and escaping his human condition. It is to the reality and sadness of man's condition that the cosmogony of the blessed Birds is addressed, and these lovely opening lines ("O suffering mankind, lives of twilight, race feeble and fleeting") are intended as a tragic counterweight to the crazy comic dream of mankind with which the play closes.

50. *tell Prodikos to go hang:* Prodikos was a sophist whom Aristophanes seems to have respected. The point here is that, wise as Prodikos may be, as a teacher of truth he is not to be compared with the Birds.

51. *laid her wind-egg there:* A wind-egg is an unfertilized pullet's egg.

54. *the poet stole his honied song:* i.e., the tragic poet, Phrynichos, famous for his lyric sweetness.

55. *Dieitrephes, our vulgar Ikaros of trade:* For Dieitrephes, see Glossary. Aristophanes, like most conservatives, is a convinced snob, and he almost never forgives a man his business background, especially if the man has succeeded, as Dieitrephes had, in making his way into the *élite* ranks of the chivalry.

56. *the poor Birds in that Aischylos play:* A reference to, followed by a quotation from, the lost *Myrmidones* of Aischylos.

56. *insult my mattress by giving it a name like Sparta:* A pun on Σπάρτη

(Sparta) and σπάρτη (a kind of broom from which rope and bed-cording were made). Euelpides detests Sparta so much that he wouldn't attach σπάρτη to his bed.

page 57. *who will guard our Storkade?* The wall which surrounded the Akropolis of Athens was usually called the Pelasgic Wall but sometimes the Pelargic Wall, both related forms. Aristophanes here uses Pelargic Wall, fancifully deriving it from πελαργός ("stork"). "Storkade" is B. B. Rogers' *trouvaille* and one which I gratefully adopt here.

58. *Hop it, man!* Pisthetairos' officiousness with Euelpides here is a stunning example of πολυπραγμοσύνη.

59. *Flutist, come in!* At these words the flutist Chairis, dressed as a Blackbird or a Crow, steps forward. Chairis' music seems to have grated intolerably on Aristophanes' ears; he is a *bête noire* in *The Acharnians* (425 B.C.) and still obnoxious by the time of *The Birds* eleven years later.

59. *propping his beak with a leather belt:* Evidently a mouth band or flutist's lip protector.

59. *the Bidding Prayer of the Birds:* This entire prayer is a parody of the customary invocation of the gods, in each case, by pun or burlesqued attributes or cult titles, linking a god with a bird. Because of the elaborateness of the puns and the obscurities of cult titles, literal translation is out of the question, and I have tried to make my own puns where I could not re-create the Greek—as I rarely could. Thus my Artemis is not a Finch but an American Phoebe, an appropriate name, I thought, for the sister of Phoibos; Kybele, Mother of Gods and Men, is not an Ostrich, as she is in the Greek, but a Dowitcher, a bird which suggested "dowager," and the Great Mother of Bustards. Those who are interested in discussion of the literal Greek should consult Roger's commentary on the passage.

60. *pray for the Chians too:* Cf. Glossary, CHIANS.

61. *as Homer hath it:* Everything about this poet is begged, borrowed, or stolen. Here he attributes lines to Homer which either are not Homeric or Homer so muddled as to be unrecognizable.

62. *O Father, Founder of Etna:* This whole passage is evidently a hideously garbled and atrociously adapted burlesque of Pindar's ode dedicated to the Syracusan tyrant Hiero on the founding of the town of Etna.

63. *Undressed amidst the nomad Skyths:* More Pindar, perhaps quoted almost verbatim, but doggerelized deliberately by me since no contemporary reader could be expected to recognize the Pindaric manner or its incongruous humor in this particular context.

64. *WHERE KORINTH KISSETH SIKYON:* That is, at Orneai. Cf. Note on p. 113, *any reference to Birds*. Itinerant prophets in Athens could live well by supplying ambiguous predictions of conquest and victory to the ambitious Athenians. This particular prophet may very well be quoting from an actual oracle which predicted the sack of Orneai and

thereby prompted the expedition; he then attempts to resell the same article, differently interpreted, to Cloudcuckooland.

page 65. *REGAL EAGLE WINGS THIS VERY DAY ARE THINE:* This is said to have been the favorite prediction of the Athenian Demos (cf. *Knights,* 1013). The Eagle, of course, symbolized supremacy and conquest.

66. *FOR THE GREATER THE FAKER:* The manuscript specifies by name two of these fakers. The first is Lampon, Athens' most renowned soothsayer; the second, Diopeithes, the accuser of the philosopher Anaxagoras.

66. *METON:* Cf. Glossary.

67. *our welkin resembles a cosmical charcoal-oven:* Meton's whole lecture is an elaborate spoof of technical "scientific" jargon of the age. But because Greek scientific jargon is almost chaste compared to our splendid modern proliferations, I have worked it up in order to create an effect analogous to that intended for Greek ears.

68. *enters an Inspector:* The Inspector, or Commissioner, was a regular Athenian official sent out from Athens to supervise subject states or to organize newly founded colonies. Their salaries seem to have been paid by the colonies they supervised, and some of them, like the Inspector here, had become rich men in the course of their careers.

69. *The Persian crisis, you know:* A free rendering. In the original the Inspector alludes loftily to his negotiations with the Persian satrap Pharnakes; he is needed at home for consultation about these weighty negotiations. Persia at this time, however, was more and more becoming a crucial factor in Greek political life.

69. *and take your ballot-boxes with you:* Wherever Athenian inspectors are found, there will also be ballot boxes, the typical device of Athenian democracy, and arbitrarily instituted throughout the empire.

69. *Enter an itinerant LEGISLATOR:* During the war the Athenian Assembly had passed so many decrees, regulations, etc., that it became virtually impossible for the subject-cities and colonies to keep abreast of them. In the circumstances the practice of peddling the latest crop of statutes became a flourishing trade.

71. *CHORUS:* The second Parabasis: The Birds eulogize themselves and the blessings they bring, issue their own proclamation, and explain to the Judges the advantages of awarding *The Birds* the first prize.

73. *shrines whose dizzy heights, like Eagle-eyries:* In Greek the word ἀετός meant (1) an Eagle, and (2) the triangular pediment which crowned the pillars.

74. *Thirty thousand Cranes whose crops were all loaded with boulders and stones:* Cranes were believed to use stones to ballast themselves; the ballast was held in the crop.

75. *Ah Feet! Ah, Feet! O, incredible Feat!* This is a common proverb with the word "feet" substituted for "hands."

page 76. *the wild steps of a military dance:* The *pyrrhichē* danced in full armor. Actually, the sentry is not dancing; the dancing is in his eyes, i.e., ablaze with martial ardor.

79. *In high tragic manner:* Iris' tragic fulmination is probably a pastiche of all the tragedians, patched out with some Aristophanic inventions.

80. *Some poor Lydian or Phrygian slave:* A direct quotation from Euripides' *Alkestis,* 675.

80. *What doth the poet say?* A quotation from the lost *Niobe* of Aischylos, incongruously incorporated into the passage without alteration. In order to clarify the deliberate incongruity (the mention of Amphion), I have intruded the line which follows the quotation.

82. *mimicry of Sokrates:* A gibe at the Spartan affectations of the Socratic circle and especially Sokrates' personal uncleanliness. To some extent this may be merely an exploitation of the common man's stereotype of the intellectual and philosopher. I remember a Princeton landlady telling me that Einstein never took a bath; this was her revenge on his genius. As for Sokrates, who knows?

82. *the* dernier cri *of human fashion:* The examples of the avine vogue which follow are all of my own invention. The Greek cannot be literally translated into English because it is based upon an untranslatable pun (*νομός*, meaning both "law" and "pasture" or "feeding-place"), designed to parody, in avine terms, the Athenian love of litigation.

84. *If I had the wings of an Eagle:* A quotation, according to the Scholiast, from the lost *Oinomaos* of Sophokles.

84. *DELINQUENT:* The Greek is *πατρολοίας*, a word which it is usual to translate as "parricide," although it means merely "father-beater." Since our young man merely *wants* to murder his father, I have made him an adolescent punk and called him Delinquent.

85. *On gossamer I go, delicately wending:* According to the Scholiast, a parody of Anakreon.

86. *our poet's craft depends completely on the clouds:* For the Clouds as patron goddesses of dithyrambic poets, cf. *Clouds,* 335 ff. Poets whose compositions are a characteristic blend of obscurity, turbid emptiness and inflated language naturally depend upon the Murky Muse for inspiration.

87. *What suspicious Birds are these:* Adapted from a poem by Alkaios.

87. *he's calling the Cuckoo to bring the spring:* In the Greek it is the Swallow who brings the Informer's Spring.

88. *to hide the holes in your coat:* Literally the manuscript has Pisthetairos say: "Are you planning to fly to Pellene?" Pellene was famous for its heavy woolen clothing, offered as prizes in the contests celebrated there.

88. *the indictment of islands for subversive activities:* By "islands" is meant the subject-states of the Athenian Empire, very largely comprised of the Aegean islands. Since the islanders were compelled to refer their more important lawsuits to the verdict of Athenian juries, they were therefore

in a disadvantageous position and easily victimized by professional informers.

page 89. *they loll around at the barbershop:* The barbershop was *par excellence* the nerve center of Athenian gossip, rumor, and political speculation.

89. *that damned Dieitrephes:* Cf. Glossary, DIEITREPHES. Dieitrephes was a notorious horse-racing enthusiast and hence in high favor with the wastrels among the Athenian *jeunesse dorée.*

90. *CHORUS:* With this strophe Aristophanes commences a series of brief Travelogues by the Birds: strange sights and marvels which their world-traveling has enabled them to visit. Actually, of course, all of the wonders are merely fabulized versions of familiar Athenian institutions and personages: the coward-sycophant Kleonymos, the thief Orestes, the psychagogue Sokrates and his accomplice Chairephon, the incredible tongue-worship of the wondrous men of Athens.

In this strophe Kleonymos is compared to a tree which grows enormous in the Spring and in winter sheds, not leaves, but shields. The Spring was the banner season for informers and sycophants, when men like Kleonymos (physically fat to begin with) were bloated with the profits of their trade. In winter the Kleonymos-tree sheds its shields, an allusion to Kleonymos' cowardice in battle (i.e., throwing down his shield and running away).

The second part of the strophe deals with the notorious footpad Orestes and concludes with a play on the name: (1) the Athenian thief, (2) his famous legendary predecessor, the son of Agamemnon. The point seems to be that those who venture out in Athens at night may meet Orestes the thief (who stripped his victims) or Orestes the heroic ghost (who paralyzed his victims—a power possessed by heroes, according to the Scholiast).

91. *Enter Prometheus:* Mankind's greatest champion and arch foe of Zeus makes his ridiculously furtive entrance on still another philanthropic mission: to warn Pisthetairos of Zeus' plans and secrets. Needless to say, he is extremely anxious to avoid observation by the gods.

94. *Say, that's clever. Prometheus all over:* Pisthetairos is impressed by the ingenuity of Prometheus' umbrella, and compliments him as deserving of his name (Prometheus meant "Foresight").

94. *All the Stone Age gods:* A free—but I thought plausible—rendering of the "barbarian gods" of the text. If Triballos is a representative of the barbarian gods, then the divinities meant are not merely uncivilized but Neolithic.

95. *Miss Universe:* The Greek gives βασιλεία, which means "sovereignty," "empire," "supreme power." Because she is an unfamiliar abstraction and not a genuine Olympian at all, I have felt free to turn her into a "sort of Beauty Queen" and to gloss her in the text as "the symbol of divine supremacy." In this play she symbolizes the logical conclusion of the Athenian (or the Birds') struggle for domination and universal

supremacy. She is what Thoukydides called ἀρχή ("empire," "domination") and what I believe Euripides everywhere in his tragedies meant by the figure of Helen: the prize for which the (Peloponnesian) War was fought.

page 95. *the inventor of the barbecue:* Because Prometheus gave fire to man.

96. *CHORUS:* The second installment of the Birds' Travelogue. The subject is Sokrates as psychagogue or psychopomp, the guide of the soul, engaged in calling up spirits from the dead in a little sacrifice which resembles that of Odysseus in Book XI of the *Odyssey*. Sokrates' Stygian assistant is his cadaverous colleague of Athenian life, Chairephon.

The scene takes place in the land of Shadowfeet (according to Ktesias, a curious web-footed tribe which lived in Libya; when they lay down for a nap, they held up their huge webfeet as awnings against the sun. To this the Scholiast adds that they had four legs, three of which were used for walking, and the fourth as a tentpole for their tentlike feet). Here, beside a Stygian swamp, haunted by terror, Sokrates summons the soul of Peisandros, an Athenian coward in search of his *psyche* (i.e., courage), by means of sacrifice; but so faint-hearted is Sokrates that he runs away in terror, leaving the bloody victim to the spectral vampire Chairephon.

100. *Dat's Stone Age for Yeah:* Cf. note on p. 125, *All the Stone Age gods.*

102. *Which makes you legally a bastard:* According to Athenian laws on citizenship, citizens must be born of Athenian fathers and mothers. Herakles, as the son of Zeus (a *bona fide* Olympian) and Alkmene (an ordinary woman, i.e., a foreigner) would be both illegitimate and ineligible for citizenship—according to Athenian law.

102. *Pallas Athene is normally referred to as The Heiress:* Because Athens was Athena's "portion," she was officially called The Heiress.

104. *CHORUS:* The concluding section of the Birds' Travelogue, a pointed satire on the Athenian worship of the Clacking Money-Making Tongue in thin anthropological disguise.

104. *of GORGIAS & SON:* To Gorgias the manuscript adds the name of Philippos, son or disciple of Gorgias the sophist. It was believed that the persuasive tongue of Gorgias served to stimulate the disastrous interest in Sicily among Athenians which culminated in the Sicilian Expedition.

105. *Enter Pisthetairos, gorgeously attired:* The culmination of the play in the apotheosis of Pisthetairos and the marriage with Miss Universe. Man's comic dream is completed; by building Cloudcuckooland and winning Miss Universe, Man becomes supreme, escapes his mortal condition, and achieves divinity. It would be blasphemous if it were not so terribly ironic a wish-fulfillment of the god-intoxicated Athenian Dream.

Glossary

AESCHYLUS, AISCHYLOS: The great Athenian tragedian (525-456 B.C.)

AESOP, AISOPOS: A writer of fables, perhaps legendary himself. He was reputed a native of Samos who flourished in the sixth century B.C.

AGAMEMNON: In mythology, commander-in-chief of the Greek forces at the siege of Troy.

AISCHINES: An indigent Athenian braggart, much given to boasting about his fabulous estates, as imaginary as Cloudcuckooland.

AKESTOR: An Athenian tragic poet. See SAKAS.

ALKMENE: Wife of Amphitryon and mistress of Zeus by whom she became the mother of Herakles.

ALOPE: Mortal woman beloved by Poseidon.

AMMON: A celebrated shrine and oracle of Zeus in Libya.

AMPHION: Musician and husband of Niobe; at the touch of his lyre the stones rose from the ground and formed themselves together to make the ramparts of Thebes.

APHRODITE: Goddess of beauty and sexual love.

APOLLO: God of prophecy, music, healing, and light; his two chief shrines were at Delphoi (q.v.) and Delos (q.v.).

ARES: God of War.

ARISTOKRATES: Son of Skellias; a prominent Athenian politician of conservative persuasion. In 421 B.C. he was one of the signers of the Peace of Nikias between Athens and Sparta. In 411 he joined the moderate conservative Theramenes in setting up the government of the Four Hundred, but later withdrew.

ARTEMIS: Goddess of chastity, childbirth, and the hunt; sister of Apollo.

ATHENE, ATHENA: Patron goddess of Athens, commonly called "owl-eyed." Although a virgin goddess, she was also a goddess of war.

BABYLON: Ancient capital of Mesopotamia, situated on the Euphrates River. It was one of the largest cities of the ancient world, and among its wonders were its great brick walls, described by the historian Herodotos.

BAKIS: A famous prophet of Boiotia, whose oracles were delivered in hexameter verse. In Aristophanes' comedies, the seers who cite Bakis are usually charlatans.

BASILEIA: The personification of Empire and Sovereign Power; in the present version she appears as Miss Universe.

CHAIREPHON: Friend and disciple of the philosopher Sokrates. His utter devotion to philosophy and the studious life and his striking pallor and emaciation made him a popular image of The Philosopher. Hence his nickname, The Bat or The Vampire.

CHAOS: The nothingness or vacancy which existed before the creation of the world. In mythology Chaos was the mother of Erebos and Night.

CHIANS: Inhabitants of the island of Chios, a state closely allied to Athens during the early Peloponnesian War and whose fidelity to the Athenian cause was rewarded by inclusion in the Athenian prayers for prosperity and success.

DARIUS, DAREIOS: King of Persia (ruled 521-486 B.C.).

DELOS: Small Aegean island sacred to Apollo.

DELPHOI, DELPHI: A town in Phokis, celebrated for its great temple and oracle of Apollo.

DEMETER: The Earth Mother; goddess of grain, agriculture, and the harvest, worshipped at her shrine at Eleusis in Attika.

DIAGORAS: Poet and philosopher of Melos. Charged with atheism in Athens and condemned to death, he fled the city.

DIEITREPHES: A notorious social climber. Of doubtful Athenian origin, he began his public career as a worker in wicker and a basketmaker, and gradually made his way upward in the military hierarchy. In 413 a detachment of Thracians under his command went amok and massacred a school full of children at Mykalessos.

DODONA: An ancient oracle of Zeus in the mountains of Epiros.

EPOPS: The Hoopoe, Tereus (q.v.).

ETNA, AITNA: A city situated on a spur of the Sicilian mountain of the same name, founded by Hiero of Syracuse.

EXEKESTIDES: Evidently a foreign slave of Karian extraction who succeeded in passing himself off as an Athenian citizen, i.e., the sort of man who would be at home anywhere.

GORGIAS: Of Leontini, a noted sophist and teacher of rhetoric.

HEBROS: A river of Thrace.

HERA: Consort of Zeus.

HERAKLES: Hero and demigod, son of Zeus and Alkmene, renowned for his great labors, prodigious strength, and equally prodigious appetite. Because Herakles is *par excellence* the monster-killer, it is particularly appropriate to swear by him when confronted by the monstrous, prodigious, freakish, or strange.

HERMES: The messenger god of Olympos; also god of thieves and the guide of the underworld.

HESTIA: Goddess of the hearth (and among Birds, goddess of the nest).

HIERO: Famous tyrant of Syracuse in Sicily, celebrated by the poet Pindar.

HIPPONIKOS: A common name in a wealthy and aristocratic Athenian family.

HOMER: The great epic poet of Greece, author of the *Iliad* and *Odyssey*.

HYMEN: God of marriage.

IKAROS: Son of the craftsman Daidalos, who escaped from Krete with his father by means of homemade wings of wax and feathers. But when Ikaros flew too high, the sun melted the wax, his wings dissolved, and he fell to his death in the sea.

IRIS: Messenger of the gods; in the earlier poets represented as a virgin.

ITYS: The son of Tereus and Prokne (q.v.), murdered by his mother in revenge for Tereus' rape and mutilation of Philomela. To the Greek ear, the name Itys seemed to form part of the refrain of the mourning nightingale.

KALLIAS: Common name in a wealthy and aristocratic Athenian family. The Kallias singled out here was a notorious profligate and spendthrift.

KINESIAS: A clubfooted dithyrambic poet of great pretensions but little ability.

KLEISTHENES: A notorious Athenian homosexual and one of Aristophanes' favorite butts.

KLEONYMOS: A corpulent glutton and part-time informer; he is Aristophanes' commonest representative of cowardice (i.e., throwing one's shield away).

KOLONOS: Small town on a hill near Athens; here the astronomer Meton (q.v.) had evidently constructed a complicated piece of engineering or clockwork.

KORINTH: Greek city allied to Sparta during the Peloponnesian War; situated on the strategic Isthmus of Korinth.

KORKYRA: Modern Corfu, a large island off the western coast of Greece. "Korkyrean wings" means "whip."

KRONOS: Father of Zeus.

KYBELE: A Phrygian Mother Goddess, worshipped as The Great Mother, "mother of gods and men."

LAURIUM, LAUREION: In southeastern Attika, famous for its silver mines. Athenian silver coins, stamped with the owl of Athena, were commonly called "owls of Laureion."

LEOTROPHIDES: An extremely fragile, delicate, and unsubstantial poet.

LEPREUS, LEPREUM: A town in Elis; it recovered its independence from Elis during the Peloponnesian War.

LETO: Mother of Artemis and Apollo.

LYDIA: A region in Western Asia Minor which provided Athens with a large number of slaves.

LYKOURGOS: An Athenian of sufficient distinction and/or oddity of appearance to have won the nickname of The Ibis. In this translation, however, he appears as The Lame Duck.

MANES: A lazy slave.

MANODOROS: A slave.

MARATHON: A plain in the eastern part of Attika; site of the famous battle (490 B.C.) in which the Athenian forces under Miltiades crushingly defeated the first Persian invasion of Hellas.

MEIDIAS: A venal and corrupt Athenian informer, evidently also a quail-breeder in his own right, whence his nickname, The Quail. For Aristophanes the propriety of the name is confirmed by Meidias' habitually dazed expression, like that of a freshly stunned quail.

MELANTHIOS: Son of Philokles and, like his father, an atrocious tragedian. Afflicted with leprosy, he seems to have been also a noted glutton (cf. *Peace,* 804).

MENELAOS: Mythological king of Sparta and brother of Agamemnon.

MENIPPOS: An Athenian horse-raiser, nicknamed The Swallow (from a pun on the word *chelidon* which means both "swallow" and the tender "hollow" in a horse's hoof).

METON: An Athenian astronomer, geometrician, and city-planner of considerable notoriety (see KOLONOS). According to Plutarch, Meton objected to the Sicilian expedition and pretended madness in order to keep his son at home.

NIKIAS: Prominent Athenian general during the Peloponnesian War. Enormously respected at Athens during his lifetime, Nikias' caution, slowness to move, stiffness, and superstitious piety were among the chief causes for the defeat of the Sicilian expedition. But as a cautious strategist and tactician, he had no equal among the Athenian generals.

ODYSSEUS: Hero of the *Odyssey* of Homer.

OLOPHYXIANS: Inhabitants of Olophyxos, a small town on the peninsula of Akte in Thrace.

OLYMPOS: A mountain in Thessaly, covered at the peak with perpetual snow and regarded by the Greeks as the abode of the gods.

OPOUNTIOS: A notorious one-eyed sycophant nicknamed The Crow.

OPOUS: A town in Lokris, whose inhabitants were called the Opuntian Lokrians.

ORESTES: A notorious burglar and highwayman; not to be confused with the heroic son of Agamemnon.

PAIAN: Manifestation of Apollo as god of healing.

PAN: Rural Arcadian god of the flocks and the woodlands.

PANDORA: Mother Earth, the giver of all gifts (*pan,* all; *dora,* gifts); not to be confused with the mythological mischief-maker and her box of human troubles.

PARIS: Prince of Troy; in the famous judgment of Paris, he was offered the most beautiful woman in the world by Aphrodite in return for awarding her the prize for beauty.

PEGASOS: The famous winged horse of mythology.

PEISANDROS: A notorious Athenian coward.

PEISIAS: Otherwise unknown, but evidently a noted traitor in his day.

PHILOKLES: Athenian tragic poet and nephew of Aischylos; among his lost plays was one which treated the story of Tereus and was evidently plagiarized from Sophokles' play of the same name. His nickname was The Lark because, according to the Scholiast, his head tapered like the pointed crest of that bird.

PHILOKRATES: An Athenian bird-seller.

PHLEGRA: A plain in Thrace said to have been the site of the great battle between the Gods and the Giants.

PHOIBOS: Apollo.

PHRYGIA: A country in central Asia Minor.

PINDAR: Great lyric poet of Thebes (518-438 B.C.).

PORPHYRION: Name of one of the Titans who fought against Zeus in the Battle of the Gods and the Giants; it is also the name of a bird, the Purple Waterhen.

POSEIDON: Brother of Zeus and god of the sea. As sea-god, he girdles the earth and has it in his power as Poseidon Earth-Shaker to cause earthquakes. In still another manifestation he is Poseidon Hippios, patron god of horses and horsemen.

PRIAM: King of Troy.

PRODIKOS: Of Keos, a famous sophist.

PROKNE: The nightingale, wife of Tereus (q.v.).

PROMETHEUS: The great Titan who championed the cause of mankind against Zeus. Because he stole fire from heaven and gave it to men, he was regarded by the gods as a traitor to Olympos. His name means Foresight and his cleverness and philanthropy were both proverbial.

PROXENIDES: An Athenian braggart and blowhard.

SAKAS: The nickname of the Athenian tragic poet Akestor (q.v.). The word Sakas seems to be a pejorative for "Skyth" and presumably Akestor, like Exekestides, was a foreigner who had managed, or was reputed to have managed, to get his name entered on the citizenship rolls of Athens.

SEMELE: Daughter of Kadmos of Thebes and mistress of Zeus, by whom she became the mother of Dionysos.

SIKYON: Greek city situated on the northeast of the Peloponnesos, adjacent to Korinth.

SIMONIDES: Of Keos, a lyric and elegiac poet (ca. 556-468 B.C.).

SKYTHS: Savage nomadic inhabitants of Skythia, a region lying roughly between the Carpathians and the river Don.

SOKRATES: The famous Athenian philosopher, ridiculed by Aristophanes for his long hair, bathlessness, and other philosophical traits.

SOLON: Greatest of Athenian lawgivers (ca. 640-561 B.C.).

SOPHOKLES: Athenian tragic poet (495-404 B.C.).

SYRAKOSIOS: An extremely garrulous Athenian orator whose loquacity earned him the sobriquet of The Jaybird.

TARTAROS: The great abyss which opened underneath Hades in the classical underworld.

TELEAS: Flighty and irresponsible Athenian bureaucrat; secretary to the Committee in charge of the Parthenon treasury.

TEREUS: In mythology, a son of Ares and king of the Daulians in Thrace. According to the legend, Pandion, king of Athens, had two daughters, Prokne and Philomela. Prokne was married to Tereus, by whom she became the mother of a son, Itys. Tereus, however, became infatuated with Prokne's sister Philomela, raped her, and cut out her tongue to keep her from informing Prokne. But Philomela managed to embroider her story in needlework and sent it to Prokne who, in retaliation against her husband, murdered her son Itys and served him up to Tereus for dinner. When he discovered the truth, Tereus pursued Prokne and Philomela but, before he could catch them, he was transformed into a Hoopoe, Prokne into a Nightingale, and Philomela into the swallow. (In the better known but less appropriate Latin version of the myth, Philomela is the nightingale and Prokne the swallow).

The story of Tereus was tragically treated by both Sophokles and Philokles.

THALES: Of Miletos, one of the Seven Sages of antiquity; renowned for his scientific genius and for having predicted an eclipse of the sun (ca. 636-546 B.C.).

THEBES: The principal city of Boiotia; during the Peloponnesian War an ally of Sparta.

THEOGENES: An Athenian braggart; probably took part with Kleon in the blockade of Sphakteria and was one of the signers of the Peace of Nikias in 421 B.C.

TIMON: The misanthrope *par excellence.*

TITANS: The race of pre-Olympian deities, born of Heaven and Earth. After the coming of the Olympians, the Titans rebelled against Zeus and were vanquished in the Battle of the Gods and the Giants at Phlegra.

TRIBALLOI: A savage people of Thrace. The name Triballos is merely an eponym of this people.

ZEUS: Chief god of the Olympian pantheon; son of Kronos, brother of Poseidon, and father of Athena. As the supreme ruler of the world, he is armed with thunder and lightning and creates storms and tempests.

The Clouds

Translated by William Arrowsmith

with sketches by Thomas McClure

CONTENTS

FOR JOHN K. COLBY

who first taught me Greek

Introduction

The Play

The original version of *The Clouds* was presented in March, 423 B.C. at the Great Dionysia, where it disappointed Aristophanes' hopes by being placed third. The First Prize was awarded to the aging Kratinos for his final comedy, *Pytine* (or *The Wineflask*) and the runner-up was Ameipsias with his *Konnos*.[1] After the success of both *Acharnians* and *Knights,* this defeat must have been a bitter blow for Aristophanes. In *Knights* of the year before he had twitted Kratinos with being a doddering drunkard whose comic talents had decayed, and the drunkard had replied by confessing his drunkenness in a play of such comic verve and gaiety —accusing Aristophanes, for instance, of being a mere "Euripidaristophanizing" plagiarist—that he completely defeated his brash young critic. Worse yet, Ameipsias' *Konnos* was, like *The Clouds,* an attack on the sophistic movement, containing a Chorus of Sophists and, evidently, satirizing Sokrates by name. All this might not have mattered had *The Clouds* been a less ambitious play, but Aristophanes regarded it as by far the finest comedy of his career to date.[2]

Probably in the hope of getting a second hearing—if only from readers —he revised the play, and the version of *The Clouds* which we now possess is not the original of 423 B.C. but a revision carried out some three or four years later. According to the Scholiast, the revision was thorough and extensive changes were made, but the chief alterations affected three sections in particular: the *parabasis,* the *agon* between the two *Logoi,* and the finale, the burning of the Thinkery. The full extent of these changes cannot be ascertained. In the *parabasis,* the original choral anapests were replaced by a passage whose meter is unique in a

[1] Konnos was the name of Sokrates' music teacher, and it is likely that the play attacked the "New Music."
[2] *The Clouds,* 522: "convinced . . . that this play was the finest of my comedies . . ."

parabasis (a probable indication that the poet had no expectation of seeing the play restaged) and in which Aristophanes takes off the customary choral mask and speaks to his readers directly in the first person. To the *agon* was added the famous, passionate defense of the Old Education, a speech clearly designed, through its power of conviction and moral seriousness, to show Aristophanes' critics that what was at stake in this play was nothing less than the fate and future of civilized Athens. About the finale no such certainty is possible, though there is some small reason to believe that in the original version it was the god Hermes, rather than Strepsiades, who fired the Thinkery.

Even in its present form, revised for readers rather than for the stage, *The Clouds* is visibly a masterpiece, a play of wonderful, ragging satire, tilted so expertly toward the preposterous and the absurd that its effect is wholly and unmistakably comic. We have, in fact, almost a *reductio ad absurdum* of the satirical intent, satire become so *buffa* and burlesque that its characters and targets, by sheer exaggeration and incongruity, survive as directly comic. In short, a splendid play, beautifully sustained and shaped, and everywhere guided by Aristophanes' genius for comic distortion and his cunning of absurdity. If not the funniest play he ever wrote, it is certainly the cleverest: clever in construction and plot, clever in its exploitation of incongruities, clever in polemic and wit. Almost, perhaps, too clever for its own good. But for Aristophanes these very qualities of cleverness and wit were precisely what made *The Clouds* superior to his own previous work and that of his "cheap and vulgar rivals": for their slapstick of situation and crude horseplay he here substitutes the ludicrous slapstick of the intellect and the better horseplay of poetry and imagination. In its structure too *The Clouds* is an improvement. Unusually tight and coherent,[3] at least by Aristophanic standards, its action is all of a piece, a continuously unfolding plot, written to be performed by a small cast, and singlemindedly devoted to the pursuit of its quarry. If it lacks the miraculous violence and vigor of *The Knights* or the exuberance of *The Acharnians,* it makes up for those qualities by the greater clarity and economy of its design and the pure lyricism of its poetry. Until *The Birds,* there is nothing in Aristophanes to match the loveliness of the poetry here assigned to the Chorus of Clouds as it enters. In this play, for the first time, we catch a glimpse of that exquisite tension between slapstick and poetry, the obscene and the sublime, which was Aristophanes' major individual contribution to

[3] In my opinion the only major structural flaw in the play is the abrupt change in the role of the Chorus. At least I find a jar when the Clouds suddenly reveal that they are actually celestial *agents provocateurs* masking as the patrons of the Sophists.

comedy and which lies at the heart of his two greatest lyrical comedies, *The Birds* and *The Frogs.*

At first blush the improbable victim of *The Clouds* seems to be the philosopher Sokrates. But actually Aristophanes is deliberately exploiting Sokrates here as a convenient comic representative of the sophistic corruption which is the play's real subject. In the illustration of that corruption, Sokrates is nothing more than the poet's cipher, a curious catchpaw of those enormous cultural polarities (Old and New, Tradition and Innovation, Country and City, Peace and War, Poetry and Prose, Custom and Logic, etc.) which Aristophanes loved to elaborate and which he presented in play after play as locked in a life-and-death struggle for the soul of Athens. Whether Aristophanes privately believed that Sokrates was a sophist or presented him that way for its comic and preposterous effect, we shall never know. But for the purposes of the play, Sokrates is merely a genial polemical emblem of the sophistic movement—if that extraordinary simultaneous flowering of individual genius, crankery, "educationism," and fraud can be called a movement at all. For Aristophanes such distinctions are academic, and to his mind the sophists are a movement only because they are something worse, a conspiracy of charlatans and humbugs. Distinctions of doctrine and belief are totally disregarded. Jumbled together in ludicrous proximity and then stuffed into the mouth of Sokrates are the doctrines of Protagoras, the pre-Socratics generally, Anaxagoras, Diagoras, Gorgias, Prodikos, and perhaps Thrasymachos. It is grotesque—and hilarious. It is polemic on the grand scale, contemptuous of niceties, careless of reputations, unfair, Procrustean, and passionately loyal to its central perception. Addressed to, and exploiting, the average man's ridiculous stereotype of philosophy and science, it remains an honest and uncompromising play.

Grant Aristophanes his premises, and his logic is ruthlessly consistent. If Sokrates is a symbol of intellectual corruption and fraud, Strepsiades represents the Old Tradition in its corruption. Far from presenting Sokrates as the indispensable corrupter, Aristophanes shows that Strepsiades can be hoodwinked only because he had been corrupted *prior* to his enrollment in the Thinkery. All Sokrates does is to complete the process—or at least he tries to. But for Aristophanes the Sophists are merely symptoms of the general corruption, not its causes; they stand to education and the life of the mind exactly as Kleon stands to politics and Euripides to tragedy. If the Sophists are strong in being unprincipled, Strepsiades is weak because he is stupid and because the principles and values that might have protected him from his own stupidity have deteriorated. He is essentially only a denser Dikaiopolis become citified and decadent; in another context he might have been a peasant hero. But transplanted to Athens from the country, cursed with an expensive aristocratic marriage and a playboy son, he is an Awful Warning on the Perils of the City and the Evils of Imperialism. According to Aristophanes, the process of corruption began with Athenian imperialism and the war fought to maintain the empire. If imperialism brought with it tyranny, luxury, litigation, and the domination of political life by demagogic rhetoric, the war was destroying the very fabric of Athenian life by ravaging the countryside and forcing the evacuation of the country population into the city. There, cut off from the earth and uprooted from the context that gave it life and value, the Old Order had decayed, and with it were being destroyed all those traditions and virtues and decencies which, for a conservative countryman like Aristophanes, were synonymous with Athenian civilization itself. Strepsiades is his comic image of this corruption and Sokrates its aggravating symptom. If the causes were irremediable, he could at least struggle with the symptoms. And no quarter asked or given.

Aristophanes and Sokrates

Why did Aristophanes select Sokrates as his spokesman for the Sophists, and was he guilty of malicious slander and moral irresponsibility in so doing?

By now these two questions have become inextricably bound up with the fortunes of the play which is, ironically, more commonly read as a perverse adjunct to The Sokratic Problem than for its satire of the sophists. No definite answer is possible in the poor state of our evidence, but the questions cannot be shrugged off, and I offer the following considerations for what they may be worth.

1. Plato's charge against Aristophanes is the serious charge of moral irresponsibility. By circulating a distorted image of Sokrates, Aristophanes created, or abetted, those slanders which Plato believed led to Sokrates' death. The official indictment read: "Sokrates is a malefactor who meddles in the matters of the heavens and the earth below, who makes the Worse Argument appear the Better and teaches others to follow his example." And the Platonic Sokrates comments to the jury: "You yourselves have seen these very things in Aristophanes' comedy—a Sokrates who is carried around in a basket and asserts that he walks upon the

air and a great many other aburdities, of which I am completely ignorant." We *may,* if we wish, doubt Plato's interpretation, but presumably the charges are accurately reported, and the implication is clear: the slanders of *The Clouds,* directly or indirectly, created the formal accusation brought against Sokrates in 399 B.C.

2. But the evidence is partisan and polemical. Plato's account is that of a devoted disciple, not a reporter, and the prejudice of Platonists is almost religious.[4]

3. Sokrates' own reaction, if Plutarch can be trusted,[5] was not that he had been slandered but that he had been teased: "I am twitted in the theater as I would be at a drinking-party."

4. Nonetheless, judging from the available evidence, the caricature of Sokrates in *The Clouds* is so distorted that it cannot be called a caricature at all. Thus Sokrates refused payment, was not an atheist, had no Thinkery, and never held the doctrines which are here put into his mouth. Worse, he consistently attacked the Sophists and their doctrines. He does, however, admit in the *Apology* that in his earlier days he had dabbled in "scientific" research.

5. That Aristophanes could not have foretold the consequence of his "slanders" is irrelevant. Slander is slander.

6. Aristophanes' private opinion of Sokrates is also irrelevant. In Plato's *Symposium,* the two men are presented as being on friendly terms, but this does not entitle us to suppose that Aristophanes really admired Sokrates or thought his views anything but pernicious. If it does, then Aristophanes was a hypocrite as well as morally irresponsible.

7. If Aristophanes was really ignorant of Sokrates' beliefs, he is equally culpable. Ignorance is no excuse for slander. But Aristophanes was anything but an ignorant man, and his refusal to allow his Sokrates to make one statement that is recognizably Sokratic seems to me to indicate strategy rather than stupidity.

8. The distortions practiced upon Sokrates are typical and not exceptional. They are, for instance, completely of a piece with Aristophanes' systematic distortion of Euripides; if Euripides' words are quoted against him, they are invariably taken from their context and parodied by willful misunderstanding. But those who are angered by the spectacle of Sokrates mocked have never lifted a finger in defense of Euripides.[6]

[4] It has even been suggested that *The Clouds* failed to win First Prize because the audience recognized—and disliked—the distorted image of Sokrates. Given what happened to Sokrates, this seems excessively naive.

[5] *De educatione puerorum* xiv.

[6] As Speaker of the House Rayburn said in a different context: "It all depends on *whose* ox is gettin' gored."

9. In any case, the treatment of Sokrates is *not,* by Aristophanic standards, harsh or "pitiless satire," as Platonists claim. It is, in fact, surprisingly mild and impersonal. (The savage attack upon Kleon in *The Knights* is an instructive comparison.) Thus, apart from a couple of gibes at Sokrates' gait and general bathlessness, his personal life is strictly avoided. We hear nothing of the shrewish Xanthippe, nothing of the fashionable pederasty of the Socratic circle (or at least nothing that implicates Sokrates), nothing about Sokrates' midwife-mother (*cf.* the treatment meted out to Euripides' mother), etc. The charges are wholly professional: Sokrates is a humbug and a charlatan.

10. Aristophanes' "slanders" are, in some real sense, dictated by convention. Comedy is the heir of the early *komos*, and the *komos* was a convention whose essential attributes were invective and abuse. Which is to say merely that the Athenian comedian was not merely given license to be abusive, but that abuse was *expected* of him. And precisely because it was conventional, was expected, it could be discounted as conventional; and presumably those who were ragged were expected to take their ragging in good part—as Sokrates did, though Kleon (and Plato) did not. Needless to say, such a convention makes the notion of "moral irresponsibility" extremely hard to assess.

11. Sokrates is presented as preposterous and this strikes me as cool and deliberate strategy—doubtless sustained by malice and even a little contempt. There is, after all, a kind of humor—the kind of humor of the *komos*, I suspect—which contrives its fun out of a total inversion of the truth. Because the humor is conventional, the exaggeration is understood *as* exaggeration and the humorist's success consists in the very size and absurdity of the distortion. The comedy lies in the disparity between the known truth and the degree of distortion achieved. This explanation might be less acceptable if it were not for the fact that Aristophanes is, of all comedians, the master of the incongruous, and that the stunning distortion is everywhere his stock-in-trade.

12. If Aristophanes has not made Sokrates preposterous because the preposterousness was funny, he has done so out of dislike and the conviction that Sokrates was dangerous. In this he was probably mistaken, but Aristophanes was a man in the livery of an Idea, and if Sokrates is distorted or satirized in the service of that Idea, it is regrettable but not culpable. Ideas distort the world and those who serve them. Platonists should understand.

Text and Acknowledgments

The texts which I have used as a basis of this translation are primarily those of Cantarella and Coulon, and I am, like every other translator of Aristophanes, indebted to B. B. Rogers' splendid notes and commentaries on individual passages. To both the University of California at Riverside and the University of Texas I owe my thanks for generous grants for the preparation of the manuscript. For help and encouragement and criticism, I am indebted to a great many people, but particularly to Douglass Parker and to my wife.

WILLIAM ARROWSMITH

Characters of the Play

STREPSIADES, *father of Pheidippides*
PHEIDIPPIDES, *a playboy*
XANTHIAS, *a slave*
STUDENTS OF SOKRATES
SOKRATES
CHORUS OF CLOUDS
KORYPHAIOS, *or Chorus Leader*
ARISTOPHANES
PHILOSOPHY
SOPHISTRY
PASIAS, *creditor of Strepsiades*
AMYNIAS, *creditor of Strepsiades*
CHAIREPHON, *disciple of Sokrates*

SLAVES, STUDENTS, WITNESSES, etc.

SCENE: *A street in Athens. On the left, the house of Strepsiades,* an old farmer compelled by the war to leave the country and take up residence in Athens; on the right the tiny, grubby, ramshackle hovel which houses Sokrates' Thinkery. On the extreme left a statue of Poseidon. Before Strepsiades' house stands a Herm, a bust of the god Hermes supported by a square pillar; in front of Sokrates' house, balancing the Herm, stands a potbellied stove with a long tapering flue and a placard which reads:* MODEL OF THE UNIVERSE ACCORDING TO THE CONVECTION PRINCIPLE.

Two cots are placed before Strepsiades' house, one occupied by Strepsiades himself, the other by Pheidippides. Huddled on the ground nearby lie several loudly snoring slaves. The time is just before dawn.

STREPSIADES

Thrashing restlessly, then throwing off his blankets and sitting bolt upright. He yawns.

Yaaaahhuuuuu.
Great Zeus Almighty, what an endless monster
of a night it's been! Won't the daylight *ever* come?
I could have sworn I heard the roosters crowing hours ago.
And listen to those slaves. Still snoring away!
By god, things around here were a long sight different
in the good old days before this war! Drat
this stinking war anyway! It's ruined Athens.
Why, you can't even whip your own slaves any more
or they'll desert to the Spartans.*
Bah.

Pointing to Pheidippides.

And as for *him,*
that precious playboy son of mine, he's worse yet.
Look at him, stretched out there sleeping like a log
under five fat blankets, farting away.
—All right,
if that's the way you want it, boy, I'll snuggle down
and fart you back a burst or two.

He burrows under the blankets for a moment, then throws them off and sits up again.

DAMN!

I'm so bitten up by all these blasted bedbuggering debts
and bills and stable-fees, I can't catch a wink.

Turning on Pheidippides.

And all because of YOU!
Yes, you and your damned horses!
Gigs, rigs, nags, ponytails*. . . . Hell,
horses everywhere! Horses in your dreams!
But *me?*
I'm bankrupt, broke, ruined, waiting for the end of the month
when all these debts come due.

Savagely kicking Xanthias awake.

—You. You there,
light me a lamp and bring me my ledger.

The slave rises, lights a flickering lamp, and brings him the ledger.

Now then,
I'll just run over this account of my debts and see
how much I owe.
Hmmmm.

Reading aloud.

TO PASIAS: *THE SUM OF THREE HUNDRED—*
Three hundred to Pasias? What in god's name for?
Of course. I remember. That gelding I bought him. Idiot!
Better I should have gelded myself.

PHEIDIPPIDES

Shouting in his sleep.

PHILO,
YOU FOULED ME! KEEP IN YOUR OWN LANE!

STREPSIADES

That's it.
That's the horsey blight that has blasted me dead.
Even in his dreams he thinks he's winning the derby.

PHEIDIPPIDES

In his sleep.

HOW MANY LAPS FOR THE STEEPLECHASE?

STREPSIADES

Laps, is it?
A fat lot of laps you've driven your poor old man!

Resuming his accounting.

Let's see now. What's the next entry after Pasias?

Reading aloud.

TO AMYNIAS: FOR GIG, BODY AND WHEELS INCLUDED, THE SUM OF—

PHEIDIPPIDES

In his sleep.

ROLL THE HORSE IN THE DUST, TRAINER, AND THEN STABLE HIM.

STREPSIADES

You've rolled *me* out of house and home, damn you!
I've lost two or three lawsuits on your account and now
the other creditors are clamoring for confiscation.

PHEIDIPPIDES

Waking up crossly.

Damn it, Dad,
why do you have to thrash around like this all night long?

STREPSIADES

Because there's a bumbailiff* in the mattress biting me,
that's why.

PHEIDIPPIDES

Oh, for god's sake, let me sleep, will you?

STREPSIADES

Go on, damn you, sleep! But I give you warning, boy.
Someday these debts will land on *your* head.

Pheidippides' only answer is a snore.

By god,
I hope that meddling matchmaker who prodded me on
to marry your mother dies a nasty death!
I used to be a farmer—the sweetest life on earth,
a lovely, moldy, unspruce, litter-jumbled life,
bursting with honeybees, bloated with sheep and olives.
And then, poor hick, what did I do but marry
your mother, a city girl, and niece of that Megakles
who was son and heir of old Blueblood Megakles* himself?
She was a pretty piece: Miss Megakles-de-luxe.
Well, so we got married and we clambered into bed—
me, a stink of wine-lees, fig-boxes, and wool-fat;
she, the whiff of spices, pure saffron, tonguekisses,
Luxury, High Prices, gourmandizing, goddess Lechery,
and every little elf, imp, and sprite of Intercourse.

But I'll say this for your mother: she was a worker.
Nothing slow about *her*. All day long she'd sit there
working away at her loom and shoving in the wool,
and then in bed at night she'd work on me
for more.
Expense meant nothing.
Clipped?
I was *shorn*.
"Madam," I said, "what do you think I am? A man
or a goat?

Suddenly the oil lamp sputters and goes out.

XANTHIAS

There's no oil left in the lamp.

STREPSIADES

Jackass!
And why in god's name did you light that guzzler of a lamp?
Come here and be whipped.

XANTHIAS

But why? What have *I* done?

STREPSIADES

Because you put in pot-bellied wicks, that's why.

He lunges at Xanthias who ducks away and disappears into the house.

Anyway, when that darling brat of ours was born
to the missus and me, we immediately started squabbling
over his name. She, of course, wanted something fancy,
some upperclass, high-horse handle with *hippos** in it—
Xanth*ippos* or Char*ippos* or Kall*ippi*des—while I naturally
wanted to give him the fine old name of Pheidonides*
in honor of his thrifty grandfather. Well, we haggled
and at last agreed on a compromise name: Pheidippides.*
She used to gush over the baby: "Just imagine. Someday
he'll be an important man, just like his Uncle Megakles,
and drive in his purple robes up to the Akropolis."
And I'd put in: "Ha, drive his goats from the hills,
you mean, dressed like his dad in a filthy smock."
Well, needless to say, he paid no heed to me
and now he's ended up by squirting his dirty horse-pox
all over my money.

Anyway, after beating my brains
all night long, I think I've finally found a way,
the *only* way out, a wonderful little chink of a loophole.
Now if I can only shove him through it, I'm saved.
But first I've got to find some way of waking him up.
I wonder what's the nicest way to wake up.
Hmmmm.

Cooing in Pheidippides' ear.

Pheidippides.
Little Pheidippides.

PHEIDIPPIDES

Waking angrily.

Damn it, Dad, what *now?*

STREPSIADES

Give your Old Man a kiss. There, now your hand, son.

PHEIDIPPIDES

Look here, what's this all about?

STREPSIADES

Tell me, my boy,
are you *really* fond of your poor old father?

PHEIDIPPIDES

Sure, Dad.
I swear it. So help me Poseidon.

STREPSIADES

No, NOT THAT!
For god's sake, none of those horse-god oaths* of yours!
Poseidon indeed! That god's the cause of all my troubles.
But if you *really* love me, my boy, I beg you, implore you,
do what I ask.
Please.

PHEIDIPPIDES

Suspiciously.

Depends. What are you asking?

STREPSIADES

Reform yourself, boy. Change your whole way of life.
Follow my advice and make a new man of yourself.
A fresh Pheidippides.

PHEIDIPPIDES

But how?

STREPSIADES

First promise.

PHEIDIPPIDES

Reluctantly.

I promise.

So help me—Dionysos.

STREPSIADES

Good. Now then, look over there.

Do you see that dirty little hovel with the dinky door?

PHEIDIPPIDES

Yes. But what are you driving at, Dad?

STREPSIADES

Awesomely.

My boy,

that little hovel is the Thinkery. Intellectuals live there,
professors who will teach you—and what's more, *prove* it—
that the whole atmosphere is actually a Cosmical Oven*
and we're not really people but little bits of charcoal
blazing away. What's more—for a fee,* of course—
they offer a course called *The Technique of Winning Lawsuits.**
Honest or dishonest, it's all one.

PHEIDIPPIDES

Who are they?

STREPSIADES

Great Scholars. Scientists.

PHEIDIPPIDES

Fine. Who are they?

STREPSIADES

Er . . .

Gentlemen. Men of Learning.

PHEIDIPPIDES

Yes, but what are their *names?*

STREPSIADES

Why . . .

PHEIDIPPIDES

Oh lord, I know those filthy charlatans you mean—
those frauds, those barefoot pedants with the look of death,
Chairephon and that humbug, Sokrates.

STREPSIADES

Scandalized.

Here, here, boy.
Hush. For shame. Don't ever let me hear you talking
so disrespectfully. What's more, if you don't want
your poor Old Man to starve, you'd better go study there
and ditch your damn horses.

PHEIDIPPIDES

By Dionysos, I *won't!*
Not on your life. I wouldn't go there if you bribed me
with every racehorse in Leogoras' stable!

STREPSIADES

My dearest boy,
I implore you. *Please* go and study at the Thinkery.

PHEIDIPPIDES

Study *what?*

STREPSIADES

I've heard that they teach two kinds of Logic.*
One of them is called Philosophical, or Moral, Logic—
whatever *that* may be. The other one is called
Sophistic, or Sokratic, Logic. Now, if you could learn
this second Logic, I wouldn't have to pay a penny
of all those debts you've saddled me with.

PHEIDIPPIDES

Count me out.
I'd rather die. Why, those vampires would suck me dry.
They'd scrape the tan right off my face. How could I
face the fellows down at the track?

STREPSIADES

Then, by Demeter,
you've had your last meal on me. Take your critturs
and pack out of this house and be damned to you!

PHEIDIPPIDES

Uncle Megakles
won't let me go horseless for long. I'll go to him.
The hell with you.

Exit Pheidippides.

STREPSIADES

I'm down, but not for long.
First I'll say a little prayer to the gods, and then
I'll go and enroll at the Thinkery myself.
But whoa:
at my age the memory is bad, the intellect dull.
How could I ever master that hair-splitting logic?
Still, I have to go, so why am I dawdling here
instead of banging on the door?

He walks over to Sokrates' house and kicks at the door.

—Hey, porter!

STUDENT

From within.

Go bang yourself.

Opening the door.

Who are you to kick our door?

STREPSIADES

Strepsiades, son of Pheidon. From Kikynna.

STUDENT

By god, the way you come here and kick in our door
I think your name should damn well be Stupidities.
Do you realize that you've just caused the miscarriage*
of a great scientific discovery?

STREPSIADES

Humbly apologetic.

Oh, please excuse me.
I didn't realize. You see, I come from the country.
But tell me, what discovery miscarried?

STUDENT

It's top secret.
Classified information. Access only to students.

STREPSIADES

You can tell *me* then. That's why I've come here,
to be a student at the Thinkery.

STUDENT

In that case, very well.
But remember, our researches are solemn mysteries.

Whispering.

Listen.
Just a minute ago Sokrates was questioning Chairephon
about the number of fleafeet a flea could broadjump.
You see, a flea happened to bite Chairephon on the eyebrow
and then vaulted across and landed on Sokrates' head.

STREPSIADES
How did he measure it?

STUDENT

A stroke of absolute genius.
First he melted some wax. Then he caught the flea,
dipped its tiny feet in the melted wax,
let it cool, and lo! little Persian bootees.
He slipped the bootees off and measured the distance.

STREPSIADES
Lord Zeus, what exquisite finesse of mind!

STUDENT
Elementary really. You haven't heard *anything* yet.
Would you like another sample?

STREPSIADES

Oh, I'd *like* that. Go on.

STUDENT
Well, it seems that Chairephon was asking Sokrates
which of two theories he held: that gnats tootled
through their mouths or, in reverse, through their tails.

STREPSIADES

Eagerly.

Gosh. Go on. What was his theory about the gnat?

STUDENT

Attend.
According to him, the intestinal tract of the gnat
is of puny proportions, and through this diminutive duct
the gastric gas of the gnat is forced under pressure
down to the rump. At that point the compressed gases,

as through a narrow valve, escape with a whoosh,
thereby causing the characteristic tootle or cry
of the flatulent gnat.

STREPSIADES

So the gnat has a bugle up its ass!
O thrice-blessèd mortals! What bowel-wisdom!
Why, the man who has mastered the ass of the gnat
could win an acquittal from any court!

STUDENT

And you know,
just the other day he was cheated of an immense discovery
because of a lizard.

STREPSIADES

Cheated by a *lizard?* But how?

STUDENT

It happened at night, during the course of his researches on the orbit
of the moon. There he stood, gaping wide-mouthed
at the sky, when a lizard on the roof let loose on him.

STREPSIADES

Ha! A lizard crapping on Sokrates! That's rich.

STUDENT

And last night there was nothing in school to eat.

STREPSIADES

Goodness,
how did he ever manage your supper?

STUDENT

A combination
of science and legerdemain.
He quickly sprinkled the table
with a fine film of powderlike ashes. Then,
deftly bending a skewer in the shape of a compass
he drew a vast arc along whose perimeter
the hook of his compass encountered somebody's cloak.
Quickly flicking his hand, he pulled back compass
and catch. He pawned the cloak; we ate the proceeds.

STREPSIADES

Why, Thales himself was an amateur compared to this!

Throw open the Thinkery! Unbolt the door
and let me see this wizard Sokrates in person.
Open up! I'm MAD for education!

The ekkyklema is wheeled about to show the whole interior court of Sokrates' Thinkery. High overhead the crane supports Sokrates in his basket busily scanning the heavens. Hanging on the walls of the Thinkery are various charts, maps, instruments, etc. In the center of the courtyard stand a number of utterly pale, emaciated students deeply engaged in a rapt contemplation of the ground.

Great Herakles,
what kind of zoo is this?

STUDENT

What's so strange about it?
What do you take them for?

STREPSIADES

Spartan prisoners
from Pylos.* But why are they all staring at the ground?

STUDENT

They're engaged in geological research:* a survey
of the earth's strata.

STREPSIADES

Of course. Looking for truffles.

To one of the students.

—You there, don't strain yourself looking. I know
where they grow big and beautiful.

Pointing to other students who are bent completely double.

Hey, and look there:
what are those fellows doing bent over like that?

STUDENT

Those are graduate students doing research on Hades.

STREPSIADES

On Hades? Then why are their asses scanning the skies?

STUDENT

Taking a minor in Astronomy.

To the students.

—Quick, inside with you.
Hurry, before the Master catches you.

STREPSIADES

No, wait.
Let them stay a little longer. I want to speak to them
on a *private* matter.

STUDENT

Impossible. The statutes clearly forbid
overexposure to fresh air.

The students disappear through a door at the rear. Strepsiades meanwhile is staring at the various maps and instruments on the walls.

STREPSIADES

Pointing to a chart.

In the name of heaven,
what's *that?*

STUDENT

That's for astronomy.

STREPSIADES

Pointing to surveying instruments.

And what are those?

STUDENT

They're for geometry.

STREPSIADES

Geometry? And what's that good for?

STUDENT

Surveying, of course.

STREPSIADES

Surveying what? Lots?

STUDENT

No. The whole world.

STREPSIADES

What a clever gadget!
And as patriotic as it is useful.*

STUDENT

Pointing to a map.

Now then, over here
we have a map of the entire world. You see there?
That's Athens.

STREPSIADES

That, Athens? Don't be ridiculous.
Why, I can't see even a single lawcourt in session.*

STUDENT

Nonetheless, it's quite true. It really is Athens.

STREPSIADES

Then where are my neighbors of Kikynna?

STUDENT

Here they are.
And you see this island squeezed along the coast?
That's Euboia.

STREPSIADES

I know that place well enough.
Perikles squeezed it dry.* But where's Sparta?

STUDENT

Sparta? Right over here.

STREPSIADES

That's MUCH TOO CLOSE!
You'd be well advised to move it further away.

STUDENT

But that's utterly impossible.

STREPSIADES

You'll be sorry you didn't,
by god.

For the first time Strepsiades catches sight of Sokrates in his basket overhead.

Look: who's that dangling up there in the basket?

STUDENT

Himself.

STREPSIADES

Who's Himself?

STUDENT

Sokrates.

STREPSIADES

SOKRATES!

Then call him down. Go on. Give a great big shout.

STUDENT

Hastily and apprehensively taking his leave.

Er . . . *you* call him. I'm a busy man.

Exit Student.

STREPSIADES

O Sokrates!

No answer from the basket.

Yoohoo, Sokrates!

SOKRATES

From a vast philosophical height.

Well, creature of a day?

STREPSIADES

What in the world are you doing up there?

SOKRATES

Ah, sir,

I walk upon the air and look down upon the sun
from a superior standpoint.

STREPSIADES

Well, I suppose it's better
that you sneer at the gods from a basket up in the air
than do it down here on the ground.

SOKRATES

Precisely. You see,
only by being suspended aloft, by dangling
my mind in the heavens and mingling my rare thought
with the ethereal air, could I ever achieve strict
scientific accuracy in my survey of the vast empyrean.
Had I pursued my inquiries from down there on the ground,
my data would be worthless. The earth, you see, pulls down
the delicate essence of thought to its own gross level.

As an afterthought.

Much the same thing happens with watercress.

STREPSIADES

Ecstatically bewildered.

You don't say?
Thought draws down . . . delicate essence . . . into watercress.
O dear little Sokrates, please come down. Lower away,
and teach me what I need to know!

Sokrates is slowly lowered earthwards.

SOKRATES

What subject?

STREPSIADES

Your course on public speaking and debating techniques.
You see, my creditors have become absolutely ferocious.
You should see how they're hounding me. What's more, Sokrates,
they're about to seize my belongings.

SOKRATES

How in the world
could you fall so deeply in debt without realizing it?

STREPSIADES

How?
A great, greedy horse-pox ate me up, that's how.
But that's why I want instruction in your second Logic,
you know the one—the get-away-without-paying argument.
I'll pay you *any* price you ask. I swear it.
By the gods.

SOKRATES

By the gods? The gods, my dear simple fellow,
are a mere expression coined by vulgar superstition.
We frown upon such coinage here.

STREPSIADES

What do *you* swear by?
Bars of iron, like the Byzantines?*

SOKRATES

Tell me, old man,
would you honestly like to learn the truth, the *real* truth,
about the gods?

STREPSIADES

By Zeus, I sure would. The *real* truth.

SOKRATES
And also be admitted to intercourse with their Serene Highnesses, our goddesses, the Clouds?

STREPSIADES
Intercourse with *real* goddesses?
Oh yes, I'd *like* that.

SOKRATES
Very well. First, however,
you must take your seat upon the mystical couch.*

STREPSIADES
I'm sitting.

SOKRATES
And now we place this sacrificial wreath on your head.

STREPSIADES
A *sacrificial* wreath?
Hey, NO!
Please, Sokrates,
don't murder me like poor Athamas* in Sophokles' play!

SOKRATES
Athamas was saved. You must mean Phrixos.

STREPSIADES
Athamas,
Phrixos—so who's a critic? Dead is dead.

SOKRATES
Courage, gaffer. This is normal procedure, required
of all our initiates alike.

STREPSIADES
Yeah? What's in it for me?

SOKRATES
Sprinkling Strepsiades from head to toe with ritual flour.
You shall be reborn, sir, as the perfect flower of orators,
a consummate, blathering, tinkling rascal.

STREPSIADES
That's no joke.
I'll be all flour the way you're powdering me.

SOKRATES

Silence!

Holy hush command your tongue. Listen to my prayer.

He stretches out his hands to heaven and prays.

O Lord God Immeasurable Ether, You who envelop the world!
O Translucent Ozone!
And you, O lightningthundered holy Clouds!
Great Majesties, arise!
Reveal yourselves to your Sophist's eyes.

STREPSIADES

Whoa, ladies, don't rain yet. Don't get me wet. Let me wrap up.

He wraps his head in his tunic.

What a damned fool! Coming without a hat.

SOKRATES

Come forth,
be manifest, majestic Clouds! Reveal your forms to me.
And whether on Olympos' snow your brooding eyrie lies,
or on the waves you weave the dance with Ocean's lovely daughters,
or dip your golden pitchers in the waters of the Nile,
or hover on Mount Mimas' snows, or over Lake Maiotis—
come forth, great Clouds!
Accept our prayers!
O hear us!
Amen.

From far off in the distance the Clouds are heard singing. As they slowly approach Athens, the singing increases steadily in volume as it rises in pitch.

CHORUS

Rise and soar
eternal Clouds!
Lift your loveliness of rain,
in sodden splendor come!
Soar from ocean's sullen swell,
rise higher to the peaks,
to the tall cliffs and trees!
Rise and soar,
while far below,
earth and shining harvest lie,
sound of god in river water,
blessèd ocean at its roar.

Arise!
For Ether's sleepless eye
now breaks with blazoned light!
Shake loose the rain,
immortal forms,
and walk upon the world!

A sustained burst of thunder is heard.

SOKRATES

O Clouds consummately blest, how clearly thy answer rumbles!

To Strepsiades.

—Did you hear that thunder crack, that *basso profundo* peal?

STREPSIADES

And how!

All hail your holyships! What a nasty jolt you gave me!
What a ratatat! You scared me so I've got to thunder too.

He breaks wind.

Sacrilege or not, I'VE GOT TO CRAP!

SOKRATES

Silence, boor!

No more of your smut. Leave filth like that to the comic stage.

A short low growl of thunder is heard.

Shhh.
Quiet.
The goddess swarm is stirring to its song.

CHORUS

Virgins of rain,
look on Pallas' shining earth,
this oil-anointed land,
country of Kekrops'
hero-breeding plain!
Holiness is here,
home of the mysteries,
whose unrevealable rites
sanctify the soul.
And here the gods have gifts.
Below the splendid gables go
processions of the blest,
and every season sees
its festivals, its crowns.

And early every Spring
Dionysos brings his joy,
the weaving of the dance,
the Muses and the flutes.

STREPSIADES

Holy Zeus, Sokrates, who were those ladies that sang that solemn hymn? Were they heroines of mythology?

SOKRATES

No, old man.

Those were the Clouds of heaven, goddesses of men of leisure
and philosophers. To them we owe our repertoire of verbal talents:
our eloquence, intellect, fustian, casuistry, force, wit,
prodigious vocabulary, circumlocutory skill—

STREPSIADES

Suddenly carried away in cloudy inspiration.

Then that's why
I suddenly tingled all over—as though I were carried up,
buoyant, exalted, swollen somehow with the flatus of philosophy:
a mist of verbal fluff, a sudden unsubstantial swelling,
a tumid bubble of wrangling words, a windbag of debate!
I seemed rent by lightning speech, ah, the thrust and parry
of opinion, of minds massively meeting . . .

In short, Sokrates,
if I could see those ladies in person, I'd LOVE to.

SOKRATES

Then look over toward Parnes. I can see them settling down ever so gently.

STREPSIADES

Where?

SOKRATES

There, a vast drifting swarm
nuzzling along through woods and valleys.

STREPSIADES

Rubbing his eyes.

I wonder what's wrong.
I can't see them.

SOKRATES

Look: just offstage.

STREPSIADES

Now I see them!

SOKRATES

You've got cataracts, friend, if you can't see them now.

Slowly and majestically, the Chorus of Clouds files in and takes up its position in the orchestra.

STREPSIADES

Ooh, what venerable ladies! They take up all the space.

SOKRATES

And you actually mean to say that it's never occurred to you that the Clouds of heaven were goddesses?

STREPSIADES

By Zeus, it's news to me.

I always used to think they were just fog and drizzle and mist.

SOKRATES

Clearly then you must also be ignorant of the fact that the Clouds are also patrons of a varied group of gentlemen, comprising: chiropractors, prophets, longhairs, quacks, fops, charlatans, fairies, dithyrambic poets, scientists, dandies, astrologers, and other men of leisure. And because all alike, without exception, walk with their heads among the clouds and base their inspiration on the murky Muse, the Clouds support them and feed them.

STREPSIADES

I see.

That's why they write*—

O downblow, dazed, of the sodden skies!

and

Ho, tresses of the Typho-headed gale! Ho, puffcheek squalls!

or

Spongy humus of the hyaline!

and

Hail, ye heaven-scudders,
sudden ospreys of the winds!

and

Come, ye wheeling cumuli,
ye clammy condensations, come!

And in return, these poets gorge themselves on the flesh of the mullet and eat of the breast of the thrush?

SOKRATES
And why not?

STREPSIADES
But what I want to know is this:
why, if these ladies are really Clouds, they look like women?
For honest clouds aren't women.

SOKRATES
Then what *do* they look like?

STREPSIADES
I don't know for sure. Well, they look like mashed-up fluff,
not at all like women. No, by Zeus. Women have . . . noses.

SOKRATES
Would you mind if I asked you a question or two?

STREPSIADES
Go right ahead.

SOKRATES
Haven't you sometimes seen a cloud that looked like a centaur?
Or a leopard perhaps? Or a wolf? Or a bull?

STREPSIADES
Often. So what?

SOKRATES
Well, the Clouds assume whatever shape they wish. Now suppose
they happened to meet some shaggy, hairy beast of a man—
Hieronymos, for instance; instantly they turn into wild centaurs
as a caricature of his lust.

STREPSIADES
I see. But what if they run into Simon,
that swindler of government funds?

SOKRATES
Presto, they turn into wolves
and catch his likeness to a T.

STREPSIADES
Oh, I see. And yesterday
because they met that coward Kleonymos, they turned into deer?

SOKRATES
Precisely. And just now, when they saw Kleisthenes in the audience,
they suddenly turned into women.

STREPSIADES

Welcome then, august Ladies!
Welcome, queens of heaven!
If ever you spoke to mortal man,
I implore you, speak to me!

A great burst of thunder.
Strepsiades cowers with fright.

KORYPHAIOS

Hail, superannuated man!
Hail, old birddog of culture!

To Sokrates.

And hail to you, O Sokrates,
high priest of poppycock!
Inform us what your wishes are.
For of all the polymaths on earth, it's you we most prefer—
you and Prodikos. Him we love for wisdom's sake, but you, sir,
for your swivel-eyes, your barefoot swagger down the street,
because you're poor on our account and terribly affected.

STREPSIADES

Name of Earth, what a voice! Solemn and holy and awful!

SOKRATES

These are the only gods there are. The rest are but figments.

STREPSIADES

Holy name of Earth! Olympian Zeus is a figment?

SOKRATES

Zeus?
What Zeus?
Nonsense.
There is no Zeus.

STREPSIADES

No Zeus?
Then *who* makes it rain? Answer me that.

SOKRATES

Why, the Clouds,
of course.
What's more, the proof is incontrovertible.
For instance,
have you ever yet seen rain when you didn't see a cloud?
But if your hypothesis were correct, Zeus could drizzle from an empty sky

while the clouds were on vacation.

STREPSIADES

By Apollo, you're right. A pretty proof.
And to think I always used to believe the rain was just Zeus
pissing through a sieve.
All right, *who* makes it thunder?
Brrr. I get goosebumps just saying it.

SOKRATES

The Clouds again,
of course. A simple process of Convection.

STREPSIADES

I admire you,
but I don't follow you.

SOKRATES

Listen. The Clouds are a saturate water-solution.
Tumescence in motion, of necessity, produces precipitation.
When these distended masses collide—*boom!*
Fulmination.

STREPSIADES

But who makes them move before they collide? Isn't that Zeus?

SOKRATES

Not Zeus, idiot. The Convection-principle!

STREPSIADES

Convection? That's a new one.
Just think. So Zeus is out and convection-principle's in.
Tch, tch.
But wait: you haven't told me who makes it thunder.

SOKRATES

But I just *finished* telling you! The Clouds are water-packed;
they collide with each other and explode because of the pressure.

STREPSIADES

Yeah?
And what's your proof for *that?*

SOKRATES

Why, take yourself as example.
You know that meat-stew the vendors sell at the Panathenaia?
How it gives you the cramps and your stomach starts to rumble?

STREPSIADES

Yes,
by Apollo! I remember. What an awful feeling! You feel sick
and your belly churns and the fart rips loose like thunder.
First just a gurgle, *pappapax;* then louder, *pappaPAPAXapaX,*
and finally like thunder, *PAPAPAPAXAPAXAPPAPAXapap!*

SOKRATES
Precisely.
First think of the tiny fart that your intestines make.
Then consider the heavens: their infinite farting is thunder.
For thunder and farting are, in principle, one and the same.

STREPSIADES
Then where does lightning come from? And when it strikes
why is it that some men are killed and others aren't even touched?
Clearly it's *got* to be Zeus. He's behind it, blasting the liars
with bolts of lightning.

SOKRATES
Look, you idiotic Stone-Age relic,
if Zeus strikes the liars with lightning, then why on earth
is a man like Simon still alive? Or Kleonymos? Or Theoros?
They're liars ten times over.
But no. Instead of doing that,
he shatters his own shrines, blasts the holiest place names
in Homer and splinters the great oaks. And why, I ask you?
Have you ever heard of an oak tree committing perjury?

STREPSIADES

Say,
you know, you've got something there. But how do you explain
the lightning?

SOKRATES

Attend.

Illustrating his lecture by means of the potbellied-stove Model of the Universe.

Let us hypothesize a current of arid air
ascending heavenwards. Now then, as this funnelled flatus
slowly invades the limp and dropsical sacks of the Clouds,
they, in turn, begin to belly and swell, distended with gas
like a child's balloon when inflated with air. Then, so prodigious
become the pressures within that the cloud-casings burst apart,
exploding with that celestial ratatat called thunder and thereby
releasing

the winds. These, in turn, whizz out at such incalculable velocities
that they catch on fire.
Result: lightning.

STREPSIADES

The very same thing that happened to me
at the great feast of Zeus!
I was roasting myself a sausage
and forgot to slit the skin. Well, suddenly it bloated up
and SPLAT!
—singed my eyebrows off and splattered my face with guts.

CHORUS

—Ah, how he hungers after learning!

To Strepsiades.

—Sir, if you can pass our test,
we guarantee that you shall be
—the cynosure of Hellas.
—Our requirements are these:
—First, is your memory keen?
—Do you hanker for researching?
—Are you subject to fatigue
from standing up or walking?
—Does winter weather daunt you?
—Can you go without a meal?
—Abstain from wine and exercise?
—And keep away from girls?
—Last, do you solemnly swear
adherence to our code?
—To wrangle
—niggle
—haggle
—battle
—a loyal soldier of the Tongue, conducting yourself always
like a true philosopher.

STREPSIADES

Ladies, if all you require
is hard work, insomnia, worry, endurance, and a stomach
that eats anything, why, have no fear. For I'm your man
and as hard as nails.

SOKRATES

And you promise to follow faithfully in my path, acknowledging no other gods but mine, to wit, the Trinity— GREAT CHAOS, THE CLOUDS, and BAMBOOZLE?

STREPSIADES

If I met another god, I'd cut him dead, so help me. Here and now I swear off sacrifice and prayer forever.

KORYPHAIOS

Then, Sir, inform us boldly what you wish. Providing you honor and revere the Clouds and faithfully pursue the Philosophical Life, you shall not fail.

STREPSIADES

Ladies, I'll tell you.

My ambition is modest, a trifling favor. Just let my muscular tongue outrace the whole of Hellas by a hundred laps.

KORYPHAIOS

Sir, you may consider your wishes granted. Never, from this time forth, shall any politician in Athens introduce more bills than you.

STREPSIADES

But I don't want to be a Senator! Listen, ladies: all I want is to escape the clutches of my creditors.

KORYPHAIOS

Your wishes are modest; we grant them. And now, Candidate, boldly commit yourself to the hands of our ministers.

STREPSIADES

Ladies, you've convinced me completely. Anyway, thanks to my thoroughbreds, my son, and my wife, I have no choice.

So I hereby bequeath you my body,
  for better, dear girls, or worse.
You can shrink me by slow starvation;
  or shrivel me dry with thirst.

You can freeze me or flay me skinless;
thrash me as hard as you please.
Do any damn thing you've a mind to—
my only conditions are these:

that when the ordeal is completed,
a new Strepsiades rise,
renowned to the world as a WELSHER,
famed as a TELLER OF LIES,

a CHEATER,
a BASTARD,
a PHONEY,
a BUM,
SHYSTER,
MOUTHPIECE,
TINHORN,
SCUM,
STOOLIE,
CON-MAN,
WINDBAG,
PUNK,
OILY,
GREASY,
HYPOCRITE,
SKUNK,
DUNGHILL,
SQUEALER,
SLIPPERY SAM,
FAKER,
DIDDLER,
SWINDLER,
SHAM,
—or just plain Lickspittle.

And then, dear ladies, for all I care,
Science can have the body,
to experiment, as it sees fit,
or serve me up as salami.

Yes, you can serve me up as salami!

KORYPHAIOS

Ah, here's a ready spirit, undaunted, unafraid!
—Sir,
complete your course with us and you shall win a glory
that towers to heaven.

STREPSIADES

Could you be a little more specific?

KORYPHAIOS

You shall pass your entire existence up in the air, among us,
strolling about with your head in the Clouds. Your life
shall be the envy of all mankind.

STREPSIADES

Ah, when shall I see that day?

KORYPHAIOS

Before long thousands of clients will stampede to your doors,
begging, pleading, imploring your service and advice
in all their lawsuits—many involving incredible sums.
I say no more.
—And now, Sokrates, take this old candidate
and test his worthiness to undergo the solemn rites of initiation.
Examine his mental powers; probe his mind and sift him.

SOKRATES

Now then, tell me something about yourself.
The information is essential if I'm to know
what strategies to employ against you.

STREPSIADES

Strategies?
What do you think I am? A military objective?

SOKRATES

No. I'm merely attempting to ask a few questions.
First, is your memory keen?

STREPSIADES

Well, it is and it isn't.
If a man owes me money, I never seem to forget it.
But if I do the owing, I somehow never remember.

SOKRATES

Well, perhaps you have some talents for speaking?

STREPSIADES
No, no talent for talk. But for larceny, lots.

SOKRATES
But how can you possibly learn?

STREPSIADES
Don't you worry.
I'll manage somehow.

SOKRATES
But look: suppose I toss you
some tidbit of higher wisdom? Could you catch it
on the fly?

STREPSIADES
What do you take me for? A puppydog
snapping up wisdom?

SOKRATES
No, a beastly old ignoramus.
In fact, I'm afraid we'll have to whip our wisdom
into your hide.
Hmmm.
Tell me, suppose someone
gave you a thrashing, what would you do?

STREPSIADES
Why,
I'd take my thrashing. Then after a little while
I'd hunt up a witness, and then a little while later
I'd bring suit for Assault and Battery.

SOKRATES
All right, old man,
undress.

STREPSIADES
Undress? But why? Have I said something wrong?

SOKRATES
No, no. But we require all candidates for initiation
to strip naked.

STREPSIADES
But I'm not a burglar,* Sokrates.
Here, search me if you want.

SOKRATES

What do you think I am?
A policeman? This is a solemn philosophical initiation.
So stop your idiot blather and get undressed.

STREPSIADES

Starting to undress with extreme reluctance.

Oh, all right.
No, wait.
First answer me this. If I study very hard
and pay attention in class, which one of your students
will I look like?

SOKRATES

Why, you'll be the spitting image of—
Chairephon.

STREPSIADES

CHAIREPHON! But he's a walking cadaver.
I'll graduate a corpse.

He feverishly whisks his cloak back on.

SOKRATES

Damnation! Stop this stalling
and GET UNDRESSED!

He pulls off Strepsiades' cloak and shoves him bodily toward the black cavelike opening at the rear of the Thinkery.

Forward, Candidate!

STREPSIADES

NO! WAIT!
I'm scared. Brr, it's as dark as a snakepit down there.
Give me a honeycake to throw to the snakes, Sokrates,
or they'll eat me alive.

SOKRATES

Forward, fool. No hesitation now!

Sokrates shoves Strepsiades before him into the opening at the rear of the Thinkery. Then he rushes back, snatches up Strepsiades' discarded cloak, smiles, tucks it under his tunic, and vanishes into the Thinkery.

CHORUS

Farewell, brave soul,
and may your future gleam as bright
as shines your courage now!
May all good fortune come to you
who, sunk in bitter age,
in the somber twilight of your years,
stride forth, undaunted, unafraid,
toward that uttermost frontier of thought
where wisdom lures you on,
O pioneer!

The Chorus turns sharply and faces the audience. From the wing appears the poet, the bald Aristophanes; he strides forth and addresses the audience directly.

ARISTOPHANES*

Gentlemen, in the name of Dionysos to whom I owe my nurture as a poet,
I intend to confront you with my personal complaints, frankly and freely,
as a poet should.
My ambitions, of course, are very simply stated:
the First Prize and a reputation for talent and wit.
Accordingly,
firmly convinced that this audience was composed of men of taste,
and that this play, THE CLOUDS, was the finest of my comedies to date,
I submitted an earlier version, expecting your pleasure and approval.
It cost me enormous anguish and labor, and yet I was forced to withdraw,
ignobly defeated by cheap and vulgar rivals. My present reproaches,
needless to say, are aimed at those self-styled critics and wits
for whom this revision has been made.
However, to the men of true taste
among you, I say this: I am, as always, your faithful friend,
and never will I willingly or knowingly abandon you or reproach you.
After all, I still remember that glorious day when the Judges—
men of whose extraordinary taste and discrimination it is a joy to speak—
awarded the First Prize to my youthful comedy, *The Banqueters.*
Now at that time, gentlemen, my Muse was the merest slip of a girl,
a tender virgin who could not—without outraging all propriety—

give birth. So I exposed her child, her maiden effort, and a stranger
rescued the foundling.* But it was you, gentlemen, whose generous
patronage
nourished my offspring, and I have never since doubted those tokens
of your exquisite taste.
And now, gentlemen, like Elektra in the play,*
a sister-comedy comes in search of you today, hoping to find
those same tokens of recognition. Let her so much as glimpse
a single curl from her brother's head, and she will know her own,
as I shall know the tokens of your approval.
She's a dainty play.
Observe, gentlemen, her natural modesty, the demureness of her dress,
with no dangling thong of leather,* red and thick at the tip,
to make the small boys snigger. Note too her delicate refinement—
her refusal to indulge in cheap cracks at the expense of baldness,
and the quiet dignity of her dancing, with nothing salacious about it.
Observe the absence of farcical slapstick and sensational situations.
Here you see no poor old man drubbing his opponents with a stick
in a futile attempt to hide the abysmal poverty of his verses.
Nor does she fling herself on stage with tragic torches blazing
and bloodcurdling fustian. No, gentlemen, my comedy comes to you
relying upon herself and her poetry.
This is what she is,
and I am the poet, her adoring father. Now I may be baldheaded
(as some of my competitors so tirelessly point out), but I am *not*
vapid;
and it has never been *my* practice to serve you up some réchauffé
of stale and tired plots. No, my fictions are always fresh,
no two of them the least alike, and all of them uproariously funny.
Observe, moreover, gentlemen, that it was *I* who punched Kleon
in the paunch in his hour of pride; yet once I had him on the ground,
I refused to kick him.
But consider my competitors; note their conduct
with poor Hyperbolos. Once they had him floored, they never stopped
grinding him down in the dirt—*plus* his mother into the bargain.
It was Eupolis, of course, who led the mass-attack upon Hyperbolos;
he gutted my KNIGHTS, botched it, and then dragged the resultant
abortion
on stage—a stunning new plagiarism entitled (of *course*) THE
PEDERAST.
Even as larceny, a complete flop: Eupolis wanted a dirty dance,*
so what did he do but introduce a drunken old hag to shake her hips?
Not that *she* was original either; he lifted her from an ancient play
by Phrynichos (who quite sensibly fed the old bitch to a sea monster).

So much for Eupolis.
After him, Hermippos opened up on Hyperbolos,
and before long every imitator in town was after Hyperbolos' hide,
and every last one of them plagiarized my celebrated simile on the eels.*
I devoutly pray that those who like such stuff are bored to death
by mine. But as for you men of taste who enjoy your Aristophanes
and applaud his talent, why, posterity will endorse your judgment.

Exit Aristophanes.

CHORUS

You, our king, we summon first.
Omnipotence, in glory throned,
look down upon our dances.
O Zeus, be with us now!

And you, steward of the sea,
whose savage trident's power
heaves the shattered world
and pries the waters up,
O Poseidon, hear our prayer!

And you, O Father Ether,
pure presence of Air,
nourisher, sustainer,
O Spirit, quicken us now!

And you whose flaring horses blaze
across the skies! O benison,
splendor whose shining spills
on earth, on heaven,
O Light, illuminate us all!

KORYPHAIOS

Gentlemen, Critics, and Clever Fellows:
YOUR ATTENTION PLEASE.
Because our agenda includes a few complaints and home truths,
we shall be blunt.
WE ARE TIRED OF BEING IGNORED.
Of all the gods
to whom this city stands in debt for benefits conferred,
no god has brought more benefits than we. Yet we alone,
forsaken and forgotten gods, receive no sacrifice at all.

But surely we need not remind you of all our loving care,
the unsleeping devotion lavished, gentlemen, on your behalf?
For example,
whenever you launch some exceptionally crack-brained project,
we promptly thunder our objection; we drizzle our displeasure.
Or look to recent history. Have you forgotten that black day
when a low tanner, a repulsive atheist nicknamed Paphlagon*
was running for election as General? And how we responded?
How we furrowed our beetling brows and rumbled with rage,
and *hard on the heels of the Levin rattled the steeds of Thunder?**
How the moon, in dudgeon, snuffed her flame amongst the rack,
and the sun in sullenness withdrew,* curling his blazing wick
back beneath his globe, refusing to shine if this Kleon
were elected?
So you elected—Kleon!
As native Athenians, gentlemen,
you are all familiar with that local brand of statesmanship
sometimes known as Blundering Through—the curious belief
which holds that, by virtue of some timely divine intervention,
all your most appalling political blunders will sooner or later
redound to the interest of Athens.
Whence the question arises:
why not make a good thing of this latest glaring example
of Blundering Through?
How?
By convicting this cormorant Kleon
of bribery and peculation. Then muzzle his omnivorous maw
and slap a yoke around his neck. Not only is such action
in perfect accord with your long tradition of Blundering Through,
but with one shrewd stroke all your bungling is redeemed
as statesmanship, manifestly furthering the noblest interests of Athens.

CHORUS

O lord of Delos, you
who haunt the cliffs and scarp,
where the ridge of Kynthos rises,
O Phoibos, be with us now!

And you of Ephesos, lady,
glory of the shrine of gold
where the Lydian women worship,
O Artemis, come to the dance!

And you, goddess on the hill,
mistress of this lovely land
beneath your aegis guarded,
O Athene, be with us now!

And you, dancer of Delphoi,
runner upon the peaks, at dark
when the trailing torches flicker
and the whirling Maenads cry their joy,
O Dionysos, dance with us now!

KORYPHAIOS

Our cluster of Clouds had gathered for the outing down to Athens
when we chanced to run into the Moon, who asked us to deliver
the following message on her behalf:

GREETINGS SALUTATIONS ETCET
TO ATHENS AND ALLIES STOP MY DEITY MORTALLY OFFENDED
BY YOUR SCANDALOUS RUDENESS DESPITE MANY SUBSTANTIAL CONTRIBUTIONS
TO WELFARE OF ATHENS STOP AM WOMAN OF ACTIONS REPEAT ACTIONS
NOT WORDS
(Signed)
THE MOON.

And the Moon has a point, gentlemen.
Thanks to her shining efforts on your behalf, your average savings
on lighting alone run more than a drachma a month. Why,
I can hear you now, instructing your slaves as you leave the house,
"No need to buy torches tonight, lad. The moonlight's lovely."
And moonlight is merely one of her many services. Nonetheless,
you brusquely refuse to devise an Accurate Lunar Calendar,
and your month is a consequent chaos,* a masterpiece of temporal confusion.
Worse still, when the gods come hungrily trudging home at night
and find they must do without their dinner because you celebrate
your festivals on the wrong day, it's the poor innocent Moon
who bears the brunt of their heavenly grumbling. What's more,
on the days when you ought to sacrifice to the gods, you're bustling
about holding trials or torturing some poor witness on the rack.

And conversely, no sooner do the gods fast or go into mourning
for Memnon or Sarpedon, than you Athenians start carousing
and boozing.
So be warned, gentlemen.
Very recently the gods
stripped Hyperbolos of his seat* on the Commission for Public Festivals
and Other Red-Letter Days—a measure designed to teach him
and all such Johnnies-Come-Lately a little respect for time.

While the Chorus resumes its customary position, the doors of the Thinkery are thrown open and Sokrates appears.

SOKRATES

Almighty Effluvium! Ozone and Chaos! Never
in all my days have I seen such peerless stupidity,
such a bungling, oblivious, brainless imbecile as this!
I no sooner teach him the merest snippets of science
than he suffers an attack of total amnesia. Still,
the Truth is my mistress and I obey.

He goes to the Thinkery door and peers into the darkness.

—Strepsiades,
where are you?
Fetch your mattress and come outside.

Strepsiades appears at the door, tugging at his mattress.

STREPSIADES

I can't come. The little bugs won't let me leave.

SOKRATES

Down with it, blockhead. Now your attention, please.

STREPSIADES

Ready.

SOKRATES

To resume then, what particular discipline
in that vast array of choices offered by your ignorance
would you especially like to acquire? For instance,
would you prefer diction or rhythm or measures?

STREPSIADES

Measures.

Why, just the other day the flourman swindled me
of half a peck.

SOKRATES

Not dry measures, dunderhead!
I want to know which *meter* you'd prefer to master—
trimeter or tetrameter.

STREPSIADES

Well, I like the yard
as well as anything.

SOKRATES

Rubbish. Palpable rubbish.

STREPSIADES

What would you like to bet that your trimeter isn't
exactly three feet?

SOKRATES

Why, you illiterate numskull!
However, perhaps you'd do better with rhythm.

STREPSIADES

Rhythm?

Will rhythm buy the groceries?

SOKRATES

Sensitivity to rhythm
confers a certain ineluctable social *savoir-faire.*
Polite society will accept you if you can discriminate, say,
between the marital anapest and common dactylic—
sometimes vulgarly called finger-rhythm.*

STREPSIADES

Finger-rhythm?

I know *that.*

SOKRATES

Define it then.

STREPSIADES

Extending his middle finger in an obscene gesture.

Why, it's tapping time
with *this* finger. Of course, when I was a boy

*Raising his phallus to the ready.**

I used to make rhythm with *this* one.

SOKRATES

Why, you lout!

STREPSIADES

But look, you goose, I don't want to learn this stuff.

SOKRATES

Then what *do* you want to learn?

STREPSIADES

Logic! Logic!
Teach me your Immoral Logic!

SOKRATES

But, my dear fellow,
one must begin by mastering the rudiments of language.
For instance, can you list me the male quadrupeds?

STREPSIADES

Pooh, I *would* be a damnfool if I didn't know *them*.
Listen: the ram, the buck, the stallion, the bull,
the duck—

SOKRATES

And now the females of the same quadrupeds.

STREPSIADES

Let's see: the ewe, the doe, the mare, the cow,
the duck—

SOKRATES

Stop right there. A gross solecism.
According to you, the word *duck* apparently applies
to both the male and female of the species.

STREPSIADES

Huh?
How do you mean?

SOKRATES

In *your* usage, they're both ducks.

STREPSIADES

Holy Poseidon, you're right! What should I have said?

SOKRATES

The male is a *duck;* the female's a *duchess.**

STREPSIADES

A *duchess?*

Bravo! Almighty Ozone, that's a good one!
For that little lesson, you can bring out your basket
and I'll fill it with seed.

SOKRATES

Oops. Another solecism.
You've made *basket* masculine, when it's feminine.*

STREPSIADES

What?

Basket is masculine? But why?

SOKRATES

Because the ending-*et*
is what in grammar we call a masculine termination.
Like the *-os* ending of *Kleonymos.*

STREPSIADES

Wait. I don't see.

SOKRATES

I repeat: *basket* and *Kleonymos* are masculine in form
and ending.

STREPSIADES

Kleonymos *masculine?* But *he*'s feminine.
Form and ending. Queer as they come.
But look,
what *should* I call a basket?

SOKRATES

Why, a *baskette,* of course.
By analogy with *toilette.*

STREPSIADES

Baskette, eh?

SOKRATES

That's it.

Now you're talking Greek.

STREPSIADES

The *baskette* of *Kleonymette?*

SOKRATES

Precisely. Which brings us to the distinction between men's names and women's names.

STREPSIADES

Oh, I know the female names.

SOKRATES

For example?

STREPSIADES

For example: Lysilla, Philinna, Demetria, Kleitagora—

SOKRATES

And now recite some masculine names.

STREPSIADES

Easy. There's thousands of them. Like Philoxenos, Melesias, Amynias—

SOKRATES

Stop, you nincompoop. I asked for men's names, not women's names.

STREPSIADES

You mean those *aren't* men's names?

SOKRATES

Not men's names at all. A transparent confusion between singular and plural. Suppose, for instance, we drop the plural *s* from Amynias, what would we have?

STREPSIADES

Why, Amynia.*

SOKRATES

You see, by dropping the plural *s*, you've made Amynias a singular woman.

STREPSIADES

Well, the draftdodger,
it serves him right. But why am I learning stuff
any damn fool knows?

SOKRATES

Fool, you flatter yourself.
However, lie down on your mattress and—

STREPSIADES

And what, Sokrates?

SOKRATES

And lucubrate upon your dilemma.

STREPSIADES

Please, no, Sokrates!
Anywhere but there. Couldn't I just go and lubricate
on the ground?

SOKRATES

Permission refused.

STREPSIADES

Ohh, what a fate!
Those little bugs are sure to crucify me now.

Strepsiades burrows under the infested sheepskins on his mattress, while Sokrates chants encouragement.

SOKRATES

First concentrate.
Then cerebrate.
Now concentrate again.

Then lucubrate.
Next, speculate
Now ruminate. And then,

if your mind gets stuck,
don't curse your luck.
Get up! Quick as a wink,

cut through the knot,
swift as a thought,
but THINK, Candidate, THINK!

Now hence, ye Syrops of Sleep! Come hither, O Pain!

STREPSIADES

Yooooooow! Yooooooow!

SOKRATES

Look here, what's biting you now?

STREPSIADES

Biting, you say?
THEY'RE MURDERING ME!
Out of the ticking
the bugs come creeping.
They're biting my ribs.
They're swilling my blood.
My balls are all sores.
My ass is a shambles.
THEY'RE MURDERING ME!

SOKRATES

There, there, old fellow. Don't take it so hard.

STREPSIADES

DON'T TAKE IT SO HARD?
When my money's gone?
When my skin's gone?
When my blood's gone?
And then what's more,
when I tried to hum
and forget these bites,
I DAMN NEAR DIED!

There is a brief interval of silence during which Strepsiades hums and thrashes under his covers. Then Sokrates picks up a sheepskin and peers under.

SOKRATES

Here, what's this? Have you stopped lucubrating?

STREPSIADES

Who, *me?*
By Poseidon, I *have not!*

SOKRATES

What thoughts have you had?

STREPSIADES
Only this: I've been thinking how much of me would be left when the bugs got through.

SOKRATES
Bah! Consume you for an ass.

STREPSIADES
I *am* consumed.

SOKRATES
Courage, gaffer. We mustn't repine.
Pull back your covers and concentrate. What we need
is some clever quibbling subterfuge with which to frustrate
and fleece your creditors.

STREPSIADES
Who's fleecing *who*, Sokrates?
That's what I'd like to know.

Another brief silence follows.

SOKRATES
Hmmm. I wonder
what he's up to now? I'll just peek under the covers.

He lifts the sheepskin.

What's this? Asleep on the job, are you?

STREPSIADES
By Apollo,
I'm *not* sleeping!

SOKRATES
Any thoughts yet?

STREPSIADES
Not a thing.

SOKRATES
Surely you've found *something*.

STREPSIADES
Well, only this thing
I've got in my hand.

SOKRATES
Buffoon! Get back to your pallet
and cogitate.

STREPSIADES

But, Sokrates, what am I cogitating *about?*

SOKRATES

A moot question, friend, whose answer lies with you.
When *you* know what *you* want, kindly illuminate *me.*

STREPSIADES

But I've told you ten thousand times already, Sokrates.
It's my debts. I want to welsh on my debts.

SOKRATES

Splendid.

Then back to your pallet.

Strepsiades dutifully crawls under his sheepskin.

And now distill your mind
to its airiest essence, allowing the subtle elixirs of thought
to permeate and penetrate every pore of the problem.
Then Analyze, Refine, Synthesize, Define—

STREPSIADES

Frantically thrashing to escape the bugs.

OUCH!

SOKRATES

Stop fidgeting!

—However, in the case of a dilemma,
defer your inquiry briefly. When refreshed, return,
sift your conclusions and knead vigorously. Then mull
the results.

STREPSIADES

Suddenly illuminated.

Ooooh, Sokrates!

SOKRATES

Yes?

STREPSIADES

EUREKA!

I've got it. A glorious dodge for ditching my debts!

SOKRATES

Aha. Expatiate.

STREPSIADES

Well, just suppose—

SOKRATES

Supposing *what?*

STREPSIADES

Just suppose I rented one of those witchwomen from Thessaly*
and ordered her to charm down the moon from the sky. And then
I snatch up the moon and I pop her into a box,
and polish her face until she shines like a mirror.

SOKRATES

And what would you gain by that?

STREPSIADES

What would I gain?
Why, think what would happen if the moon never rose.
I wouldn't have to pay interest.

SOKRATES

No interest? But why?

STREPSIADES

Because interest falls due on the last day of the month,
before the New Moon, doesn't it?

SOKRATES

A superlative swindle!
Now then, let me propose a somewhat thornier case.
You are threatened, we assume, with a suit for five talents.
Problem: how do you quash the verdict?

STREPSIADES

How? *I* don't know.
I'd have to meditate on *that*.

SOKRATES

By all means meditate;
but beware of immuring your mind with excessive introspection.
Allow your intellect instead to sally forth upon her own,
as though you held a cockroach on a leash.

STREPSIADES

Suddenly illuminated.

Ooh, Sokrates, I've found a glorious bamboozle! I've got it!
Admit it, it's wonderful!

SOKRATES

Kindly expound it first.

STREPSIADES

Well, have you ever noticed in the druggists' shops
that beautiful stone, that transparent sort of glass
that makes things burn?

SOKRATES

A magnifying glass, you mean?

STREPSIADES

That's it. Well, suppose I'm holding one of these,
and while the court secretary is recording my case,
I stand way off, keeping the sun behind me,
and scorch out every word of the charges.*

SOKRATES

By the Graces,
a magnificent Bamboozle!

STREPSIADES

Whew, and am I glad
to get *that* suit quashed!

SOKRATES

Now then, try your teeth
on this little teaser.

STREPSIADES

Shoot.

SOKRATES

This time imagine
that you find yourself a defendant without a witness.
Your case is absolutely hopeless. Problem: to prevent
your opponent's suit from coming to trial.

STREPSIADES

Pooh,
nothing to it at all.

SOKRATES

Elaborate.

STREPSIADES

But it's a pushover,
Sokrates. While they were trying the case before mine,
I'd go hang myself.

SOKRATES

Preposterous!

STREPSIADES

It's *not* preposterous.

You can't sue a corpse.

SOKRATES

Poppycock. Palpable rubbish.

As your tutor, I hereby resign. And now, GET OUT!

STREPSIADES

You resign? But why?

Falling on his knees in supplication.

Oh, please. I implore you, Sokrates . . .

SOKRATES

But you forget everything as fast as you learn it, numskull!
Tell me, what was the first lesson?
Well, speak up.

STREPSIADES

Let me think.
The first lesson?
The *first* lesson?
Ummm. That whoozit you put seeds in!
For god's sake,
what *is* it called?

SOKRATES

Why, you blithering bungler!
You senile incompetent! You . . . you mooncalf! Clear out!

STREPSIADES

Sweet gods in heaven, what's to become of me now?
I'm a goner unless I master those sleights-of-tongue.

Falling on his knees before the Chorus.

O most gracious Clouds, please advise me. Tell me
what to do.

KORYPHAIOS

Our counsel, reverend sir, is this.
Have you a grown-up son perhaps? Then send him off
to study in your place.

STREPSIADES

It's true, ladies, I have a son,
but he's a gentleman, you see, with a true gentleman's
natural distaste for learning. So what can I do?

KORYPHAIOS

Is he the boss?

STREPSIADES

Well, he's a strapping, sturdy boy,
and there's a bit of eagle-blood on his mother's side.
Still, I'll go fetch him anyway. If he refuses
to learn his lessons, by god, he'll never set foot
in my house again!

To Sokrates.

—I won't be gone a moment.

Exit Strepsiades into his house.

CHORUS

Now, sir, you see
what blessings we,
the Clouds, have brought to pass.

E.g. this fool-
ish, willing tool,
this frantic, eager ass.

But seize your prey.
Avoid delay.
No matter how well hooked,

your fish is not
fried fish till caught—
and goose is better cooked.

Exit Sokrates. Enter Strepsiades, dragging Pheidippides.

STREPSIADES

Out with you! By Condensation, you won't stay here!
Go cut your teeth on Megakles' money!

PHEIDIPPIDES

But Father,
what's the matter with you? Are you out of your head?
Almighty Zeus, you must be mad!

STREPSIADES

"Almighty Zeus!"

What musty rubbish! Imagine, a boy your age
still believing in Zeus!

PHEIDIPPIDES

What's so damn funny?

STREPSIADES

It tickles me when the heads of toddlers like you
are still stuffed with such outdated notions. Now then,
listen to me and I'll tell you a secret or two
that might make an intelligent man of you yet.
But remember: you mustn't breathe a word of this.

PHEIDIPPIDES

A word of what?

STREPSIADES

Didn't you just swear by Zeus?

PHEIDIPPIDES

I did.

STREPSIADES

Now learn what Education can do for *you:*
Pheidippides, there is no Zeus.

PHEIDIPPIDES

There is no Zeus?

STREPSIADES

No Zeus. Convection-Principle's in power now.
Zeus has been banished.

PHEIDIPPIDES

Drivel!

STREPSIADES

Take my word for it,

it's absolutely true.

PHEIDIPPIDES

Who says so?

STREPSIADES

Sokrates.

And Chairephon too. The famous expert on fleafeet.

PHEIDIPPIDES

Are you so far gone on the road to complete insanity
you'd believe the word of those charlatans?

STREPSIADES

Hush, boy.
For shame. I won't hear you speaking disrespectfully
of such eminent scientists and geniuses. And, what's more,
men of such fantastic frugality and Spartan thrift,
they regard baths, haircuts, and personal cleanliness generally
as an utter waste of time and money—whereas *you,*
dear boy, have taken me to the cleaner's so many times,
I'm damn near washed up. Come on, for your father's sake,
go and learn.

PHEIDIPPIDES

What do they teach that's worth knowing?

STREPSIADES

Worth knowing? Why, the accumulated wisdom of mankind.
For instance, what a blockhead and numskull you are.
Hmmm.
Wait here. I'll be right back.

Strepsiades darts into his house.

PHEIDIPPIDES

Gods in heaven,
what should I do? My father's gone completely balmy.
Should I hale him into court on charges of insanity
or notify the undertakers?

Strepsiades reappears with a pair of ducks. He holds up first one and then the other.

STREPSIADES

Now then, what's this called?

PHEIDIPPIDES

That? A duck.

STREPSIADES

Excellent. Now what do you call this?

PHEIDIPPIDES

Why, another duck.

STREPSIADES

Another duck? You stupid boy.

From now on you must learn to call them by their right names.
This one is a duck; that one's a duchess.

PHEIDIPPIDES

A *duchess!*
So this is the glorious wisdom you've picked up
from those walking corpses!

STREPSIADES

Oh, there's lots more too,
but I'm so old everything I learn goes in one ear
and right out the other.

PHEIDIPPIDES

Ah. Doubtless that explains
how you lost your cloak.

STREPSIADES

I didn't lose it. I swapped it.
For thoughts.

PHEIDIPPIDES

And where have your sandals gone, you idiot?

STREPSIADES

In the words of Perikles himself when they asked him
where the money went: *Expended as required.*
*No comment.**
And now, inside with you, boy.
Humor me in this and you can make an ass of yourself
in any way you like. Ah, how well I remember those days
when you were six, and I had to humor your tantrums.
Why, the very first pay I ever drew as a juror
went to buy you a cart at the fair.

PHEIDIPPIDES

All right, Dad.
But someday you'll be sorry.

STREPSIADES

Ah, good dutiful boy.
—Hallo there, Sokrates!
Hey, Sokrates, come outside.
I've brought my son along—no damn thanks to him.

Enter Sokrates from the Thinkery.

SOKRATES

Why, he's still a baby. How could a toddler like this
possibly operate our Hanging Baskets?

PHEIDIPPIDES

As for you,
why don't you hang yourself and skip the basket?

STREPSIADES

Here,
for shame! You'd insult the Master?

SOKRATES

Imitating Pheidippides.

"Thkip the bathket."
Dear me, what adorable, childish prattle. And look
at those great sulking lower lips. How in the world
could this fumbling foetus ever master the arts
of Verdict-Quashing, False Witness, Innuendo,
and Character Assassination? On the other hand, however,
the case is not without precedent. *Even* Hyperbolos,*
after all, somehow mastered the tricks of the trade.
The fee, of course, was prodigious.

STREPSIADES

Now don't you worry,
Sokrates. The boy's a born philosopher. Yes, sir,
when he was just a mite of a shaver, *so* high,
he used to make the cleverest things you ever saw.
Why, there were dollhouses, sailboats, little pushcarts
from scraps of leather, and the sweetest little frogs
carved from fruit peel. He's a scholar, all right.
So tutor him in your two logics—traditional Philosophical Logic
and that flashy modern sophistic logic they call Immoral
because it's so wonderfully wicked. In any case,
if he can't master both logics, I insist that he learn
the Immoral Kind of argument.

SOKRATES

Philosophy and Sophistry*
will instruct your son in person. And now, gentlemen,
if you'll excuse me, I must leave.

STREPSIADES

But remember, Sokrates:
I want him able to make an utter mockery of the truth.

Exit Sokrates. After his departure the doors of the Thinkery are thrown open and Philosophy and Sophistry are rolled forward in great gilded cages. From the shoulders down, both are human; from the neck up they are fighting-cocks. Philosophy (or the Traditional Logic) is a large, muscular rooster, powerful but not heavy, expressing in his movements that inward harmony and grace and dignity which the Old Education was meant to produce; his plumage is so simple and dignified as to seem almost dingy. Sophistry, by contrast, is comparatively slight, with sloping shoulders, an emaciated pallor, an enormous tongue and a disproportionately large phallus. His body is graceless but extremely quick-moving; his every motion expresses defiant belligerence, and his plumage is brilliant to the point of flashiness. The debate itself should be conducted at top speed with much scratching and spurring. As the Attendants open the cages, the fighters step out and circle each other warily, jockeying for position.*

PHILOSOPHY
Front and center, you Feathered Impertinence.
Take your little bow before the audience.
You like to swagger.

SOPHISTRY
Why, you Pompous Lump,
with all my heart. The bigger the crowd,
the better I'll rebut you.

PHILOSOPHY
You'll rebut *me?*
Who are *you,* runt?

SOPHISTRY
A Logic.

PHILOSOPHY
You,
A Logic? Why, you cheap, stunted Loquacity!
You pipsqueak Palaver!

SOPHISTRY

I may be called
Mere Sophistry, but I'll chop you down
to size. I'll *refute* you.

PHILOSOPHY

Refute *me?* How?

SOPHISTRY

With unconventionality. With ultramodernity.
With unorthodox ideas.

PHILOSOPHY

For whose present vogue
we are indebted to this audience of imbeciles
and asses.

SOPHISTRY

Asses? These sophisticated gentlemen?
These wits?

PHILOSOPHY

I'll *invalidate* you.

SOPHISTRY

Invalidate *me?*
How, fossil?

PHILOSOPHY

My arguments are Truth and Justice.

SOPHISTRY

Then I'll disarm you and defeat you, friend.
Your Justice doesn't exist.

PHILOSOPHY

What? No Justice?
Preposterous!

SOPHISTRY

Then show it to me. Where is it?

PHILOSOPHY

Where is Justice? Why, in the Lap of the Gods.

SOPHISTRY

In the Lap of the Gods? Then would you explain
how Zeus escaped punishment after he imprisoned
his father?* The inconsistency is glaring.

PHILOSOPHY

Aaaagh.
What nauseating twaddle. It turns my stomach.

SOPHISTRY

Why, you Decrepitude! You Doddering Dotard!

PHILOSOPHY

Why,
you Precocious Pederast! You Palpable Pervert!

SOPHISTRY

Pelt me with roses!

PHILOSOPHY

You Toadstool! O Cesspool!

SOPHISTRY

Wreath my hair with lilies!

PHILOSOPHY

Why, you Parricide!

SOPHISTRY

Shower me with gold! Look, don't you see
I welcome your abuse?

PHILOSOPHY

Welcome it, monster?
In my day we would have cringed with shame.

SOPHISTRY

Whereas *now* we're flattered. Times change.
The vices of your age are stylish today.

PHILOSOPHY

Repulsive Whippersnapper!

SOPHISTRY

Disgusting Fogy!

PHILOSOPHY

Because of *you* the schools of Athens
stand deserted; one whole generation
chaffers in the streets, gaping and idle.
Mark my words: someday this city
shall learn what you have made her men:
effeminates and fools.

SOPHISTRY

Ugh, you're squalid!

PHILOSOPHY

Whereas you've become a Dandy and a Fop!
But I remember your beggared beginnings,
playing as Telephos,* grubby and shifty,
tricked out in Euripidean rags and tatters
and cramming your wallet with moldy leavings
from Pandaletos' loaf.*

SOPHISTRY

What a prodigy of wisdom
was there!

PHILOSOPHY

And what a prodigy of madness here—
your madness, and madder still than you,
this maddened city which lets you live—
you, corrupter and destroyer of her youth!

SOPHISTRY

Throwing a wing about Pheidippides.

Why, you Hoary Fossil! This is one student
you'll never teach!

PHILOSOPHY

Pulling Pheidippides back.

Teach him I *shall*—
unless he's prepared to devote his career
exclusively to drivel.

SOPHISTRY

Bah, rave to yourself.
—Come here, boy.

PHILOSOPHY

You touch him at your peril.

KORYPHAIOS

Intervening.

Gentlemen, forego your wrangling and abuse,
and each present his arguments in turn.
Describe how *you* taught the men of the past,
and *you,* Sir, your New Education.

PHILOSOPHY

I second
your proposal.

SOPHISTRY

As do I.

KORYPHAIOS

Excellent.
Who will speak first?

SOPHISTRY

Let him begin.
I yield the floor. But when he's done,
I'll smother him beneath so huge
a driving hail of Modern Thought
and Latest Views, he cannot speak—
or if he does, my hornet words
and waspish wit will sting him so,
he'll never speak again.

CHORUS

—At last!
—The Great Debate begins!
—Between these two
contending, clever speakers,
—matched so fairly,
—who
will win, is anybody's guess.
—Both are subtle,
—both facile, both witty,
—both masters of rebuttal
—and abuse.
—The stake? Wisdom.
—Wisdom is the prize.
—For her they fight.
—For her their rival hackles rise.
—So listen well.
—Upon their skill, the destinies of Lang-
uage, Intellect, and Educated Athens hang.

KORYPHAIOS

To Philosophy.

Come, Sir, I summon you—you who conferred your crown of virtue
upon the Older Generation—to take the stand. Be bold; rise
and with clarion tongue tell us what you represent.

PHILOSOPHY

Gentlemen,
I propose to speak of the Old Education,* as it flourished once
beneath my tutelage, when Homespun Honesty, Plainspeaking, and
Truth
were still honored and practiced, and throughout the schools of Athens
the regime of the three D's—DISCIPLINE, DECORUM, and
DUTY—
enjoyed unchallenged supremacy.
Our curriculum was Music and
Gymnastic,
enforced by that rigorous discipline summed up in the old adage:
BOYS SHOULD BE SEEN BUT NOT HEARD. This was our
cardinal rule,
and when the students, mustered by groups according to region,
were marched in squads to school, discipline and absolute silence
prevailed.
Ah, they were hardy, manly youngsters. Why,
even on winter mornings when the snow, like powdered chaff,
came sifting down, their only protection against the bitter weather
was a thin and scanty tunic. In the classes, posture was stressed
and the decencies firmly enforced: the students stood in rows,
rigidly at attention, while the master rehearsed them by rote,
over and over. The music itself was traditional and standard—
such familiar anthems and hymns as those, for instance, beginning
A Voice from Afar or *Hail, O Pallas, Destroyer!**—and the old modes
were strictly preserved in all their austere and simple beauty.
Clowning in class was sternly forbidden, and those who improvised
or indulged in those fantastic flourishes and trills so much in vogue
with the degenerate, effeminate school of Phrynis, were promptly
thrashed
for subverting the Muses.
In the gymnasium too decorum was demanded.
The boys were seated together, stripped to the skin, on the bare ground,
keeping their legs thrust forward, shyly screening their nakedness
from the gaze of the curious. Why, so modest were students then,
that when they rose, they carefully smoothed out the ground beneath
them,
lest even a pair of naked buttocks leaving its trace in the sand
should draw the eyes of desire. Anointing with oil was forbidden
below the line of the navel, and consequently their genitals kept
their boyish bloom intact and the quincelike freshness of youth.
Toward their lovers their conduct was manly*: you didn't see *them*

mincing or strutting, or prostituting themselves with girlish voices
or coy, provocative glances.
At table courtesy and good manners
were compulsory. Not a boy of that generation would have dreamed
of taking so much as a radish or the merest pinch of parsley
before his elders had been served. Rich foods were prohibited,
raucous laughter or crossing their legs forbidden. . . .

SOPHISTRY

Ugh,
what musty, antiquated rubbish. It reeks of golden grasshoppers,
all gewgaws and decaying institutions!

PHILOSOPHY

Nonetheless, these were the precepts
on which I bred a generation of heroes, the men who fought
at Marathon.

To Sophistry

And what do *you* teach?
Modesty?
No, vanity and softness,
and the naked beauty of the body muffled in swirling clothes,
gross and unmanly. Why, at Panathenaia now it sickens me
to see the boys dancing, ashamed of their own bodies, effetely
forgetting their duty to the goddess while they screen their nakedness
behind their shields.
Bah.

To Pheidippides.

No, young man, by your courage
I challenge you. Turn your back upon his blandishments of vice,
the rotten law courts and the cheap, corrupting softness of the baths.
Choose instead the Old, the Philosophical Education. Follow me
and from my lips acquire the virtues of a man:—
A sense of shame,
that decency and innocence of mind that shrinks from doing wrong.
To feel the true man's blaze of anger when his honor is provoked.
Deference toward one's elders; respect for one's father and mother.
To preserve intact, unsullied by disgrace or stained with wrong,
that image of Manliness and Modesty by which alone you live.
Purity:—to avoid the brothels and the low, salacious leer
of prostituted love—which, being bought, corrupts your manhood
and destroys your name. Toward your father scrupulous obedience;
to honor his declining years who spent his prime in rearing you.
Not to call him Dotard or Fogy—

SOPHISTRY

Boy, if you follow his advice,
you'll finish by looking like one of Hippokrates' sissified sons.
They'll call *you* Mollycoddle Milksop.

PHILOSOPHY

Rubbish. I promise you,
not contentious disputations and the cheap, courtroom cant
of this flabby, subpoena-serving, shyster-jargoned de-generation,
but true athletic prowess, the vigor of contending manhood
in prime perfection of physique, muscular and hard, glowing
with health.

Ah, I can see you now, as through an idyl moving—
you with some companion of your age, modest and manly like you,
strolling by Akademe perhaps, or there among the olives,
sprinting side by side together, crowned with white reed,
breathing with every breath the ecstasy of Spring returning,
the sudden fragrance of the season's leisure, the smell of woodbine
and the catkins flung by the poplar, while touching overhead,
the leaves of the linden and plane rustle, in love, together.
So follow me, young man, and win perfection of physique. To wit—

Demonstrating each attribute individually.

BUILD, Stupendous.
COMPLEXION, Splendid.
SHOULDERS, Gigantic.
TONGUE, Petite.
BUTTOCKS, Brawny.
PECKER, Discreet.

But follow my opponent here, and your reward shall be, as follows:

BUILD, Effeminate.
COMPLEXION, Ghastly.
SHOULDERS, Hunched.
TONGUE, Enormous.
BUTTOCKS, Flabby.
PECKER, Preposterous!

(but thereby insuring you an enormous and devoted political following.)
What is worse, you shall learn to make a mockery of all morality,
systematically confounding good with evil and evil with good,
so plumped and pursy with villainy, sodomy, disgrace, and perversion,
you resemble ANTIMACHOS himself.

Depravity can sink no lower.

CHORUS

—Bravo!
—What brilliance!
—What finesse!
—*This* is wisdom
at its noble best!
—Such Modesty,
—such Decorum
in every lovely word distilled!
—Ah, lucky they
—whose happy lives were lived
—beneath your dispensation,
—by all the ancient virtues blessed!

To Sophistry.

—So, sir,
—despite your vaunted subtlety and wit,
—take care:
—Your rival's speech has scored.
—Some crushing *tour de force,*
—some master stroke,
—is needed now.
—The stage is yours.

KORYPHAIOS

Unless your strategy is shrewdly planned and your attack ferocious,
then your cause is lost. We'll laugh you out of court.

SOPHISTRY

At last!
A few minutes more and I would have exploded from sheer impatience
to refute him and demolish his case.
Now then, I freely admit
that among men of learning I am—somewhat pejoratively—dubbed
the Sophistic, or Immoral, Logic. And why? Because I first
devised a Method for the Subversion of Established Social Beliefs
and the Undermining of Morality. Moreover, this little invention of mine,
this knack of taking what might appear to be the worse argument
and nonetheless winning my case, has, I might add, proved to be
an *extremely* lucrative source of income.
But observe, gentlemen,
how I refute his vaunted Education.

To Philosophy

Now then, in your curriculum
hot baths are sternly prohibited. But what grounds can you possibly adduce
for this condemnation of hot baths?

PHILOSOPHY

What grounds can I adduce? Why,
they're thoroughly vicious. They make a man flabby and effeminate.

SOPHISTRY

You can stop right there, friend. I have you completely at my mercy.
Answer me this: which of the sons of Zeus was the most heroic?
Who suffered most? Performed the greatest labors?

PHILOSOPHY

In my opinion,
the greatest hero who ever lived was Herakles.

SOPHISTRY

Very well then.
But when we speak of the famous Baths of Herakles,* are we speaking
of hot baths or cold baths? Necessarily, sir, of hot baths.
Whence it clearly follows, by your own logic, that Herakles was
both flabby and effeminate.
Q.E.D.

PHILOSOPHY

Q.E.D.! This is the rubbish I mean!
This is the logical claptrap so much in fashion with the young!
This is what fills the baths and empties the gymnasiums!

SOPHISTRY

Very well,
if you like, consider our national passion for politics and debating,
pastimes which you condemn and I approve. But surely, friend,
if politics were quite so vicious as you pretend, old Homer—*
our mentor on moral questions—would never have portrayed Nestor
and those other wise old men as politicians, would he? Surely
he would not.

Or take the question of education in oratory—
in my opinion desirable, in yours the reverse. As for Moderation and Decorum,
the very notions are absurd. In fact, two more preposterous
or pernicious prejudices, I find it hard to imagine. For example,

can you cite me *one* instance of that profit which a man enjoys
by exercising moderation? Refute me if you can.

PHILOSOPHY

Why, instances abound
Er . . . Peleus,* for example. His virtue won him a sword.

SOPHISTRY

A sword,
you say? What a charming little profit for the poor sucker!
Look at our Hyberbolos: nothing virtuous about *him,* god knows,
and yet, what with peddling lamps—plus a knack for swindling—
he piled up a huge profit. All cold cash. No swords for him.
No sir, Hyperbolos and swords just don't mix.*

PHILOSOPHY

Furthermore,
Peleus' chastity earned him the goddess Thetis for his wife.

SOPHISTRY

Precisely,
and what did she do? Promptly ditched him for being cold,
no passion for that all-night scrimmage between the sheets
that lusty women love.
Bah, you're obsolete.

To Pheidippides.

—Young man,
I advise you to ponder this life of Virtue with scrupulous care,
all that it implies, and all the pleasures of which its daily practice
must inevitably deprive you. Specifically, I might mention these:
Sex. Gambling. Gluttony. Guzzling. Carousing. Etcet.
And what on earth's the point of living, if you leach your life
of all its little joys?
Very well then, consider your natural needs.
Suppose, as a scholar of Virtue, you commit some minor peccadillo,
a little adultery, say, or seduction, and suddenly find yourself
caught in the act. What happens? You're ruined, you can't defend
yourself
(since, of course, you haven't been taught). But follow me, my boy,
and obey your nature to the full; romp, play, and laugh
without a scruple in the world. Then if caught *in flagrante,*
you simply inform the poor cuckold that you're utterly innocent
and refer him to Zeus as your moral sanction. After all, didn't he,
a great and powerful god, succumb to the love of women?

Then how in the world can you, a man, an ordinary mortal,
be expected to surpass the greatest of gods in moral self-control?
Clearly, you can't be.

PHILOSOPHY

And suppose your pupil, by taking your advice, is promptly convicted of adultery and sentenced to be publicly reamed up the rectum with a radish?* How, Sir, would you save him from *that?*

SOPHISTRY

Why, what's the disgrace in being reamed with a radish?

PHILOSOPHY

Sir, I can conceive of nothing fouler than being buggered
by a radish.

SOPHISTRY

And what would you have to say, my friend,
if I defeat you on this point too?

PHILOSOPHY

What *could* I say?
I could never speak again for shame.

SOPHISTRY

Very well then.
What sort of men are our lawyers?

PHILOSOPHY

Why, they're all Buggers.

SOPHISTRY

Right!
What are our tragic poets then?

PHILOSOPHY

Why, they're Buggers too.

SOPHISTRY

Right!
And what of our politicians, Sir?

PHILOSOPHY

Why, Buggers to a man.

SOPHISTRY

Right!
You see how stupidly you spoke?
And now look at our audience.
What about them?

PHILOSOPHY

I'm looking hard.

SOPHISTRY

And what do you see?

PHILOSOPHY

By heaven,
I see an enormous crowd of people,
and almost all of them Buggers.

Pointing to individuals in the audience.

See there? That man's a Bugger,
and that long-haired fop's a Bugger too.

SOPHISTRY

Then how do we stand, my friend?

PHILOSOPHY

I've been beaten by the Buggers.

Flinging his cloak to the audience.

O Buggers, catch my cloak
and welcome me among the Buggers!

With a wild shriek Philosophy disappears into his cage and is wheeled away into the Thinkery, just as Sokrates comes out.

SOKRATES

Well, what are your wishes? Will you take your son home,
or shall I instruct him in the Pettifogger's Art?

STREPSIADES

Teach him—
and flog him too. But remember: I want his tongue
honed down like a razor. Sharpen him on the left side
for piddling private suits, but grind him on the right
for Grand Occasions and Affairs of State.

SOKRATES

Sir,
you may depend upon me. I promise I'll send him home
a consummate little sophist.

PHEIDIPPIDES

God, what a picture of misery—
a nasty, pasty-faced, consummate little stinker!

Exeunt Sokrates and Pheidippides into the Thinkery.

KORYPHAIOS

Very well, go in.

To Strepsiades.

—You, Sir, shall live to regret your decision.

Exit Strepsiades into his own house, as the Chorus turns sharply and faces the audience.

CHORUS

And now, Gentlemen of the Jury, a few brief words about the Prize
and the solid benefits you stand to gain by voting for *THE CLOUDS*—
as you certainly should anyway.
First of all, when the season sets
for Spring and plowing time has come, we guarantee each judge's fields
the top priority in rain. Let others wait. Furthermore,
for his vineyards and orchards, we promise, perfect growing-weather:
no drought shall touch them, no flooding rains destroy.
However,
if some presuming mortal dares dishonor our divinity,
let him savor his punishment:
His acres, hard, dry, and barren,
shall see no harvesting. No wine, no fruit, shall ripen for *him.*
And when the olives sprout, and the season's green festoons
the vines, *his* shall wither, battered by our ratatat of rain.
And when he's busy baking bricks, we'll snuff his kiln with water
and smash his tiles with cannonades of hail. If he, his friend,
or relatives should celebrate a wedding, we'll send a DELUGE down
and drown the wedding night in rain!
By god, we'll make him say
he'd rather be roasting in Egypt than have voted wrong today!

Enter Strepsiades from his house, counting on his fingers.

STREPSIADES

Five days, four days, three days, two days, and then
that one day of all the days of the month

I dread the most, that makes me fart with fear—
the last day of the month, Due date for debts,*
when every dun in town has solemnly sworn
to drag me into court and bankrupt me completely.
And when I plead with them to be more reasonable—
"But PLEASE, sir. Don't demand the whole sum now.
Take something on account. I'll pay you later."—
they snort they'll never see the day, curse me
for a filthy swindler and say they'll sue.
                                        Well,
let them. If Pheidippides has learned to talk,
I don't give a damn for them and their suits.
                                        Now then,
a little knock on the door and we'll have the answer.

He knocks on Sokrates' door and calls out.

Porter!
        Hey, porter!

Sokrates opens the door.

SOKRATES

Ah, Strepsiades. Salutations.

STREPSIADES

Same to you, Sokrates.

He hands Sokrates a bag of flour.

Here. A token of my esteem.
Call it an honorarium.* Professors always get honorariums.

Snatching back the bag.

But wait: has Pheidippides learned his rhetoric yet—
that swindling Rhetoric that performed for us just now?

SOKRATES

Taking the bag.

He has mastered it.

STREPSIADES

O great goddess Bamboozle!

SOKRATES

Now, sir, you can evade any legal action you wish to.

STREPSIADES

Really? Even if I borrowed the money before witnesses?

SOKRATES

Before ten thousand of them. The more the merrier.

STREPSIADES

In parody.

Then let my loud falsetto peal
*with gladsome paeans plangent!**
Mourn, O ye lenders of money,
weep, O principals! Gnash your teeth,
O ye interests compounded.
For lo, within mine halls
a son hath risen,
a son with burnish'd tongue,
yea, with double edges lambent!
Hail, O hero of my halls,
who delivered my domicile,
who fractur'd mine enemies
and drowned a father's dolor!
Ho, fetch forth mine son
forthwith! O my son,
*debouch from mine abode!**
O heed thy father, prithee!

Pheidippides, the very image of "modern youth," slouches contemptuously out of the Thinkery.

SOKRATES

Behold the man!

STREPSIADES

O joy! My boy!

SOKRATES

Take him and go.

STREPSIADES

O my son! O! O!
O! O! O! O!
Oh, how gladly I behold thy pasty face,
that negative and disputatious look! And see there,
how there blossoms on his lips our national rejoinder,
"Huh? G'wan!" How perfectly he is the rogue,
but looks the victim through and through. And on his face
that utter pallor, ah, that true Athenian look!
—All right, Son, you ruined me, so it's up to you
to save me.

PHEIDIPPIDES

What's eating *you,* Dad?

STREPSIADES

Your damn debts.
And the date. That's what. Your debts are due today.
Today's Dueday.*

PHEIDIPPIDES

Today's two days? Or two Duedays?
But how can one day be two days?

STREPSIADES

How should *I* know?
It just *is!*

Resuming more calmly, patiently explaining.

Today's Dueday, son. *This* is the day
when creditor's are required by law to post their bond*
in court in order to obtain a summons against their debtors.
No bond, no summons.

PHEIDIPPIDES

Ergo, they will forfeit their bond.
By definition, one day cannot be two days.

STREPSIADES

It *can't* be?
But why not?

PHEIDIPPIDES

Because it's a logical impossibility, numskull.
If one day were two days, then *ipso facto* a woman
could be simultaneously a young girl and an old hag.
Which she can't be.

STREPSIADES

But it's the law!

PHEIDIPPIDES

In that case,
I suspect the law on debt has been profoundly misinterpreted.

STREPSIADES

Misinterpreted? But how?

PHEIDIPPIDES

Enigmatically.

Old Solon loved the people.

STREPSIADES

And what in god's name has that got to do with the Duedate?

PHEIDIPPIDES

Solon's sympathies lay with the debtor, not with the creditor.

STREPSIADES

And so?

PHEIDIPPIDES

And so, when Solon promulgated his law on debt,
he carefully specified *two* distinct Duedates
for debts, not *one,* as the current interpretation has it.
Prima facie, a summons *could* be issued on either day,
though in practice this was impossible, since the creditor's bond
could be paid only on the second Duedate.

STREPSIADES

But why did Solon
set two Duedates?

PHEIDIPPIDES

Read between the lines, moron.
Solon intended that the debtor should present himself in court
on the first date and declare himself absolved of his debts
on the grounds of the creditor's failure to issue a summons.
He won by default. *If,* however, the debtor failed
to take advantage of the deliberate ambiguity of the law,
he had to account to his creditors in court the next day.
Not an attractive prospect.

STREPSIADES

But wait. If that's the law,
then how do you account for the glaring fact that the magistrates
actually demand that the creditor's bond be paid on the first day
and not on the second?

PHEIDIPPIDES

Precisely because they *are* magistrates.*
Ipso facto, their greed is magisterial and their gluttony
uncontrollable. And because they can't wait to get their fingers
in the pie, they have quietly connived among themselves

to set the Duedate back a day earlier. Their procedure, of course, is utterly illegal.

STREPSIADES

Still perplexed.

Huh?

But suddenly illuminated.

Hey!

Haw, that's good!

Turning to the audience.

Well, numskulls, what are *you* gawking at?
Yes, *you* down there!
You dumb sheep with the pigeon faces!
Cat's-paws for cleverer men! Any sophist's
suckers!
O shysterbait!
Generation of dupes!
Poor twerps, poor silly saps!
O Audience of Asses,
you were born to be taken!
—And now, gentlemen, a song.
A little ditty of my own, dedicated to me and my son,
offering us warmest congratulations on our success.
Ready,
everybody?

Singing and dancing.

Oh, Strepsiades, Strepsiades,
there's no one like Strepsiades!
He went to school with Sokrates
who taught him all his sophistries!
He's smarter than
Euripides,
for only he's,
yes, only he's
Pheidippides'
Old Man!

By god, if ever I heard a hit, that's it!

To Pheidippides.

Once you finish off my creditors' suits, the whole town
will go green with envy of Strepsiades.
And now, son,
I'm throwing a dinner in your honor. So let's go in.

Exeunt Strepsiades and Pheidippides into the house. An instant later Pasias arrives, accompanied by his Witness, with a summons against Strepsiades. A notorious spendthrift, drunkard, and glutton, Pasias is grotesquely fat. Essentially a good-natured man, he has prepared himself for a difficult ordeal, and comes equipped with a wine flask from which he periodically fortifies himself.

PASIAS

Well,
what am I supposed to do? Throw my hard-earned money
down the drain?

Something in his own words reminds him that he needs a drink, a stiff one.

Playboy Pasias, is it?
Nossiree.
Bah! Me and my great big heart! Soft-touch Pasias.
But I should have known. You've got to be a bastard.
Hard as nails.

He hardens himself with a drink.

If I'd sent him packing when he tried
to put the touch on me, I wouldn't be in this fix now.
What a mess!

To Witness.

I have to drag you around to stand witness,
and what's more, I'll make an enemy of Strepsiades for life.

He fortifies himself with still another drink.

Well, I'll sue him anyway.
Yessiree.
Athens expects it,
and I won't have it said that Pasias ever besmirched
the National Honor.*
Nossiree.

Shouting into the house.

—Strepsiades! I'm suing you!

STREPSIADES

Appearing at the door.

Somebody want me?

PASIAS

I do. Today's the Dueday.

STREPSIADES

To the audience.

Gentlemen, you're all witnesses: he distinctly mentioned *two* days.

To Pasias.

—What are you suing me for?

PASIAS

What *for?* Why, the money you borrowed from me to buy that horse.

STREPSIADES

Horse? *What* horse? Everybody knows I'm allergic to horses. Ask the audience.

PASIAS

By god, you swore you'd pay me! You swore it by the gods.

STREPSIADES

Well, by god, now I swear I won't. Anyway, that was before Pheidippides learned the Science of Unanswerable Argument.

PASIAS

And *that*'s why you won't pay me?

STREPSIADES

Can you think of a better reason? I'm entitled to some return on his education, aren't I?

PASIAS

And you're prepared to perjure yourself on an oath sworn by the gods?

STREPSIADES

By the gods?

What gods?

PASIAS

What gods?

Why, Zeus, Poseidon, and Hermes.

STREPSIADES

Damn right
I would. And what's more, I'd do it again. Gratis,
by god!
I *like* perjury.

PASIAS

Why, you barefaced swindler!
You damnable liar!

STREPSIADES

Prodding Pasias in the belly.

Boy, what blubber!
—You know,
that paunch of yours ought to make someone a mighty dandy
wineskin . . .

PASIAS

By god, that's the last straw!

STREPSIADES

Hmmmm. Yup,
five gallons, I'd guess offhand.

PASIAS

So help me Zeus!
So help me every god in heaven, you won't get away
with this!

STREPSIADES

You know, you and your silly gods tickle me.
Zeus is a joke to us Thinking Men.

PASIAS

By god, someday
you'll regret this.
Now then, for the last time,
will you pay me or won't you? Give me a straight answer
and I'll be off.

STREPSIADES

Don't you budge. I'll be right back
and bring you my final answer.

Strepsiades rushes into the house.

PASIAS

To his Witness.

I wonder what he's doing.

Do you think he'll pay me?

STREPSIADES

Reappearing from the house; in his hands he holds a large basket.

Now where's that creditor of mine?

Holding up the basket in front of Pasias.

—All right, you, what's this?

PASIAS

That? A basket.

STREPSIADES

A *basket?*

And a stupid ignoramus like you has the nerve to come around
badgering me for money? By god, I wouldn't give a cent
to a man who can't even tell a basket from a baskette.

PASIAS

Then you won't pay me back?

STREPSIADES

Not if *I* know it.

Look here,
you Colossus of Lard, why don't you quietly melt away?
Beat it, Fatboy!

He threatens to beat him with his baskette.

PASIAS

I'm going. Yessiree. And by god,
if I don't post my bond with the magistrates right now,
my name's not Pasias.

Nossiree.

STREPSIADES

Tch tch. Poor Pasias.
You'll just lose your bond on top of all your other losses.
And, personally speaking, I wouldn't want to see you suffer
just because your grammar's bad.

Beating Pasias over the head with his baskette.

Remember?

Baskette!

Exit Pasias at a run pursued by Strepsiades. An instant later, hideous wails and shrieks are heard offstage, and these are followed by the pathetic entrance of the notorious effeminate and gambler, Amynias. He has just had an accident with his chariot, and his entrance is a picture of misery: his head is covered with blood, his clothes torn, and his language, a delirious compound of tragic rhetoric and a marked lisp, is almost unintelligible.

AMYNIAS
Alackaday!
Woe is me!
Alas! Alas!

STREPSIADES
Gods in heaven,
what a caterwauling!
—Look, who *are* you?
The way you whine
you sound like some poor blubbering god from a tragedy
by Karkinos.*

AMYNIAS
Wouldst hear how I am hight? Know then:
a wretched wight in woe am I, Adversity
yclept.

STREPSIADES
Then hit the road, Buster.

AMYNIAS
O Funest Doom!
O Darkling Destiny!
How fell the fate by which I fall,
ah, Pallas!
O all unhors'd! O human haplessness
I am!

STREPSIADES
I get it. You're an actor, and you want me to guess
what part you're practicing.
Hmm.
Must be a female role.
But of course!
You're Alkmene in the play by Xenokles,
and you're mourning your brother . . .

AMYNIAS

You're *such* a tease, you naughty man.
Now then, be a dear, and ask Pheidippides
to pay me my money. You see, I'm in the most frightful way.
You simply can't *imagine!*

STREPSIADES

Money? What money?

AMYNIAS

Why, the money
Pheidippides borrowed.

STREPSIADES

Hmmm. You *are* in a frightful way.
You simply can't *imagine*.

AMYNIAS

But I *can*. You see, on my way,
I was thrown from my chariot. Literally *hurled* into the air.
It was *too* awful.

STREPSIADES

It fits. You must have hurt your head.
That would explain that gibberish about money.

AMYNIAS

What's gibberish
about wanting my money?

STREPSIADES

Obvious case of delirium.
Brain damage too, I suspect.

AMYNIAS

Brain damage?

STREPSIADES

Yup.
You'll probably be queer the rest of your life. That's how
I see it.

AMYNIAS

Pay me my money, or I'll sue you! That's how
I see it.

STREPSIADES

Is that so?

All right, let me ask you a question.
I'm curious to know which theory on rainfall you prefer.
Now then, in your considered opinion, is the phenomenon of rain
best explained as a precipitation of *totally* fresh water,
or is it merely a case of the same old rainwater
in continuous re-use, slowly condensed by the Clouds
and then precipitated once more as rain?

AMYNIAS

My *dear* fellow,
I really couldn't care less.

STREPSIADES

Couldn't care less, eh?
And a sophomore like you, completely ignorant of Science,
thinks he's got the right to go around pestering people
to pay him money?

Boy, some nerve!

AMYNIAS

Look here,
if you're temporarily short of cash, then let me have
the interest.

STREPSIADES

Interest? What the devil's interest?

AMYNIAS

Why, interest
is nothing more than the tendency of a cash principal
to reproduce itself by increments over a period of time.
Very gradually, day after day, month after month,
the interest accrues and the principal grows.

STREPSIADES

Dandy.
Then in your opinion there's more water in the ocean now
than last year? Is that right?

AMYNIAS

But, of course, it isn't.
Oceans *can't* grow, you silly man. It's against the Law
of Nature.

STREPSIADES

Then what about you, you unnatural bastard?
If the ocean, with all those rivers pouring into it,
doesn't grow, then who the hell are you to expect your money
to grow?
And now CLEAR OUT! Go peddle your subpoenas
somewhere else.

Amynias stands firm and Strepsiades calls out to his slave.

—Bring me my horsewhip.

The slave brings the whip and Strepsiades cracks it threateningly at Amynias.

AMYNIAS

Appealing in terror to the audience.

—Gentlemen,
you're my witnesses!

STREPSIADES

Still here, are you?

He flicks Amynias with the whip.

Giddeap!
Gallop, you gelding!
Gee!

He flicks Amynias again with his whip, this time in the rear.

AMYNIAS

A hit! A hit!
A palpable hit!

STREPSIADES

Raising his phallus to the ready.

Git, dammit, or I'll sunder your rump
with my ram!

With a wild whinny of fright, Amynias rushes offstage.

Going, are you?
A damned good thing.
And don't come back here nagging me about your money,
or I'll badger your bum!
You'll get the ride of your life!

Strepsiades re-enters the house to resume his interrupted dinner with Pheidippides.

CHORUS

Individually

—Such is wickedness,
—such its fatal fascination:
—this senile amateur of fraud,
—by greed and guile obsessed,
—frantic to disown his debts
—(and,
—such his luck,
—apparently
—succeeding).
—BUT please take note:
—soon,
—perhaps today,
—this poor man's Sokrates must learn his lesson,
—*viz.*
—CRIME DOES NOT PAY.
—Dishonesty comes home to roost.
—It's Poetic Retribution!
—But *now,* poor fish!
—he thinks he's sitting
—pretty.
—Success at last!
—For hasn't his Pheidippides become
—so voluble a speaker,
—so specious a sophist,
—a shyster so vicious,
—that he's now
—ABSOLUTELY INVINCIBLE?
—So he gloats.
—But wait!
—Take note:
—the time will come—

Strepsiades howls in pain offstage.

—in fact, it's coming now—
—when poor Strepsiades
will wish to god
—Pheidippides were
—DUMB!

With a bellow of pain and terror, Strepsiades plunges out of his house, hotly pursued by Pheidippides with a murderous stick.

STREPSIADES
OOOUUUCH!!!
HALP!
For god's sake, help me!

Appealing to the Audience.

Friends!
Fellow-countrymen! Aunts! Uncles! Fathers! Brothers!
To the rescue!
He's beating me!
Help me!
Ouuch!
O my poor head!
Ooh, my jaw!

To Pheidippides.

—You great big bully,
Hit your own father, would you?

PHEIDIPPIDES
Gladly, Daddy.

STREPSIADES
You hear that? The big brute *admits* it.

PHEIDIPPIDES
Admit it? Hell,
I *proclaim* it.

STREPSIADES
You cheap Cutthroat!
You father-beating Bastard!
You Turd!
You . . . you . . . you—

PHEIDIPPIDES
Carry on. Don't you know
you're complimenting me?

STREPSIADES

Why, you . . . you . . . you Palpable Pervert!
You Pederast!

PHEIDIPPIDES

Roll me in roses, Daddy!

STREPSIADES

You Bugger!
Hit your own father, would you?

PHEIDIPPIDES

Damn right I would.
God knows, I had good justification.

STREPSIADES

Justification, you say?
Why, you Dunghill, what justification could there *ever* be
for hitting your own father?

PHEIDIPPIDES

Would a logical demonstration
convince you?

STREPSIADES

A logical demonstration? You mean to tell me
you can *prove* a shocking thing like that?

PHEIDIPPIDES

Elementary, really.
What's more, you can choose the logic. Take your pick.
Either one.

STREPSIADES

Either *which?*

PHEIDIPPIDES

Either *which?* Why,
Sokratic logic or pre-Sokratic logic. Either logic.
Take your pick.

STREPSIADES

Take my pick, damn you? Look,
who do you think paid for your shyster education anyway?
And now you propose to convince *me* that there's nothing wrong
in whipping your own father?

PHEIDIPPIDES

I not only propose it;
I propose to *prove* it. Irrefutably, in fact. Rebuttal
is utterly inconceivable.

STREPSIADES

By god, *this* I want to hear!

CHORUS

Old friend, WATCH OUT.
Upon this bout
may hang your own survival.

What's more, unless
I miss my guess,
the odds are on your rival.

That curling lip,
that sneer's a tip,
and you'd be wise to heed it.

The tip? A trap.
But, *verbum sap.*
I wish you luck. *You*'ll need it.

KORYPHAIOS

To Strepsiades.

And now, Sir, I suggest you brief the Chorus. Begin at the beginning
and describe your little fracas exactly as it happened.

STREPSIADES

Yes'm.
The whole damn dirty squabble from start to finish.
As you know,
we both went in to celebrate. Well, Ladies, a custom's a custom,*
after all, and there's nothing like a little music, I always say,
to get a party off to a good start. So naturally I asked him
to get down his lyre and sing a song. For instance, Simonides'
*Shearin' o' the Ram.**
Well, you know what the little stinker answered?
That singing at table was—Obsolete,
Old Hat,
Lowbrow,
Bullshit!
Strictly for grandmothers.

PHEIDIPPIDES

You damn well got what you deserved.
Asking me to sing on an empty stomach! What is this anyway?
A banquet or a cricket-concert?

STREPSIADES

You hear that?
A cricket-concert!
His exact words.
And then he started sneering at Simonides!
Called him—get this—Puny Pipsqueak Hack!
Was I *sore?*
Brother!
Well, somehow I counted to ten, and then I asked him
to sing me some Aischylos.
Please.
And you know what he replied?
That he considered Aischylos "a poet of colossal stature:"—
Yup,
"the most colossal, pretentious, pompous, spouting, bombastic bore
in poetic history."*
I was so damn mad I just about went through the roof.
But I gritted my teeth together, mustered up a sick smile
and somehow managed to say, "All right, son, if that's how you feel,
then sing me a passage from one of those highbrow modern plays
you're so crazy about."
So he recited—you can guess—Euripides!
One of those slimy tragedies* where, so help me, there's a brother
who screws his own sister!
Well, Ladies, *that* did it!
I jumped up,
blind with rage, started cursing at him and calling him names,
and he started screaming and cursing back and before I knew it,
he hauled off and—*wham!*—he biffed me and bashed me and clipped
me
and poked me and choked me and—

PHEIDIPPIDES

And, by god, you had it coming!
Knocking a genius like Euripides!

STREPSIADES

Euripides!
A GENIUS??
That . . .
That . . . that . . !

Pheidippides raises his stick threateningly.

HALP! He's hitting me!

PHEIDIPPIDES

You've got it coming, Dad!

STREPSIADES

Got it coming, do I?
Why, you ungrateful brat, I *raised* you!
When you were a baby I pampered you! I waited on you hand and foot!
I understood your babytalk. You babbled GOO and I obeyed. Why,
when you whimpered WAWA DADA, who brought your water?
DADA did.
When you burbled BABA, who brought your Baby Biscuits?
DADA did.
And when you cried GOTTA GO KAKA DADA, who saved his shitty darling?
Who rushed you to the door? Who held you while you did it? Damn you,
DADA did!
And in return you choked me,
and when I shat in terror,
would you give your Dad a hand,
would you help me to the door?
No, you left me there alone
to do it on the floor!

Yes, to do it on the floor!

CHORUS

YOUR ATTENTION, PLEASE!
Pheidippides
now makes his demonstration—

a proof which will,
I'm certain, thrill
the younger generation.

For if this lad
defeats his Dad,
there's not an older man

or father in
this town, whose skin
is worth a Tinker's Damn!

KORYPHAIOS

And now that Doughty Champion of Change, that Golden-Tongued Attorney
for Tomorrow, that Harbinger of Progress
—PHEIDIPPIDES!

To Pheidippides.

Remember, Sir,
we want the truth
—or a reasonable facsimile.

PHEIDIPPIDES

Gentlemen, Eloquence
is sweet, sweeter than I ever dreamed! This utter bliss of speech!
This rapture of articulation! But oh, the sheer Attic honey
of subverting the Established Moral Order!
And yet when I look back
on those benighted days of pre-Sokratic folly, upon the boy
I used to be, whose only hobby was horses, who could not speak
three words of Greek without a blunder, why . . .
words fail me.
But *now,* now that Sokrates has made a fresh Pheidippides of me,
now that my daily diet is Philosophy, Profundity, Subtlety,
and Science, I propose to prove beyond the shadow of a doubt
the philosophical propriety of beating my Father.

STREPSIADES

For the love of Zeus,
go back to your damn horses! I'd rather be stuck with a stable
than be battered by a stick.

PHEIDIPPIDES

I ignore these childish interruptions
and proceed with my demonstration.
Now then, answer my question:
did you lick me when I was a little boy?

STREPSIADES

Of course I licked you.
For your own damn good. Because I loved you.

PHEIDIPPIDES

Then *ipso facto,*
since you yourself admit that loving and lickings are synonymous,
it's only fair that I—for your own damn good, you understand?—
whip you in return.
In any case, by what right do you whip me
but claim exemption for yourself?
What do you think I am? A slave?
Wasn't I born as free a man as you?*
Well?

STREPSIADES

But . . .

PHEIDIPPIDES

But what?
Spare the Rod and Spoil the Child?
Is that your argument?
If so,
then I can be sententious too. *Old Men are Boys Writ Big,*
as the saying goes.
A fortiori then, old men logically deserve
to be beaten more, since at their age they have clearly less excuse
for the mischief that they do.

STREPSIADES

But it's unnatural! It's . . . *illegal!*
Honor your father and mother.
That's the law.
Everywhere.

PHEIDIPPIDES

The *law?*
And who made the law?
An ordinary man. A man like you or me.
A man who lobbied for his bill until he persuaded the people
to make it law.
By the same token then, what prevents me now
from proposing new legislation granting sons the power to inflict
corporal punishment upon wayward fathers?

Nothing vindictive,
of course.
In fact, I would personally insist on adding a rider,
a Retroactive Amnesty for Fathers, waiving our right to compensation
for any whippings we received prior to the passage of the new law.
However, if you're still unconvinced, look to Nature for a sanction.
Observe the roosters, for instance, and what do you see?
A society
whose pecking-order envisages a permanent state of open warfare
between fathers and sons. And how do roosters differ from men,
except for the trifling fact that human society is based upon law
and rooster society isn't?

STREPSIADES

Look, if you want to imitate the roosters,
why don't you go eat shit and sleep on a perch at night?

PHEIDIPPIDES

Why? Er . . .
because the analogy doesn't hold, that's why. If you don't believe me,
then go ask Sokrates.

STREPSIADES

Well, whatever your roosters happen to do,
you'd better not lick me. It's your neck if you do.

PHEIDIPPIDES

My neck?
How so?

STREPSIADES

Because look: I lick you. All right, someday you'll have a son
and you can even the score with me by licking the hell out of him.
But if you lick me, then your son will follow your precedent
by licking you. If you have a son.

PHEIDIPPIDES

And if I don't have a son?
You've licked me, but where am I? I'm left holding the bag,
and you'll go to your grave laughing at me.

There is a long tense silence as the full force of this crushing argument takes its effect upon Strepsiades.

STREPSIADES

What?

But how . . .?

Hmm,

by god, you're right!

To the Audience.

—Speaking for the older generation, gentlemen,

I'm compelled to admit defeat. The kids have proved their point: naughty fathers should be flogged.

PHEIDIPPIDES

Of course, I nearly forgot.

One final matter.

STREPSIADES

The funeral?

PHEIDIPPIDES

Far from it. In fact,

it may even soothe your feelings.

STREPSIADES

How to be licked and like it, eh?

Go on. I'm listening.

PHEIDIPPIDES

Well now, Misery Loves Company, they say.

So I'll give you some company:

I'll horsewhip Mother.

STREPSIADES

You'll *WHAT*???

HORSEWHIP YOUR OWN MOTHER?

But this is worse! Ten thousand times worse!

PHEIDIPPIDES

Is that so? And suppose I prove by Sokratic logic the utter propriety of horsewhipping Mother?

What would you say to that?

STREPSIADES

What would I *say*?

By god, if you prove *that*,

then for all I care, you heel,

you can take your stinking Logics
and your Thinkery as well
with Sokrates inside it
and damn well go to hell!

To the Chorus.

—You Clouds got me into this! Why in god's name
did I ever believe you?

KORYPHAIOS

The guilt is yours, Strepsiades,
yours and yours alone. The dishonesty you did
was your own choice, not ours.

STREPSIADES

But why didn't you warn me
instead of luring a poor old ignoramus into trouble?
Why did you encourage me?

KORYPHAIOS

Because this is what we are,
the insubstantial Clouds men build their hopes upon,*
shining tempters formed of air, symbols of desire;
and so we act, beckoning, alluring foolish men
through their dishonest dreams of gain to overwhelming
ruin. There, schooled by suffering, they learn at last
to fear the gods.

STREPSIADES

Well, I can't say much for your methods,
though I had it coming. I was wrong to cheat my creditors,
and I admit it.

To Pheidippides.

—All right, boy, what do you say?
Let's go and take revenge on Sokrates and Chairephon
for swindling us. Are you game?

PHEIDIPPIDES

What? Raise a finger
against my old Philosophy professor? Count me out.

STREPSIADES

Show a little respect for Zeus.

PHEIDIPPIDES

Zeus?

You old fogey,
are you so stupid you still believe there's such a thing
as Zeus?

STREPSIADES

Of course there's a Zeus.

PHEIDIPPIDES

Not any more
there isn't. Convection-Principle's in power now.
Zeus has been deported.

STREPSIADES

That's a lie! A lot of cheap
Convection-Principle propaganda circulated by those windbags
in the Thinkery!

I was brainwashed! Why, they told me
that the whole universe was a kind of potbellied stove

Pointing to the model in front of the Thinkery.

like that model there, an enormous cosmical barbecue,
and the gods were nothing but a lot of hot air and gas
swirling around in the flue. And I swallowed it,
hook, line, and sinker!

PHEIDIPPIDES

Rave to yourself, Madman.
I'm leaving.

Exit Pheidippides.

STREPSIADES

O Horse's Ass, Blithering Imbecile,
Brainless Booby, Bonehead that I was to ditch the gods
for Sokrates!

He picks up Pheidippides' stick and savagely smashes the potbellied model of the Universe in front of the Thinkery. He then rushes to his own house and falls on his knees before the statue of Hermes.

—Great Hermes, I implore you!

Be gracious,
lord! Forego your anger and give me your compassion.
Pity a poor old codger who was hypnotized with hogwash,

drunk on drivel.
O Hermes, give me your advice,
tell me what to do.
Should I sue?

He puts his ear close to the god's mouth as though listening to whispered advice.

What?
Ummm.
Good.
Got it.
DON'T SUE . . .
Go on.
Yes?
BURN DOWN THE THINKERY . . . SMOKE OUT THE CHARLATANS . . .
INCINERATE THE FAKES!
Aye aye, Sir!

Shouting to his slave.

—Xanthias! come here!
Quick, get me your ladder!
Bring me an axe!

Xanthias runs up with a ladder and an axe.

Now
scramble up there on the Thinkery and rip up the tiles
until the roof caves in.
Shoo, boy!

Xanthias sets his ladder against the Thinkery, clambers up, and starts chopping at the tiles and prying them up with his axe.

—Quick,
bring me a torch!

Another slave runs up with a blazing torch.

By god, I'll fix those fakes
for what they did to me or my name's not Strepsiades!
Let's see if they can fast-talk their way out of this.

He bounds up the ladder to the roof, furiously firing the rafters and beams with his torch, while Xanthias pries at the tiles with the axe. The smoke billows up in clouds and the whole roof begins to glare luridly, while inside the Thinkery are heard the first signs of alarm and confusion.

FIRST STUDENT

From within.

FIRE! ! FIRE! !
HELP!

STREPSIADES

Scorch 'em, Torch!
Go get 'em!

When Xanthis stops to stare at the holocaust, Strepsiades tosses him the torch, snatches up the axe, and starts slashing furiously at the rafters.

FIRST STUDENT

Rushing out of the Thinkery and peering up to the roof.

—Sirrah, what dost?

STREPSIADES

Dust? That's chips,
Buster. I'm chopping logic with the rafters of your roof.

SECOND STUDENT

From within.

Who roasteth our rookery?

STREPSIADES

A man without a coat.

SECOND STUDENT

Rushing outside.

But we're burning alive!

STREPSIADES

Hell, I'm freezing to death!

FIRST STUDENT

But this is Arson! Deliberate Arson! We'll die!

STREPSIADES

Splendid. Exactly what I had in mind—

He narrowly misses his leg with the axe and then teeters dangerously on the roof.

oops!—
so long as I don't split my shins with this axe
or break my neck in the process.

Wheezing, hacking, and gagging, Sokrates scuttles out of the Thinkery, closely followed by an incredible procession of emaciated, ghostlike Students, all gibbering with terror. Finally, at the very rear, squawking and clucking like two frightened roosters, come Philosophy and Sophistry.

SOKRATES

You there, sirrah!
What is thy purpose upon my roof?

STREPSIADES

Ah, sir,
I walk upon the air and look down upon the sun
from a superior standpoint.

SOKRATES

Choking on the smoke and almost incoherent with rage.

Why, you—
agh!
I'm gagging . . .
argh
I . . .
grhuahg . . .
CAN'T . . .
TALK! !
Arrggghhh . . . .

As Sokrates collapses into a spasm of choked coughing, Strepsiades and Xanthias come scrambling down the ladder from the roof. Then Chairephon, totally covered with soot and cinders and his cloak smouldering, streaks from the holocaust of the Thinkery.

CHAIREPHON

Yiyi!
HALP!
It's like an oven in the Thinkery! I'm burnt to a crisp.
I'm a cinder.

STREPSIADES

Belaboring him with a stick as Xanthias lashes Sokrates.

Then why did you blaspheme the gods?
What made you spy upon the Moon in heaven?

KORYPHAIOS

Thrash them,
beat them, flog them for their crimes, but most of all
because they dared outrage the gods of heaven!

Strepsiades and his slaves thrash Sokrates and his followers, until the whole herd of thinkers, followed by Philosophy and Sophistry, stampedes madly toward the exit. Here they meet—and flatten—Pasias and Amynias returning to the Thinkery armed with summonses and accompanied by their witnesses.* Exeunt omnes *in a general rout. Behind them the Thinkery with an enormous crash collapses into blazing ruin.*

CHORUS

Now ladies, let us leave
and go our way.
Our dances here are done,
and so's our play.

Slowly and majestically, the Chorus files out.

Notes

page 11. *Strepsiades:* A name derived from στρέψις (turning, twisting, wriggling). That is, Strepsiades is etymologically The Debtdodger and his name is played upon throughout the play.

11. *desert to the Spartans:* The annual invasions of Attika by the Spartans and their allies during the first few years of the Peloponnesian War meant that maltreated or discontented Athenian slaves could easily desert to the enemy, and the fear of desertion was common in Athens.

12. *ponytails:* Pheidippides wore his hair long and curling in the style affected by the younger knights.

13. *bumbailiff:* B. B. Roger's solution, perhaps too English for American ears; but the pun is almost untranslatable. The Greek word here translated as bumbailiff is δήμαρχος, inserted as a surprise in place of the expected "bedbug" or "flea."

13. *Blueblood Megakles:* Megakles was a common male name of the Alkmaionid family, one of the oldest and most aristocratic in Athens. It is largely because of the prominence of Alkmaionid names in the play that Pheidippides has frequently—and not improbably—been regarded as a caricature of Alkibiades, also an Alkmaionid and notorious for his dissolute youth.

Strepsiades' marriage to an Alkmaionid wife is, of course, a *mésalliance* between a prosperous farmer and a daughter of the dissolute and luxurious city nobility. Presumably, such alliances were not uncommon in the late fifth century, and Aristophanes clearly intends to show the progress of corruption in Strepsiades, ruined by his playboy son and his luxurious wife.

14. *hippos:* "Horse." A common component in artistocratic names, since in early Athens the ownership of a horse automatically meant membership in the military cavalry or the social chivalry.

14. *Pheidonides:* The name means Parsimonious.

14. *Pheidippides:* The compromise means Parsimonious Chevalier or The Scrimping Aristocrat.

15. *horse-god oaths:* As Poseidon Hippios, Poseidon was the patron god of horsemen. Cf. *Knights* 551 ff.

page 16. *Cosmical Oven:* The theory advanced in this passage is of uncertain provenience. In *Birds* 1001, Aristophanes attributes it to Meton, though the comedian Kratinos attributed it to Hippo in his *Panoptai,* and both Herakleitos and Parmenides held that the heavens were made of Fire. Here, however, it is probably best taken as a representative—and, for Aristophanes, representatively ridiculous—example of contemporary physical theory. Some of the Sophists may have held something like it; so far as we know, Sokrates did not.

But the metaphor of the Cosmical Oven is central to the play, and for this reason Aristophanes has placed a visible model of it in front of the Thinkery (cf. 11. 1473-74). Moreover, unless I am mistaken, the metaphor is a surprisingly consistent one, whose every detail and principle would have been instantly understood by an Athenian—but not an American—audience. For the principle here is that of an ordinary, humdrum, home-made charcoal-burner's "kiln," used incongruously as a diagram of highfalutin' Socratic physics, and it is in the appreciation of the details that the humor of the finale lies. It is, according to Aristophanes, a kiln designed for very slow heat and very little air (i.e., a πνιγεύς); in shape it is like an inverted bowl (i.e., a δῖνος—cf. 1. 1473), bellied at the bottom and tapered at the top; set inside it are charcoals (i.e., ἄνθρακες—1. 97) and *above* the charcoals are the swirling heated gases and flames (i.e., αἰθέριος δῖνος—1. 380) under whose steady heat wood becomes charcoal. Translated into the physics of the Aristophanic Sokrates, the humble charcoal-burner's oven becomes the Universal Crucible, in which the gods are the lightning and the slow, downward-burning heat of the heavens, the forces which slowly carbonize the world and the creatures below; in which living is a form of burning and the dead are only ashes. Against this background, with only minor modifications, Sokrates' student can demonstrate to Strepsiades the cosmical principles involved in the gnat's buzz and Sokrates can explain the thunder as elemental farting. And it is, of course, the same metaphor which informs the finale of the play where the Thinkery itself becomes an enormous blazing kiln. Sokrates chokes on the smoke (ἀποπνιγήσομαι—1. 1504), Chairephon is roasted alive (κατακαυθήσομαι—1. 1505), while Strepsiades, like a blazing god, fires the roof *above* them.

Such, I believe, is Aristophanes' meaning. Because, however, charcoal kilns are unfamiliar nowadays, I have been compelled to make the Cosmical Oven an ordinary potbellied stove and to introduce a pseudo-scientific equivalent for Δῖνος, i.e., Convection-Principle.

16. *for a fee:* The perennial gibe. The Sophists expected to be paid for the instruction they gave, an attitude which seemed mercenary to the wealthy Plato and which Platonists since have never tired of condemning. Doubtless many of the Sophists were mercenary and several were rich men, but the mere fact of accepting a salary for professional services

rendered does not—except in artistocratic societies where cash payments are regarded as vulgarizing those who receive them—convict a man of intellectual dishonesty. But perhaps I am prejudiced. In any case, the sophistic movement made headway in Athens, not because the Sophists were greedy mountebanks in a gullible age, but because there was a rising class with a desperate need for new skills and techniques and for this class the existing education was worse then useless. If the New Education began by being *vocational*—offering precisely those legal and verbal skills which were so urgently required for the conduct of Athenian imperialism—it ended by being genuinely *revolutionary,* that is, by systematically questioning and overturning all the established beliefs of the old order. It could never have become this, however, had not the fact of payment *freed* the Sophists from the old order as much as it *bound* them to the new. Hence the hostility and open contempt of such conservatives as Aristophanes and Plato.

Sokrates, it is true, did *not* accept payment, and this is Sokrates' glory. But Sokrates' glory is not necessarily the Sophists' shame.

page 16. *The Technique of Winning Lawsuits:* Literally, "to overcome the truth by telling lies," i.e., the familiar accusation that the Sophists made "the worse cause appear the better." It was precisely this charge that was brought against Sokrates by his accusers later, and Aristophanes may be responsible for the suspicion. That some Sophists professionally claimed this ability is beyond dispute. Equally, however, the sophistic attack upon traditional beliefs must have seemed both perverse and illogical to staunch conservatives. Passionately held convictions tend, i.e., to defend themselves by their look of being self-evident: those who question them are *ipso facto* guilty of dishonesty or faulty reasoning. And this is especially true of an age when logic was in a state of comparative infancy. Plato, for instance, constantly attacks the Sophists for their devotion to specious logic (i.e., sophistry), and yet his own *Republic* contains dozens of logical fallacies and grotesque equivocations that even a schoolboy could detect. And presumably these are honest mistakes. But the Sophists normally receive no mercy.

17. *two kinds of Logic:* i.e., the so-called Just (or Major or Better) Logic and the Unjust (or Minor or Weaker) Logic, here rendered as Philosophy and Sophistry respectively.

The originator of the Doctrine of the Two Logics (or *Antilogoi*) was Protagoras of Abdera. If we are right in assuming that Protagoras' famous dictum ("Man is the measure of all things") means that the truth is subjective, then the same statement also implies that a proposition can be simultaneously both true and false. And it is a fact that Protagoras taught his students to argue *both* sides of a given statement with equal plausibility—presumably as an exercise in forensic virtuosity. The very willingness of Athenian courts to consider matter that would now be regarded as inadmissible supports the view that these exercises were practical in scope and not deliberate attempts to subvert justice. But for Aristophanes the *Antilogoi* are transparent sophistry, humbug on a huge scale, and he accordingly makes the debate between the two *Logoi* the climax of the comedy.

It is customary, of course, to translate Λόγος as "Logic" or "Argument," and this is the literal meaning of the word. But the issue here is larger, and to translate this way tends to obscure the fact that Aristophanes is talking, not about systems of formal logic, but about a whole system of Reason, discursive and nondiscursive alike. Λόγος also means Reason; but Reason includes several modes of discourse ranging from the work of the imagination to moral reason and strictly logical reason in the narrow sense. The so-called Just Argument, for instance, is not really an argument or a logical system at all; it is a personification of the kind of Reason spoken by a certain kind of society before logic, strict logic, existed: a Reason which expressed itself in education, in morals, in imagination, in the criteria of values and the justifications offered for those values. As opposed to the Unjust Argument, it represents the rational power of poetry—and the peculiar logic of poetic imagination—against the rational power of prose and formal logic (and for this very reason Aristophanes lets the Just Argument speak in splendid anapests while the Unjust Argument uses prosy iambics). In ethics, it represents the power of rational suasion—by means of models and parallels drawn from the great body of lyric and epic poetry—in contrast to a system of ethics, just as rational but rational in a different way, sanctioned by inferences drawn from Nature and animal existence (cf. Pheidippides' inferences from the life of the rooster, 11. 1427-29). In culture, it is the rational guidance of Custom (not Blind Custom), the corrective rightness of traditional experience as against the restless innovations and risky isolation from experience and history of the pure intellect. It is not what the modern world normally means by Reason, and certainly not what Protagoras meant, but it is, I think, what Aristophanes meant and what most Greeks would have understood him to mean. But for this very reason, because his *Logos* is not a logic but a prelogical discourse of the whole human reason, the Just Argument is helpless against his opponent. His case cannot be expressed logically, and yet it remains rational.

All this may seem like compounding old humbug with new, but it is the justification I make for translating Δίκαιος Λόγος as Philosophy and Ἄδικος Λόγος as Sophistry. Sophistry, of course, should be taken in the strict sense of the word, Philosophy in the loose and unprofessional sense (as in the catchphrase, "a philosophy of life").

page 18. *miscarriage:* Probably a conscious echo of Sokrates' claim to be a midwife of ideas.

page 21. *Spartan prisoners from Pylos:* Cf. Glossary, under *Pylos.* After their imprisonment, the Spartans must have been considerably emaciated.

21. *geological research:* Literally, "they are exploring the things under the earth." This was, in fact, one of the accusations brought against Sokrates by his accusers in 399 B.C. In substance the charge implies that scientific research is blasphemous, insofar as the very act of investigating Nature suggests that the inquirer has doubts about the received cosmology. In the *Apology,* Sokrates admits to having dabbled in scientific research in his earlier days; the later Sokrates, Plato implies, had quite outgrown such nonsense.

23. *And as patriotic as it is useful:* During the years preceding the Peloponnesian War, Athens sometimes confiscated the territory of rebellious subject cities. The land so confiscated was then divided by lot and portioned out among the poorer citizens of Athens. Such allotments, needless to say, were enormously popular—at least in Athens.

24. *a single lawcourt in session:* The Athenian love of litigation was notorious, and Aristophanes never misses a chance of hitting it. Cf. *Wasps.*

24. *Perikles squeezed it dry:* Cf. Glossary: EUBOIA.

26. *Bars of iron, like the Byzantines?:* Sokrates' statement that the gods are an expression coined by vulgar superstition causes Strepsiades to think of a less vulgar sort of coinage. And so he comes up with the Byzantines who, alone in the Greek world, used coins made of iron.

27. *the mystical couch:* Probably a very battered settee. The reader should perhaps be aware that the whole scene of Strepsiades' admission to the Thinkery and introduction to the Clouds is an elaborate "philosophical" initiation rite, probably paralleling initiation into one of the many Greek mysteries. Thus Sokrates' researches are *mysteries;* Sokrates powders Strepsiades as a *purification;* Strepsiades wears a *chaplet* and is forced to strip *naked* (like a candidate at the Eleusinian Mysteries) before entering the *cave* at the rear of the Thinkery (which reminds him of the cave of the oracular Trophonios, a Theban seer). After his entrance he must undergo an *ordeal* (whippings, bedbugs, etc.) before being vouchsafed rebirth as a *new man.*

27. *poor Athamas:* Cf. Glossary: ATHAMAS. Athamas attempted to kill his son Phrixos; when sentenced to be sacrificed for the attempt, he was saved by Herakles. The point here is that Strepsiades' mythology is inaccurate and his literary education has been neglected. But since no conceivable modern audience can be expected to know—or even to care—whether Athamas was killed or saved, I have deliberately intruded the two succeeding lines in the hope of making them seem Aristophanic and the situation a little clearer.

31. *That's why they write:* Presumably all the effusions which follow this are genuine examples of what happened when the Murky Muse inspired a dithyrambic soul.

page 41. *But I'm not a burglar:* According to the Scholiast, this line is explained by the customary Athenian procedure for searching a house in which stolen goods might have been hidden. The searcher was required to strip so that he could not, under pretense of carrying out his search, convey into the house of the accused the goods presumed to have been stolen. Sokrates' reply in the following line is an intruded gloss of my own manufacture, designed to give the situation a possible point for a contemporary audience.

43. *ARISTOPHANES:* In the Greek text the speech which I have here assigned to Aristophanes is given to the Chorus in accordance with the normal convention of the *parabasis.* But if the Chorus in a normal *parabasis* speaks *on behalf of* the poet, the parabasis of *Clouds* is unique in having the Chorus speak, in the first person, *as* the poet himself. Doubtless in the original version of this play, the *parabasis* was spoken by the Chorus on the poet's behalf; but in the revision Aristophanes has laid aside the mask and speaks directly for himself. In the circumstances it seemed unnatural to give the Chorus the poet's lines, and I have therefore brought Aristophanes on stage to speak for himself in person.

45. *a stranger / rescued the foundling:* Aristophanes had produced his comedy *The Banqueters* under the name of Kallistratos. His reason for so doing, he claims, was natural modesty and observation of Athens' neglect and mistreatment of her comic poets (cf. *Knights* 514-45); more likely, he was too young to enter the contest under his own name.

45. *Elektra in the play:* Cf. Glossary: ELEKTRA.

45. *dangling thong of leather:* The comic phallus. Despite the almost unanimous consensus of scholars that Aristophanic characters did *not* wear the phallus, and Aristophanes' explicit denial here, I am nonetheless convinced they did. My only argument is the text and the near impossibility of explaining the dramatic action of numerous scenes in the absence of the phallus. In *Clouds,* Strepsiades' little play on "finger-rhythm" (652 ff.) literally requires the phallus, as does his parting threat to Amynias 1299-1302). The masturbation-jingle in *Knights* (24 ff.) is unactable without it; the Wasps are stingless, etc., etc. Nor am I in the least deterred by Aristophanes' denial—the prize evidence of those who deny the phallus in Aristophanes—simply because it would be the height of ingenuousness, I think, to take Aristophanes' word for it, especially here. *The Clouds* may very well be a daintier, wittier play than the comedies of Aristophanes' rivals, but the disclaimers here are slyly contradicted by the play: several scenes are pure slapstick, Strepsiades beats his opponents with a stick, etc.

45. *a dirty dance:* That is, the *kordax.* Cf. Glossary: KORDAX.

46. *my celebrated simile* on the / *eels:* Cf. *Knights* 864-67.

47. *Paphlagon:* Cf. Glossary: PAPHLAGON.

page 47. *hard on the heels of the Levin rattled the steeds of Thunder:* A quotation from Sophokles' (lost) *Teukros.*

47. *How the moon, in dudgeon, snuffed her flame amongst the rack, and the sun in sullenness withdrew:* An eclipse of the moon took place in October 425, and a solar eclipse in March 424, just before the election of Kleon as general.

48. *your month is a consequent chaos:* An allusion to the confusion created in the Hellenic calendar by the Athenian astronomer Meton. Instituted in 432 B.C. and then gradually adopted throughout Greece, the Metonic calendar changes made for initial difficulties. Because the reform was not uniformly adopted throughout Greece, the same festivals in different places would fall on different dates, etc.

49. *stripped Hyperbolos of his seat:* Hyperbolos (cf. Glossary) had been appointed Athenian delegate to the Amphictyonic Council of Delphoi in 424 B.C. The Council was a religious and juridical federation of Greek city-states whose primary concerns at this time would have been the war and infractions of such "international law" as existed at the time. Presumably, this Council would have been responsible for smoothing the way to general Greek adoption of the Metonic calendar. Exactly what happened to Hyperbolos is not known; the Chorus says that it "stripped him of his crown"—which may mean, as Rogers suggests, that the wind blew off the sacred chaplet which he wore in his official capacity. From the animosity of the Clouds, it can be reasonably assumed that Hyperbolos had supported the Metonic reform.

51. *vulgarly called finger-rhythm:* δάκτυλος in Greek means both "finger" and "dactylic meter."

52. *Raising his phallus to the ready:* Cf. note on p. 120: *dangling thong of leather.*

53. *the female's a duchess:* An anachronistic pun of my own invention; the Greeks had ducks but no dukes. Literally, the Greek says "the male is a rooster (ἀλέκτωρ), the female a roosterette (ἀλεκτρύαινα)."

53. *You've made basket masculine, when it's feminine:* "Basket" is my own contribution. In the Greek, the word is κάρδοπος, "a kneading-trough," whose -ος termination is normally the sign of the masculine gender, though κάρδοπος is in fact feminine. This pun, of course, leads directly to discussion of Kleonymos, another instance of a masculine ending for an actual effeminate.

54. *Why, Amynia:* In the original, this whole passage is based upon a play on the Greek vocative (whereby the nominative *Amynias* becomes *Amynia*—which has the -α termination of the feminine nominative). Because English has no vocative, I have recast the play here as a confusion between singular and plural. For Amynias, cf. Glossary: AMYNIAS.

59. *witchwomen from Thessaly:* Throughout antiquity, Thessaly was famous

for its red-headed witches. Cf. Apuleius *Metamorphoses* I; Plato *Gorgias* 513 a.

page 60. *scorch out every word of the charges:* The charges would have been written down on a wax tablet.

65. *Expended as required. / No comment:* When asked to account for the expenditure of several talents (actually used to purchase the withdrawal of the Spartans), Perikles answered only: "I spent them as required."

66. *Even Hyperbolos:* Hyperbolos had evidently studied under the sophists for a fee of one talent—a large sum.

66. *Philosophy and Sophistry:* Cf. note on p. 117: *two kinds of Logic.*

67. *from the/neck up they are fighting-cocks:* According to a Scholiast, the Logics were garbed as fighting cocks and brought out in cages. This statement has rarely won the approval of scholars, who are quick to point out that it is contradicted by the references throughout the debate to hands, clothing, and other parts of the *human* anatomy. If I am right, the Logics wore rooster masks and a few feathers with perhaps a great vivid bustle of tail feathers; but from the neck down they were visibly human. After their adoption by the Birds, Pisthetairos and Euelpides appear garbed in this very way (cf. *Birds*). Such a solution allows Aristophanes to present the Logics as fighting cocks or as wrestlers as his dramatic needs required, and the text seems to me to support this.

69. *how Zeus escaped punishment after he imprisoned/his father:* Zeus dethroned his father Kronos and bound him in chains. The same argument is used by Euthyphro (cf. Plato *Euthyphro*) to justify his prosecution of his own father. But the argument here is interesting because it shows clearly the mythological rationale of the Old Education and the way in which the New Education refuted it. For the Old Education, mythology was a rational corpus of heroic behavior and morality was taught in mythological terms, quite despite the fact that the morality of mythology was incompatible in many instances with the operative moral values of the fifth century. The greatest artists of the older generation—Aiskhylos and Pindar—had in fact attempted to reconcile myth and moral behavior by rewriting the offensive myths and expelling their crudities or giving them new—and moral—interpretations. The exponents of the New Education quite naturally turned their characteristic invention—formal logic—against the Old Education by pointing out the inconsistencies of its morality and mythology. The same purpose informs many of Euripides' tragedies, and for this reason he incurred the suspicion and contempt of Athenian conservatives—quite despite the fact that his own artistic intentions were really very much like those of Aiskhylos, an attempt to harmonize mythology and morality. But because the morality was relatively new—or looked that way—and was supported by a logic which was destructive of the old morality, he was not understood by conservatives. Few artistic feuds seem, in fact, more futile than Aristophanes' with Euripides, since—

apart from dramatic differences—the two men basically believed the same things.

page 71. *Telephos:* Cf. Glossary: TELEPHOS.

71. *Pandaletos' loaf:* Cf. Glossary: PANDALETOS.

73. *the Old Education:* Readers interested in knowing more about the conflict between different views of education in fifth-century Athens and the rationale of the Old Education should consult the relevant chapters of Werner Jaeger's *Paideia.* Suffice it to say here that it was basically a curriculum comprising two major fields called respectively Music and Gymnastic. By Music was meant the education of the inward man; the schooling not merely of the mind, but of the emotions, the "soul," the feelings and the thoughts in their rational ensemble. The basic instrument of this inward education was poetry joined to music, a blend in which poetry taught by means of example and emulation and was sustained by music which was believed to inculcate the moral virtues. Gymnastic was, of course, vigorous and disciplined athletics. The intended product of this theory of education was a disciplined reason in a disciplined body, an outward grace which expressed the grace and harmony within, the whole person embodying the classical virtues: self-control, decorum, respect for others, piety toward the gods, moderation in all things, dignity and courage. It was, in short, far more what we would call moral education, education in "character," than intellectual training. It was also, for obvious reasons, the education of a restricted and exclusive class. It taught no skills, prepared for no career, and was obviously impractical for Athenian society of the late fifth century. For these reasons, it has always appealed to the exponents of "education of character," British public schools and their American imitators. Aristophanes put his whole heart into its exposition here, and I have done my best to overcome my own repugnance, though probably unsuccessfully.

It would, of course, have been a pleasure to modernize the debate and present it in topical terms as a struggle between the views of education represented—less than ideally, of course—by American universities and that preposterous pretence of education perpetrated by the professional "educationists" in the secondary schools of America. But this is a suggestion which might be adopted by a producer in search of a topical Aristophanes; for a translation, it is out of the question.

73. *A Voice from Afar* or *Hail, O Pallas, Destroyer!:* According to the Scholiast, the second of these hymns is ascribed to Lamprokles of Athens; the first to Kydeides of Hermione.

73. *their conduct was manly:* The point is precisely the manliness. The fashionable homosexuality of the Athenian upper classes was essentially borrowed from Sparta, where homosexuality was not only tolerated but even encouraged as a military virtue (because "lovers" would fight well for each other). Hence the contempt with which Philosophy regards the

effeminate homosexuals of the Athenian New Education. Only among the Athenian lower classes was homosexuality viewed with contempt. The modern image of an Athens populated exclusively by happy philosophical pederasts is largely due to the fact that the surviving literature is a leisure-class production; poor men were very rarely Platonists.

page 77. *Baths of Herakles:* Greeks normally named hot baths everywhere the Baths of Herakles. Another example of specious logic against which Philosophy is helpless.

77. *old Homer:* This argument must have hurt. Of all the poets, Homer was regarded by the Old Education as the greatest, the Bible of true belief. And now, like the devil, Sophistry quotes scripture.

78. *Peleus:* Cf. Glossary: PELEUS.

78. *Hyperbolos and swords just don't mix:* Because Hyperbolos presumably attempted to avoid military service.

79. *reamed/up the rectum with a radish:* The poetic punishment meted out to adulterers in Athens.

82. *Due date for debts:* Strepsiades does not actually say this. What he says is that the day he fears is "the-Old-and-The-New." By this he means the effective last day of the lunar month, the day on which both the last of the waning Old Moon and the first of the waxing New Moon could be seen. The-Old-and-The-New, in short, was the normal name given to the last day of the month, the day on which debts were payable. And this nomenclature continued to be used even when the calendar was no longer lunar. The term is, to modern ears, grotesquely unfamiliar, but it is also crucial to an understanding of the action, and for this reason I have had considerable misgivings about altering it. But upon reflection it seemed to me that "Due date" might just possibly do, and I have so rendered it. But see the note on this page: *Today's Dueday.*

82. *Call it an honorarium:* Aristophanes, that is, hints that Sokrates was not above receiving "tokens of esteem" from his disciples. This may be pure satirical malice, but then again it may not be. Sokrates' students were mostly rich aristocrats; he himself was poor. And in the circles which Plato frequented, a distinction was probably drawn between a payment and a "gratuity"—the common sophistry of "good society." But this is guesswork.

83. *with gladsome paeans plangent:* An echo, according to the Scholiast, from the *Satyrs* of Phrynichos—or Euripides' *Peleus.* Probably the latter.

83. *debouch from mine abode:* A very slight modification of Euripides' *Hekabe* 173 ff.

84. *Today's Dueday:* Cf. note above: *Due date for debts.* For a more literal rendering of Pheidippides' sophistic analysis of the-Old-New-Day in the following lines, readers should consult any prose translation of the play. I have preferred to use the "Dueday—two day" pun because it made the equivocation instantly visible as glib hocus pocus, though it also

meant a necessary change—a slight one—in the interpretation of Solon's legislation which Pheidippides offers. But I suppose most readers of the *Clouds* to be more interested in a comedy than in the details of Athenian debt legislation.

page 84. *to post their bond:* Before commencing a legal action against a defaulting debtor, a creditor had to post with the prytanies, as caution money to defray court expenses, the sum of 10 per cent of the amount of the debt.

85. *Precisely because they* are *magistrates:* A deliberate distortion of the literal meaning of the Greek. The text actually says: "They act like Foretasters; in order to devour the meal as quickly as possible, they have the deposits paid a day in advance." The Foretasters seem to have been officials responsible for sampling the dishes to be served at a public feast the following day.

87. *the National Honor:* The National Honor (and, one might add, the public interest) of Athens required that every citizen be as litigious as possible.

91. *tragedy / by Karkinos:* Karkinos was a frigid, fourth-rate tragedian with an apparent penchant for introducing querulous beggar-gods in his plays. Most of the fustian which follows is presumably the work of Karkinos or his son Xenokles. Talent did not run in the family.

100. *a custom's a custom:* The festive custom of *paroinia,* acording to Rogers, an old convivial tradition of singing at table.

100. *Shearin' o' the Ram:* Krios (which also means "Ram") was a wrestler, probably the victim of an overwhelming defeat in a wrestling match, and hence the "Shorn Ram." Simonides' poetry was very highly regarded by the older generation.

101. *bombastic bore / in poetic history:* The charge was common in antiquity. In an age of discursive prose and colloquial poetry, the gorgeousness of Aischylos and his extravagant metaphorical bravura made him look like a drunken lord of language. For Aristophanes, of course, Aischylos is the Model Poet who "makes men better citizens" as opposed to the Arch-Corrupter, Euripides. Cf. *Frogs.*

101. *One of those slimy tragedies:* A reference to Euripides' (lost) *Aiolos.*

104. *Wasn't I born as free a man as you?:* A parody of Euripides' *Alkestis* 691.

107. *the insubstantial Clouds men build their hopes upon:* This line and most of the two which follow it are Arrowsmith, not Aristophanes. I have intruded them in order to give just a little more resonance to the meaning of the Clouds. For although English has idioms in plenty which more or less parallel the Greek—to "have one's head in the Clouds," "to build on the clouds," "castles in the clouds," etc.—a little further rounding out seemed necessary. The Clouds are the patrons of visionaries and woolgatherers the world over; here they are cloudy deceivers, the shining hopes that deceive Strepsiades.

page 113. *Pasias and Amynias:* The Greek plays, of course, have come down to us without footnotes or stage directions other than what the Scholiasts tell us. And I admit that there is no textual justification for bringing back Pasias and Amynias here, nor is it suggested by any Scholiast. They are here because Pasias threatened to pay his bond and return with a summons, and because I think Aristophanes would have liked them to be foiled again, even at Strepsiades' moment of truth.

Glossary

AISCHYLOS, AESCHYLUS: The great Athenian tragedian (525-456 B.C.).

AKADEME, ACADEMY: Originally a precinct sacred to the hero Akademos and afterward used as a gymnasium and recreation area. The general Kimon planted it with groves of olives and plane trees. Only in the fourth century, after becoming the haunt of the philosopher Plato and his followers, did the once athletic Akademy become academic in the modern sense of the word.

AKROPOLIS, ACROPOLIS: The citadel of Athens.

ALKIBIADES: An Athenian politician (*ca.* 450-404) of great ability and brilliance. Of aristocratic Alkmaionid descent, he was related to Perikles and was, for some time, a devoted disciple of Sokrates. Distinguished by wealth, birth, and spectacular personal beauty, he spent his youth in lavish display and debauchery (Pheidippides in *The Clouds* has been thought to be a caricature of Alkibiades). After the death of Kleon in 422, Alkibiades became chief of the belligerent anti-Spartan party in Athens in opposition to the more conservative Nikias and was one of the primary advocates of the disastrous Sicilian expedition.

AMYNIAS: Son of Pronapes and one of Strepsiades' creditors in *The Clouds*. He was not, however, a professional moneylender but a notorious effeminate and wastrel, probably addicted to gambling.

ANTIMACHOS: A homosexual on a prodigious scale.

APOLLO: God of prophecy, music, healing, and light; his two chief shrines were at Delphoi (q.v.) and the island of Delos (q.v.).

ARTEMIS: Goddess of the hunt and the moon, sister of Apollo (q.v.).

ATHAMAS: King of Orchomenos and the legendary subject of a (lost) play by Sophokles. Having attempted to murder his son Phrixos (q.v.),

Athamas was sentenced to be sacrificed. He was crowned with a sacrificial wreath and dragged before the altar, but just before being dispatched, was saved by the sudden intervention of Herakles.

ATHENA, ATHENE: Goddess of wisdom and war and patroness of Athens. On her breast she wore the aegis, a goatskin plated with scales and a Gorgon's head in the center.

BACCHOS: See DIONYSOS.

BYZANTION: A city on the Bosporos and a subject-city of the Athenian Empire. Its siege by the Athenians under Kimon in 469 was celebrated.

CHAIREPHON: A pupil and disciple of Sokrates; his scrawniness and emaciated pallor are constantly ridiculed by Aristophanes.

DELOS: Small Aegean island sacred to Apollo.

DELPHOI, DELPHI: A town in Phokis, celebrated for its great temple and oracle of Apollo.

DEMETER: The Earth-Mother; goddess of grain, agriculture, and the harvest, worshipped in her shrine at Eleusis in Attika.

DIONYSOS: God of vineyards, wine, and dramatic poetry; also called Bacchos, Evios, Bromios, etc.

ELEKTRA: Daughter of Agamemnon and Klytaimnestra; with her brother Orestes she murdered her mother for having killed her father. In the *parabasis* of *The Clouds,* Aristophanes alludes to the famous scene in Aischylos' *Choephoroe,* when Elektra recognized that her brother Orestes had returned to Argos from the lock of hair left on Agamemnon's tomb.

EPHESOS: A city in Asia Minor (Ionia), site of a famous temple of Artemis.

EUBOIA: A large and fertile island northeast of Attica. In 457 Perikles planted an Athenian colony on the island and otherwise exploited it. As a result the island revolted in 445 and had to be resubjugated. This time, however, Perikles' treatment of the island was so severe that it was commonly said (at least by his enemies) that he had "stretched Euboia on the rack of torture."

EUPOLIS: An Athenian poet of the Old Comedy and a rival of Aristophanes. Eupolis claimed that Aristophanes had imitated him in *The Knights,* and Aristophanes countered by charging that Eupolis' *Marikas* was a plagiarism of his own *The Knights.*

EURIPIDES: Athenian tragedian (480-406 B.C.) whose character and plays were constantly ridiculed by Aristophanes. Euripides' mother may have been (though this is uncertain) a marketwoman who sold chervil, and Aristophanes never tires of twitting the tragedian about his mother's vegetables.

HERAKLES: Hero and demigod, son of Zeus and Alkmene; renowned for his great labors, his prodigious strength, and his gluttonous appetite.

HERMES: God of messengers and thieves; in Athens in every doorway stood a statue of Hermes (i.e., a herm, usually a pillar surmounted by a bust of the god), protector of the door and guardian against thieves—presumably because it takes a thief to keep another thief away.

HIERONYMOS: A dithyrambic poet and tragedian, notorious for his extraordinary shagginess, bestial appearance, and pederasty.

HIPPOKRATES: Athenian general and nephew of Perikles; his three sons, it seems, were all distinguished for their stupidity and were popularly nicknamed "The Pigs."

HYPERBOLOS: An Athenian demagogue, successor to Kleon on the latter's death in 422. Of servile origins, he seems to have been a peddler of lamps and then to have studied with the Sophists in order to advance himself politically. (At least these are the charges made against him by Aristophanes.) He was later ostracized and finally murdered by the oligarchical leaders in Samos.

KARKINOS: An Athenian tragic poet whose poetry and three sons are all ridiculed by Aristophanes. Karkinos' name means "Crab."

KEKROPS, CECROPS: Legendary first king of Attika and reputed founder of Athens. Hence "country of Kekrops" is equivalent to "Athens," and "son of Kekrops" to "Athenian." He is usually represented as twi-form, i.e., with the head and upper trunk of a man, but serpent-shaped below (symbolizing his earthborn origin).

KIKYNNA: An Athenian deme of the tribe of Akamantis.

KLEON: Son of Kleainetos; the most notorious and powerful of all Athenian demagogues. After the death of Perikles in 429 B.C., Kleon became, until his own death in 422, the leader of the radical democracy and the anti-Spartan extremists in Athens. An impressive speaker and a thoroughly unscrupulous and venal politician, he was bitterly loathed and attacked by Aristophanes. In 424 B.C., thanks to his coup in capturing the Spartan hoplites at Sphakteria, he reached the height of his power; so unchallengeable was his position that he was able to persuade the Athenians not to accept the handsome terms offered by Sparta in an attempt to recover her imprisoned hoplites. Filled with confidence in his military ability and tempted by the hope of further glory, Kleon took command of an Athenian army in Thrace, where, in 422, he was defeated and killed by the Spartan forces under Brasidas.

In Aristophanes' *The Knights,* Kleon is only slightly masked under the name of Paphlagon (q.v.).

KLEONYMOS: A corpulent glutton and part-time informer; Aristophanes' commonest butt for cowardice (i.e., throwing one's shield away).

KORDAX: A salacious dance commonly used in Athenian Old Comedy.

KRONOS: Father of Zeus, Hera, and Poseidon. Deprived of his rule by Zeus. Synonymous with "old fogy."

KYNTHOS: A mountain on the island of Delos, sacred to Apollo.

LEOGORAS: A wealthy Athenian gourmet, addicted to horse raising (or possibly to pheasant-breeding). Father of the orator Andokides.

LYDIA: A district of Asia Minor; under its greatest king, Kroisos (Croesus), it included almost all of Asia Minor from the river Halys to the Ionian coast. Its wealth and effeminacy were proverbial among Greeks.

MAENADS: The frenzied female worshippers (Bacchantes) of Dionysos (q.v.).

MAIOTIS: An inland sea (the modern Sea of Azov), northern arm of the Black Sea.

MARATHON: The famous battle (490 B.C.) in which the Athenian forces under Miltiades crushingly defeated the first Persian invasion of Hellas.

MEGAKLES: A name belonging to the Alkmaionid family, one of the proudest and most distinguished aristocratic families of Athens.

MEMNON: Famous hero, son of Tithonos and Eos (Dawn); killed in the Trojan War at the hands of Achilleus.

MIMAS: A mountain on the coast of Ionia.

NESTOR: King of Pylos and a hero of the Trojan War, famous for his wisdom and eloquence.

OLYMPOS: Mountain (app. 9700 feet, alt.) in Thessaly, covered at the summit with perpetual snow and reputed by the Greeks to be the abode of the gods.

PALLAS: The goddess Athena (Pallas Athene).

PANATHENAIA: The great Athenian festival in honor of Athena.

PANDALETOS: A professional informer.

PAPHLAGON: Aristophanes' (and presumably Athens') nickname for the demagogue Kleon (q.v.). The name is intended to suggest: (1) that Kleon came of slavish and foreign stock—i.e., was not an Athenian but a Paphlagonian—and (2) the sheer volume and violence of Kleon's rhetorical assaults (from Greek *paphlazein,* to froth, bluster, storm).

PARNASSOS: A high mountain to the north of Delphoi (q.v.); one of the chief haunts of Apollo and the Muses, but frequented also by Dionysos.

PARNES: A mountain in the northeast of Attika, forming part of the boundary between Attika and Boiotia. Near its foot was situated the deme of Acharnai.

PASIAS: One of Strepsiades' creditors; evidently a grotesquely fat man and probably a drunkard to boot.

PELEUS: Hero of mythology, husband of Thetis and father of Achilleus. According to legend, Astydamia, wife of Akastos, fell in love with Peleus but was rejected by him. Angered, she denounced him to her husband for having attempted to seduce her. Akastos thereupon invited Peleus to a hunting expedition on Mt. Pelion, stripped him of his weapons, and left him to be torn to pieces by the wild animals. When Peleus was almost on the point of death, however, the god Hermes brought him a sword.

PERIKLES: Greatest of Athenian statesmen of the fifth century, and from 461 B.C. until his death in 429, the almost unchallenged leader of the radical Athenian democracy. Of one of Athens' most aristocratic families (the Alkmaionids), he was nonetheless the politician most responsible for the creation of the extreme democracy of the late fifth century. To Aristophanes' critical and conservative eyes, it was Perikles who was responsible for the corruption of Athens, and Aristophanes never tires of contrasting the Athens of the Persian War period with the Athens of Perikles—corrupt, effete, cruelly imperialistic, avaricious, at the mercy of Sophists, clever orators, and impostors, cursed with a system (e.g., the law courts) which practically guaranteed further excesses and injustices. Worst of all in Aristophanes' eyes was Perikles' belligerent war policies (e.g., the famous Megarian Decree of 432) and the fact that, after 429, Athens was left to the mercies of men like Kleon and Hyperbolos who lacked Perikles' restraint and political genius. Like almost all the comic dramatists, Aristophanes was a conservative (*not* an oligarch), and although he distinguishes clearly between Perikles and his corrupt successors, he nonetheless holds Perikles responsible for creating the political system in which men like Kleon could thrive.

PHOIBOS: Apollo (q.v.).

PHRIXOS: Son of Athamas (q.v.); on the point of being sacrificed to Zeus, he was rescued by his mother Nephele.

PHRYNICHOS: The famous early Athenian tragedian.

PHRYNIS: Of Mytilene, a famous citharist and musician of the fifth century; his innovations shocked and angered contemporary conservatives.

POSEIDON: Brother of Zeus and god of the sea. As god of the sea, he girdles the earth and has it in his power, as Poseidon the Earthshaker, to cause earthquakes. In still another manifestation, he is Poseidon Hippios, patron god of horses and horsemen.

PRODIKOS: Of Keos, the famous sophist and friend of Sokrates.

PYLOS: Town of the southwestern coast of Messina whose siege and capture, along with the neighboring island of Sphakteria in 425-24, became a *cause célèbre* of the Peloponnesian War and the major source of Kleon's prestige and power in Athens. As a result of their defeat at Pylos and the capture of their hoplites, the Spartans were forced to sue for peace; every overture, however, was met by the determined refusal of Kleon, eager for the war to continue.

SARPEDON: Legendary hero, son of Zeus and Europa; killed by Patroklos during the Trojan War.

SIMON: A swindler, the details of whose peculations are unknown.

SIMONIDES: Of Keos, the great sixth-century lyric poet.

SOKRATES: (*Ca.* 469-399 B.C.) The great Athenian philosopher and teacher of Plato. In appearance he was almost grotesquely ugly; with his bulging eyes, fat lips, and a round paunch, he looked like nothing so much as a Satyr or Silenos. This, combined with his practice of strolling about the marketplace and accosting citizens with questions about truth, justice, beauty, etc., made him an apt target for ridicule, all the more since it is doubtful whether the majority of Athenians could, in fact, distinguish between Sokrates and the average Sophist. That this is the case can be inferred from *The Clouds* and Aristophanes' extremely sophistic presentation of Sokrates.

SOLON: Famous Athenian legislator (*ca.* 638-588 B.C.), whose achievement it was to have ended debt-slavery in Athens.

SOPHOKLES: The Athenian tragedian (495-404 B.C.).

TELEPHOS: Legendary king of Mysia and the subject of tragedies by Aischylos, Sophokles, and Euripides. Wounded by Achilleus while defending his country, Telephos was informed by an oracle that only the weapons which had given him his wound could cure him. Thereupon, disguised as a beggar, he made his way to Argos where, with the connivance of Klytaimnestra, he covertly took the young Orestes hostage. When the gathered Greeks were condemning Telephos for his hostility to their cause, the disguised hero made a speech in his own defense, but with such warmth and eloquence that the Greeks recognized him. When Achilleus demanded his death, Telephos threatened to kill the infant Orestes. Finally, Achilleus relented and agreed to give Telephos the weapon which had wounded him and which would cure him.

THALES: Of Miletos (*ca.* 636-546 B.C.), one of the Seven Sages of antiquity; renowned for his scientific genius and for having predicted an eclipse of the sun.

THEOROS: Flatterer, perjurer, sycophant of Kleon.

THESSALY: A large district in northern Greece, renowned throughout antiquity for its abundant supply of witches.

THETIS: The sea nymph, mother of Achilleus by Peleus (q.v.). Courted against her wishes by Peleus, she changed herself successively into a bird, a tree, and a tigress. But Peleus, acting on the instructions of the centaur Cheiron, countered by holding her fast until she assumed human form and consented to marry him.

TLEPOLEMOS: Hero and son of Herakles, the subject of a tragedy by the dramatist Xenokles, one of the sons of Karkinos (q.v.). In the play one of the characters describes how his brother was killed by Tlepolemos.

TROPHONIOS: King of Orchomenos, worshipped as a hero after his death. His oracle in a cave in Boiotia was celebrated throughout Hellas, and those who consulted him made it their practice to take honeycakes with which to appease the snakes who frequented the cavern.

TYPHO, TYPHON: A fire-breathing giant, frequently represented as a hurricane.

XANTHIAS: A common servile name.

XENOKLES: An Athenian tragedian, son of Karkinos (q.v.).

XENOPHANTES: Father of Hieronymos (q.v.).

ZEUS: Chief god of the Olympian pantheon; son of Kronos, brother of Poseidon and father of Athena. As the supreme ruler of the world, he is armed with thunder and lightning and creates storms and tempests.

The Wasps

Translated by Douglass Parker

with sketches by Geraldine Sakall

CONTENTS

PARENTIBUS SUIS

HAS LITTERAS

PRO EPISTULIS

INTERPRES

D. D. D.

Introduction

The Play

The Wasps is not a favorite of modern readers. For two-thirds of its length, its subject matter is felt to be obscure except to specialists, while the final third concludes in a fashion that even specialists lament as unconnected, or else try to explain away on the grounds of a built-in flaw in the form of Old Comedy. The first of these objections can be met with a brief explanation: Athenian law, a far different entity than modern American law, found its characteristic judicial expression in courts where guilt and, on occasion, sentence were decided by the majority vote of huge juries, sometimes composed of as many as 1001 citizens. These dicasts (a word which may be glossed, in view of their functions, by either "judges" or "jurors") were daily chosen to serve from the six thousand citizens who constituted the annual panel. Before the mid-fifth century, dicasts performed this service gratis, but Perikles instituted a small salary, probably in 462, and the demagogue Kleon increased it to three obols per man per jury day in 425 or 424. The buying power of this amount cannot be firmly expressed in modern equivalents; it could pay for a pigeon, or three salted fish, or the cleaning of a cloak. In any case, it was barely enough to sustain life in a small family, and, as a result, jury duty seems to have attracted mainly those who had no other income or chance of any. Primarily the old. Such a system does not necessarily contain within itself the assurance of justice to all; to a conservative playwright, however, the case was clear and fast: the jurors were inevitably the creatures of Kleon and the other demagogues to whom they owed their pay, and were further, because of their poverty, fair game for bribery.

It was with an attack on this state of affairs that Aristophanes returned to political comedy at the Lenaia of 422, offering *The Wasps*. Here the protagonist, old Philokleon the demon dicast, is weaned from his boss-ridden, jury-going ways by his virtuous son, Phobokleon (as here translated), with successive applications of force, logic, and what we might call therapy—the home trial of a dog for stealing the cheese. At length, a full cure from litigiousness is effected—and 500 lines still remain in the play.

Which brings us to the second objection to *The Wasps*. What is the ending doing there, anyway? Why the long scene in which Phobokleon attempts to make his father a gentleman, the wild drunk scene with the nude flute-girl, the utterly unrelated dance? To those who regard Aristophanes as a pamphleteer, the answer is either clumsiness (he was, after all, still young) or a [necessary] constraint inherent in the form ("every Old Comedy must end with wild farce and a festive procession"), coupled with a not-too-laudable desire to please the groundlings. More perceptive critics attempt to see the play as a whole, and sometimes offer a line from Horace in summation of the plot: *Naturam expellas furca, tamen usque recurret*—roughly rendered, "You can't fight human nature." Philokleon reformed is worse than Philokleon the unreconstructed juryman.

Now, this is good, so far as it goes, but it stops short of a final solution. Behind the judging attacked in *The Wasps* we can see another judgment festering, the judgment which the year before had rejected Aristophanes' favorite child, his comedy of ideas, *The Clouds*. The extensive revision of the earlier play has not prevented critics from noting the basic similarity of the two comedies. In both, the protagonist changes his ways under the force of instruction to the point where he completely reverses his former behavior. But in *The Clouds,* the instruction was in what Aristophanes regarded, let us say, as a vice; in *The Wasps* it is in virtue—and the result is hopeless. This is more than a simple warping of the plot; it is an inversion: both the moral and the aesthetics set forth in the Grand Experiment of 423 are flung down and, quite literally, danced upon. Further, we have an obvious allegory, rather more thoroughgoing than usual. Philokleon, the litigious old man, has obvious affinities with Demos, the "Uncle Sam" of *The Knights,* and is the Athenian people viewed in the practice of its characteristic weakness; Phobokleon—the young reformer, the idealist with purely altruistic motives, the Kleon-hater who is thereby accused of subversive antidemocratic leanings—is Aristophanes himself; and the play is a dramatic presentation of what he sets forth explicitly in the Parabasis—the failure of his teaching to change his fellow-citizens for the better.

Indeed, the whole play is a calculated insult to the audience's intelligence. Not only does it break every rule of good comedy formulated by Aristophanes in *The Clouds* 537 ff. (though this may have been written later), but it contradicts its own program, expounded by Xanthias in lines 57-63. We have an avowedly slapstickless play that wallows in knockabout farce; a professedly nonpolitical play whose principals are "Kleon-Lover" and "Kleon-Hater"; a play which avoids attacking Euripides by bringing him on stage (so I believe) in an advanced stage of disrepair; a chaste play whose Chorus is distinguished by a phallic peculiarity. And so forth. And, in the final wild dance, Philokleon, once juryman, now jury-bait, has progressed from Phrynichos the elder to Phrynichos the younger, has been rejuvenated according to comic formula—and still prefers indecent spectacle to sense. His triumph in the dance is his defeat as a rational being. Aristophanes, with an overt contempt for his audience's taste rarely matched elsewhere (the Introduction to Ben Jonson's *Bartholomew Fair* affords some comparison), has given the people what they want—and, in giving, damned them for wanting.

But there is one more turn of the screw. Happily ignorant of the present-day criticism which damns his *dramatis personae* as a clutch of two-dimensional types, Aristophanes has complicated his characters beyond mere allegory, however ironic. Philokleon is more than the Old Reprobate, more than a symbol of Athens' excesses—he is violently himself. Utterly immoral, completely loveless, distinguished by the most thoroughgoing lack of *sophrosune* in Greek drama, he is yet driven to his reprehensibilities by a fierce inner integrity which is somehow wholly admirable. He knows who he is, and will prove it in any environment, at any cost. And does, over and over again. Opposite him is his son Phobokleon—the voice of the author, his virtues undoubted, altruistic to his father's selfishness. More fundamental, however, is a much less admirable form of altruism: Phobokleon is, at bottom, a snob; his virtues are not self-impelled, but generated *ad hoc* by his concern for appearances, for the good opinion of the Right People. He is no hypocrite, but his basic inadequacy blooms after the Parabasis, when, having achieved the Good Life for his father, he can only define it as the approved paradise of those rakehells who comprise his peer-group. In one sense, then, our choice lies between doing the right things for the wrong reason (Phobokleon) and doing the wrong things for the right reason (Philokleon). Not an easy choice, and the despair of the seeker after black and white—but an intensely comic polarity.

Thus is irony ironized beyond pamphleteering, incident endowed with the cross-welter of meanings, the coexistence of mutual exclusives, which marks great drama of any sort. Aristophanes has expanded his pique at the failure of *The Clouds* into a funny play, and counterpointed it into a fine one. It would be satisfying to report to lovers of poetic justice that this play carried off the first prize, but such does not seem to be the case. The account of the competition is confused, but it would appear that Aristophanes entered two plays at the Lenaia of 422, and defeated his *Wasps* with his *Rehearsal*. Poetic justice is rarely simple.

Translation

The Wasps, with its scholia, is our greatest single source of knowledge for the minute workings of the Athenian jury system—but this translation is not. Had Aristophanes written a didactic *De Iuris Natura* in Greek, the translator's aim would be, of course, to reproduce it; but he wrote a comedy, and nothing kills comedy or poetry like a niggling antiquarianism. Thus, with the initial statement above concerning the basic difference between Athenian and American jury practice, I consider the reader prepared; other significant facts can be gained from the text, where necessary intruded glosses have, on a very few occasions, been amplified by notes. Points of little or no importance for the appreciation and understanding of the play have been swallowed up in modern analogues and legal diction. In this connection, I have regretfully kept at a minimum Latin, still even in America the hallmark of the law. No translator of Aristophanes can avoid anachronism, or wants to, but there are limits.

For the rest, the principles stated in the Introduction to *The Acharnians* apply, with a few additional observations. *The Wasps* is not a play which depends vitally on rhetorical tension and contrast, and expansion in that line is much less here. On the other hand, stage directions, or intruded glosses to supplant them, are much more common, as befits a play in which the slapstick element is quite large. Unison choruses—to state a principle which applies to *The Acharnians* as well—should be conceived of as *sung, not chanted,* and, in the unlikely event of production, music should be provided. The modern rendition of stasima via that bastard form of noncommunication known as Choral Speaking may impart a bogus patina of ritual to tragedy, but has no conceivable excuse for appearing in a comedy.

A word on staging. The proscenium stage requires the entrance of the Chorus from the wings, an entrance which I have thus tried to slow down; the motivation is not far to seek, happily. The house has inevitably been located center stage, in the Greek fashion, though there is little *dramatic* reason for this. Further consideration has brought me to conclude that it might with profit be located at the left, with the Chorus making its entrance from the right. This would allow freer movement on a modern stage. In any event, the Chorus' presence on stage is felt, if not seen, from its initial appearance until the play's end. One other suggestion should be noted: the front door might possess a wicket, or some such device, through which Philokleon can be seen when necessary.

Text

Though my basic text has been Coulon's (1924), supplemented by Cantarella's (1954), I have made so many minor changes, particularly in line assignments, that it would be pointless to record them. I wish, however, to set down my demurral at one triumph of modern scholarship: both Coulon and Cantarella, out of obscure fealty to Wilamowitz, to that will-of-the-wisp called the "Three-Actor Law," and to a woolly-brained scholiast with pretensions to literary criticism, refuse to name the principal slaves, and deny the "First Servant" (i.e., Sosias) any independent utterance after line 137, giving the balance of the slave speeches in the opening scene to the "Second Servant" (i.e., Xanthias), who also receives every word of lines 54-135. I refuse, for my part, to share in the fruits of this victory of method over intelligence; I have gone back to earlier texts, picked and chosen, and reinstated Sosias at the expense of the "Second Servant" or "A Servant" in several places, notably 1292 ff. At least one slave in *The Wasps* has a well-defined character: he is a coward and a blusterer—and his name, in this version, is Sosias. In this connection, my adoption of Van Leeuwen's *oise* for the MSS *Chroise* (Wilamowitz *Kroise*) should be noted at 1251. Other important deviations are commented on as they occur. I have derived aid and comfort—and an occasional pun—from the editions of Starkie (1897), Rogers (2d. ed., 1915), and Van Leeuwen (2d. ed., 1909).

Acknowledgments

Again, gratitude is due the University of California, for typing grants; Donna Lippert, for typing; the indefatigable triumvirate of Donald Johns, William Sharp, and Marshall Van Deusen, for perceptive patience. More inexpressible thanks fall to William Arrowsmith, for his thoroughgoing, masterful critiques and his healthy, bracing differences of opinion (some of them not resolved at this writing); and to my wife, not only for putting up with all this, but for putting in her three obols' worth, time and again, to my great profit. I am especially in the debt of the Welsh poet Will Fletcher, who has helped me more than, under the circumstances, he can ever know.

DOUGLASS PARKER

Characters of the Play

SOSIAS, XANTHIAS } *Slaves of Phobokleon*

PHOBOKLEON, *son of Philokleon*

PHILOKLEON, *an elderly Athenian juror*

FIRST KORYPHAIOS

SECOND KORYPHAIOS

CHORUS *of elderly Athenian Jurors* (*WASPS*)

FIRST LITTLE BOY

SECOND LITTLE BOY

FLEAHOUND, *a dog*

CHOWHOUND, *a dog*

A FLUTE-GIRL

A BANQUET GUEST

MYRTIA, *proprietress of a bakery*

CHAIREPHON

THE MAN WHO LOOKS LIKE EURIPIDES

A WITNESS

SLAVES

ASSORTED KITCHEN UTENSILS

PUPPIES

OUTRAGED GUESTS AND SMALL TRADESMEN

THREE SONS OF KARKINOS

SCENE: *A street in Athens. In the background, center, the house of Philokleon and Phobokleon, a two-storied dwelling with a front door, a side door, and a second-story window. A huge net covers the entire façade, draped so that the doors are free. Over the front door, a wreath. Phobokleon is asleep on the flat roof. On guard before the house, armed with long iron spits, are the two slaves, Sosias and Xanthias. They are very weary. Xanthias, in fact, is asleep. The time is shortly before dawn.*

SOSIAS

Shaking Xanthias.

Xanthias!

No answer. He shakes again.

What the hell do you think you're doing?

XANTHIAS

I'm studyin'. How to Relieve the Watch. One easy lesson.

He goes back to sleep.

SOSIAS

You're aching for trouble. Have you forgotten what we're guarding? A MONSTER!

XANTHIAS

Scares me so much
I'm afraid to stay awake.

Back to sleep again.

SOSIAS

Okay, it's your neck. . . .
Go ahead, see if I care. . . . Why should I care?
I can hardly keep *my* eyes open.

He snuggles down.

Delicious!

He goes to sleep; then, after a moment or two of silence, begins to thrash around wildly, kicking Xanthias awake.

XANTHIAS

Now what? Have you gone crazy? Or did you join those holy-rolling Asiatic Korybants?*

SOSIAS

Neither.

But it *was* a divine visitation. *And* from Asia.
Bacchos descended and filled me with his presence.

He produces a wine bottle and drinks. Xanthias, after a look, produces his *bottle and drinks.*

XANTHIAS

A fellow-worshipper! The real afflatus—Phrygian
liquid sleep. One thing about Oriental religion—
it's *restful.*

He drinks again.

Except, it made me dream just now—
incredible!

SOSIAS

Me, too. A highly abnormal nightmare. . . .
You tell yours first.

XANTHIAS

I seemed to see an eagle
swoop down, massive and vast, upon the city,
clench in his claws a brazen buckler, bear it
aloft to heaven—

and turn into Kleonymos, and throw
the shield away.

SOSIAS

Say what you want about Kleonymos,
he's a wonderful riddle.

XANTHIAS

How so?

SOSIAS

It can win you a drink:
"What animal defends itself by shedding *its armor?"*

XANTHIAS

That dream—what an omen!

SOSIAS

Don't worry. It can't mean anything
disastrous.

XANTHIAS

Kleonymos can't mean anything *but*.
—It's your turn; you tell your dream.

SOSIAS

Mine's a big one.
It concerns the whole hull of the Ship of State.

XANTHIAS

Then get a move on, man, and lay the keel.

SOSIAS

I'd no sooner gone to sleep than I dreamed about sheep,
all members of the Assembly, meeting on the Pnyx. *Dressed* sheep—
they all were carrying canes and wearing cloaks.
Up front, I saw a greedy, rapacious whale
haranguing these poor sheep in a booming bellow,
the bloated blatting of a swollen sow.

XANTHIAS

Pew!

SOSIAS

What's wrong?

XANTHIAS

You can stop right there. Whales, sows—
your nightmare stinks of rotten leather; it reeks
of that tanner Kleon.*

SOSIAS

Then this filthy whale
took up a bag and filled it with lumps of fat.

XANTHIAS

Oh, god, it *is* Kleon! He's sacking Greece!

SOSIAS

Squatting on the ground beside the whale
I saw Theoros. He had a crow's head. At least,
that's what *I* said it was. But Alkibiades—he was
in my dream—*he* said Theoros was a sapsucker.*
Alkibiades isn't much on birds.

XANTHIAS

Maybe not.

He *is* a pretty good judge of character, though.

SOSIAS

But isn't that mysterious, Theoros turning into a crow?

XANTHIAS

No mystery at all. Best thing that could happen.

SOSIAS

How?

XANTHIAS

How? He's a man, then suddenly he becomes a crow—
the interpretation's obvious. Your dream means that Theoros
will soar away from us—

SOSIAS

And what?

XANTHIAS

—and CROAK!*

He ducks as Sosias, disgusted, swings wildly, then picks up the two iron spits and chases him around the stage.

SOSIAS

Stop, you subtle soothsayer! Come here, you two-bit
prophet—I want to give you your pay: two spits!

XANTHIAS

Hold it! Let me tell the audience the plot.

The chase stops. He turns to the audience.

First, Gentlemen, a few preliminary remarks.
Don't look for anything too high-brow from us;
or for any slapstick smuggled out of Megara.
We haven't got those two slaves chucking chestnuts
out of a basket to keep the audience happy,
or Herakles to be swindled out of his supper again.
As for the aesthetic bit—that's out. We won't
bring on Euripides to get another working over.
Now Kleon's illustrious, thanks to luck*—no matter,
we won't chop him up into hash *again:* No Politics.

We merely have a little plot with a moral—
not too refined and dainty for *you,* of course,*
but rather more intelligent than smutty farce.
So look—

Pointing at Phobokleon.

that's our master there—asleep
topside—the big fellow—the one up on the roof.
He's locked his father indoors, and set us two
on sentry duty so the old man can't go out.
The father's sick with a baffling, unnatural disease,
so strange that none of you would ever guess it
unless I told you . . .

Listening to some imaginary voice from the audience.

You don't believe me? Try it!

Listening again and pointing.

There's Pronapes' son Amynias.—You say the old man's
sick with *dice*-addiction?

SOSIAS*

Dice-addiction!
He's judging from his own disease. —Dead wrong, Amynias!

XANTHIAS

Not quite.—Take fifty per cent, Amynias. Addiction
is half of the affliction.

Jerking a thumb at Sosias, who is beckoning to someone in the audience.

Sosias is telling Derkylos
the old man's addicted to *drink.*

SOSIAS

I certainly am not!
That's a gentleman's disease. What would *he* know about it?

XANTHIAS

Pointing again.

You have a theory, Nikostratos? He's a *sacrifice*-addict—
a religious fanatic? No. Oh, then you say
he's a *hospitality*-addict?

SOSIAS

You mean like Philoxenos, the Perfect
Host? Perfect to a fault—he's a bugger. NO!

XANTHIAS

To the audience in toto.

These feeble guesses are futile—you'll never find out.
If you really want to know, then quiet down,
and I'll tell you the master's disease in just a minute.

He pauses and waits for silence.

He's a JURY-addict! Most violent case on record.
He's wild to render verdicts, and bawls like a baby
if ever he misses a seat on the very first bench.
He doesn't get any sleep at night, not a wink.
Or, if he closes his eyes a speck, he's in Court—
all night his mind goes flapping around the water-clock.
You know those pebbles that the Jurors drop into the urns
marked *Guilty* and *Not Guilty,* to record their votes on the verdict?
Well, he's squeezed *his* pebble so often and so hard
that when he wakes up, he has three fingers stuck together,
like someone putting incense on the festival altar.
And worse. Let him see the name of a fathead faggot
scrawled on a wall—*"I letch for Demos; he's a doll"*—
and he scratches beside it, *"I itch for the Jury; it's a jewel."*
Once his rooster didn't crow till sundown. Know
what he said? "That cock's corrupt! The officials under investigation
bribed him to wake me up too late for Court!"
Now he shouts for his shoes right after supper;
he's over there *way* before dawn, and goes to sleep
clutching a courtroom column just like a barnacle.
And nasty—watch him in action! When he takes his tablet
to fix the penalty, he always draws the Long Line:*
everyone gets the maximum sentence from him!
Then off for home like a bee—or a *bumble*-bee—
wax just plastered underneath his fingernails.
He's petrified that he might run out of those pebbles
he uses for voting; so he keeps a *beach* in the house.
In sum, he's insane; the more we reason with him,
the more he judges everybody else. Absolutely
hopeless. Incurable.
So now we've locked him up
with bolts, and watch to be sure he doesn't go out.
The son, you see, takes his daddy's disease quite hard.
First, he tried the Word Cure. Gently he wheedled
and pleaded the old man to put away his cloak
and stay home.

Didn't work. So next, the Water Cure.
Dunked him and dosed him.
No dice.
Then Applied Religion.
Made him a Korybant.
Tambourine and all, his daddy
banged his way into court for more drumhead justice.
Finally, as a last recourse, he turned to Pure Prayer.
One night he grabbed the old man, sailed over to Aigina,
and bedded him down for the cure in Asklepios' temple . . .
and up he popped at dawn by the jury-box gate!
Since then, we never let him out of the house.
At first, he kept sneaking out the pipes and drains
and running away. And so we plugged up all
the holes with hunks of rag, and sealed them tight.
He reacted rather like a jackdaw—kept banging pegs
in the wall, running down, and hopping off.
At last we took these nets and draped them around
all over the house—and *now* we keep him in.
One more thing about the old man—he's a KLEON-addict!
—I mean it! That's his name, in fact: PHILOKLEON!
His son takes the opposite tack. In this and everything.
He *hates* Kleon. And that's *his* name: PHOBOKLEON!*
He's sort of a snooty, snorty, holier-than-thou-er . . .

PHOBOKLEON

Awake.

Xanthias! Sosias! You asleep?

XANTHIAS

Oh-oh!

SOSIAS

What's up?

XANTHIAS

Phobokleon.

PHOBOKLEON

Pointing at the side door.

One of you get over here right away!

Xanthias obeys.

Father's gone and got into the stove. He squeaked in somehow, and now he's skittering around like a mouse.
—*You* see that he doesn't slip out the bathtub drain.

Sosias runs to the house.

—*You* keep leaning on that door.

XANTHIAS

Yessir! Yessir!

Silence. Then the trapdoor on the chimney is slowly raised from within.

PHOBOKLEON

Almighty Poseidon, what's that creaking in the chimney?

Philokleon's head begins to emerge cautiously from the chimney.

Hey, who are you?

PHILOKLEON

I'm smoke, and I'm issuing forth.

PHOBOKLEON

Smoke? That's nice. What wood are you from?

PHILOKLEON

I'm peach wood.*

He starts to clamber out. Phobokleon shoves him back.

PHOBOKLEON

Impeacher-wood? Too acrid. Back you go!

He shoves Philokleon all the way back into the chimney, and slams the trapdoor over the opening, then lifts a large log over it.

Peace to your ashes. I'm putting the damper down—
with a log on top. Think up another one.

He drops the log on the chimney with a crash.

I don't have troubles enough—now I'll be famous—
son of a smudgepot, a smokestack for my family tree!

The front door shakes violently.

SOSIAS

Somebody at the door.

PHOBOKLEON

Push hard! Squeeze tightly!
Show what you're made of!

The slaves strain against the front door.

I'll be down and help you.
Watch out—keep an eye on that door bar. You know what he's like.
He'll probably chew the nut right off the bolt.

He disappears into the house.

PHILOKLEON

From behind the locked front door.

What are you up to? Damn you, let me out to judge!
Do you want Drakontides to be *acquitted?*

SOSIAS

Would that bother you?

PHILOKLEON

BOTHER? The oracle at Delphoi warned me once:
"Thy first acquittal bringeth thy final summons!"

SOSIAS

Apollo preserve us from prophecies like that one!

Phobokleon emerges from the side door and puts his shoulder to the front door.

PHILOKLEON

Please let me out—I'll bust!

PHOBOKLEON

The answer is NO!

PHILOKLEON

Then I'll—I'll gnaw the net through with my teeth!

PHOBOKLEON

You don't *have* any teeth.

PHILOKLEON

Consarn it all!
How can I kill you? How? Give me my sword!
Or—quick! Bring me a tablet—I'll *sentence* you!

PHOBOKLEON

I'm afraid the old man's plotting something desperate.

PHILOKLEON

Me? I wouldn't think of it.

I only want

to bring the donkey out and sell him. That's all.

It's market day, you know.

PHOBOKLEON

Oh, come, now. *I*

can sell the donkey.

PHILOKLEON

Not as good as *I* can!

PHOBOKLEON

Better, by god!

PHILOKLEON

Will you *please* let the donkey out?

SOSIAS

He's a slippery old cuss. And talk about excuses!

Just to get out of the house!

PHOBOKLEON

And what good did it do?

All that angling and not a single bite.

Still, I'd better go in and get that donkey;

we can't have Papa popping out again.

He unbars the door, enters the house, and leads out the donkey. Philokleon is hanging underneath it, as Odysseus hung under the Kyklops' ram, face up, but has miscalculated a little; his head is directly under the donkey's rear. The donkey appreciates this not at all, and hee-haws piteously.

Packass, why all the tears? Don't you *want* to be sold?

Get a move on!

The donkey stands stock-still and bawls louder.

Why all the noise? Are you carrying

an Odysseus—something like that?

SOSIAS

Peeking under the donkey and espying Philokleon.

By god, he *is!*
One of those snuck under him right back here!

PHOBOKLEON

What's that? Let me see.
—There he is, all right. What *is* this?
Pardon me, sir, but who might you be?

PHILOKLEON

Nobody.

PHOBOKLEON

Nobody? Hmmm. From what country?

PHILOKLEON

Ithaka. Son of
Skedaddle.

PHOBOKLEON

A likely story. Well, Nobody, no bloody
fun for you!

To Sosias.

Drag him out of there! Hurry!

As Philokleon's head emerges from between the donkey's rear legs.

That old dunghill—of all the places to hide!
what do I tell my friends?
"Oh, that old foal
is my father. He's the biggest man in the Borough."

PHILOKLEON

Clinging to the donkey and fending off Sosias.

You let me alone, or there's going to be a fight!

PHOBOKLEON

You'll have to fight us both—what's so important?

PHILOKLEON

I'll lose my ass!

He is dragged out.

PHOBOKLEON

You're rotten—all tricks and no scruples.

PHILOKLEON

Rotten? Me? You're badly mistaken, son.
Why, a man like me's just at his tastiest—well hung,
right in my prime. Wait till you see the stake
I'm going to leave you.

PHOBOKLEON

Take that ass and shove it—
and yourself—back in the house!

PHILOKLEON

As he and the donkey are forced back in.

Help!
Colleagues! Jurors! Kleon! Somebody!
HALP!

PHOBOKLEON

Slamming the door shut after Philokleon.

Shout to your heart's content—this door stays locked!
—Sosias, pile lots of rocks against the door—
then stick the pin back into the bar again,
and shove the beam against *that*. Then both of you
find that bowl—the huge one—and roll it up.
And please show a little speed!

The slaves obey in a flurry of action. Suddenly Sosias, near the house, gives a jump.

SOSIAS

Ouch! They got me!

Rubbing his head, as the others turn to him increduously.

Honestly—some plaster hit me!
Where'd it come from?

XANTHIAS

There's probably a mouse up there. *It* hit you.

SOSIAS

Looking up.

A mouse?
Up where?

Philokleon's head appears at the edge of the roof.

That's no mouse.
But I see something
that tunneled under the tiles.

To Phobokleon.

You'd better hurry
and sell this house, Boss—it's got *Jurors!*

PHOBOKLEON

Seeing his father.

Again?
Why do these things happen to me? Now he's a sparrow,
all set to fly away! Where did I put that net?

He grabs a long-handled net and waggles it at Philokleon.

Shoo! Back in there! Shoo!

Philokleon's head disappears. Phobokleon looks around hopelessly.

I swear to god,
I'd rather be up north with the army, and freeze
myself blue, blockading Skione, than try
to keep this idiot father of mine at home.

SOSIAS

Well, I guess we've scared him off for good.
All the holes are plugged—he can't sneak out.
What about a nap?

Phobokleon frowns at him.

Not a *long* one—

He produces his bottle again.

just a—
just a drop?

PHOBOKLEON

Are you crazy? Father's friends are coming—
the other Jurors! In just a minute or two,
they'll be along to summon him.

SOSIAS

A minute or two?
It won't be light for an hour!

PHOBOKLEON

I know. They must
have got up late today. They usually stagger by
this street just at midnight, carrying lamps.
They summon father by mumbling and moaning those ancient,
sticky-sweet, Asiatic songs by Phrynichos.*

SOSIAS

So?
It's just a bunch of old men—what's the worry?
If they make any ruckus, we can throw a few rocks.
That'll shake them up.

PHOBOKLEON

This is *not* "just a bunch of old men,"
you cretin! These are authentic Athenian Jurors,
choked with pride, crammed with spleen and venom.
Shake *them* up, anger *them*—and you'll discover
you've annoyed a nest of maddened wasps.
A sting,
keen and sharp, projects from each one's loins.
When they're aroused, they spring with wild cries
and sting, and jump, and judge like fiery sparks.

He returns to the roof.

SOSIAS

I say don't worry. Give me my rocks, and I
can eradicate any wasps' nest—jurors or not.

In spite of Phobokleon's injunctions, he and the two slaves go to sleep almost immediately—and, as will appear, quite soundly. A short pause, and the Chorus of Wasps*—that is, of Old Men who sit on juries—staggers on. They are divided into two Semichoruses, each led by a Koryphaios and a little boy with a lamp. They wear tattered cloaks and, in the place of the normal comic phalluses, enlarged representations of wasps' stings.* Their chief characteristic is age: they are impossibly old and crabbed, and walk bent, scanning the ground, in a painful shuffle that contrasts sharply with the exhortations of the First Koryphaios.*

FIRST KORYPHAIOS

Forward, boys—brisk's the word!

To one dodderer who is not moving appreciably slower than the rest.

Hey, Komias, you're dragging!
Once you whipped us along. Now look at you—rotten leather.
Charinades here makes better time!

To the Second Koryphaios.

Hey, there, Strymodoros!
Euergides—did he make it? Did Chabes come in from Phlya?

SECOND KORYPHAIOS

They're all here—the last of the Boys of the Old Brigade.

He stops, lost in reminiscence.

Byzantion—how long ago? Why, it's nearly fifty years!
And what a wild bunch we were! Remember that baker's wife?
You and I, we went halves. We slipped off watch and split her
breadboard up for kindling. Mad?—Those were the days!

FIRST KORYPHAIOS

Fine, fine—but let's hurry to Court!

—Put some muscle in it!
Laches gets it today! He's up for survey. They say
he's loaded—got pots of money—squeezed Sicily dry.*
And the Boss—Kleon—was mighty insistent yesterday:
"Be EARLY!" he said. "Bring a triple ration of ANGER!" he said.
"Whatever you do, CONVICT that criminal!"—That's what he said.
So we'd better rush and be there, boys, before it gets light.

SECOND KORYPHAIOS

Yes, move along, but look sharp—that's what the lamps are for.
Watch out for pebbles—we can't have Jurors taking the rap!

SECOND LITTLE BOY

To the Second Koryphaios.

Daddy, Daddy, there's mud ahead—right there! Watch out!

SECOND KORYPHAIOS

Stopping and peering.

Dratted lamp—can't see. Take a twig and push up the wick.

SECOND LITTLE BOY

No, Daddy—I can push it up better with this. See?

He inserts his finger into the lamp.

SECOND KORYPHAIOS

Oh, you've got a head on *you*—waggle the wick with your finger—
and slosh all the oil—that expensive, hard-to-get-oil—
you IDIOT!
It's no skin off *your* nose when I have to pay those prices!

He hits the Second Little Boy.

There, that'll teach you!

SECOND LITTLE BOY

Any more lessons like that, Daddy,
and we'll blow out our lamps and go home. See how you like it alone—
you'll stumble and fumble and muck around like ducks in the dark.

SECOND KORYPHAIOS

I punish bigger and better men than you, sonny,
every. . . .

He slips.

Oops! the mud! I'm up to my knees in GUCK!
And look at all that snuff on the wicks—sure sign of a cloudburst
in three-four days. Oh, it's good for the crops—what's left of them.
Nothing like oceans of rain and a good, stiff, chilly North wind.

FIRST KORYPHAIOS

Well, here's Philokleon's house. Wonder what happened to him?
I don't see him waiting around to join the group. That's odd.
Never had to rout him out before. He was always first—
head of the line, singing the old songs. He's mad for music. . . .
That's an idea: we can . . .

Suddenly to the Chorus, which is about to plod right by.

HALT!

The Chorus halts.

. . . *sing* him out to work.
—Places, men! Strike up a song; make it a good one!
Let's bring our crony out as fast as he can crawl!

FIRST SEMICHORUS

Singly.

Where's the old man? Why doesn't he come
to the door? Or at least say hello?
Do you suppose he lost his shoes?
That's sad. He could stub a toe.
Sprain an ankle. Strain a vein.
Rupture himself—you never know.

Tutti.

He's the nastiest man on the jury—
malign, marblehearted, and mean!
Though others may yield to defendants' appeals,
he thinks that acquittal's obscene!

SECOND SEMICHORUS

Singly.

What discomposed him? Yesterday's
false Friend of Democracy.
Our bogus Secret Agent in Samos?*
The defendant we let go FREE?
It infected our colleague. Fever. Colic.
Mercy is bad for his allergy.

Tutti, to the house.

Recover your health in the jury—
we're serving a traitor from Thrace.*
He's fat and he's flush and the pickings are plush!
Come down and we'll set you a place!

A pause. Silence from the house.

FIRST KORYPHAIOS

All right, boy, let's move along.

The First Little Boy steps to the center of the stage, then stops.

Come on, start up.

The First Little Boy starts up, not the procession, but a double duet with the Koryphaioi, molto con espressione, *in which the Boys parody the impossibly pathetic youngsters whom Euripides would occasionally deprive of their mothers (as in the* Alcestis) *or feed to the Minotaur (as in the lost* Theseus).

FIRST LITTLE BOY

O Father, gentle Father,
I beg of thee a boon.

FIRST KORYPHAIOS

Name me the toy; I'll buy it,
O best-belovèd Son.

FIRST LITTLE BOY

Not toys. I faint with famine;
a Fig to make me whole?

FIRST KORYPHAIOS

A fig's too damned expensive,
you glutton! Go to hell!

FIRST LITTLE BOY

We'll refuse to light your way!

FIRST KORYPHAIOS

I struggle every day,
buying wood, and grain, and meat
for the three of us to eat
from my petty jury pay,
you miserable pigs—
Oh! Woe!
And you want Figs!

SECOND LITTLE BOY

O Father dear, a query:
Suppose they should decree
No Court Today—where, Father,
would that leave you and me?

SECOND KORYPHAIOS

We wouldn't have the money
to buy the food we want—
before we could afford it,
we could ford the Hellespont!

SECOND LITTLE BOY

Poor Mother, why was I
born into this world to diet on wrangles and disputes,
bitter writs and sour suits?
Oh, the fruitless mimicry
of my foodless little sack!
Alas! Alas!
My life's a lack!

The Little Boys dissolve into sobs, and the Chorus seems about to follow suit. The threatened inundation is staved off, however, by the appearance of Philokleon at the window, behind the net. Quaveringly he breaks into song, a song which bears a rather horrid resemblance to the monody of a shackled Euripidean heroine—Andromeda, say, or Danae.

PHILOKLEON

Aye weary do I waste at this aperture
lusting to list to your overture,
but heark for no hymns from me, Belovèd—
I cannot sing.
Whence, oh whence my deliverance?
They fence me pent 'neath dire surveillance
in durance vile, the while I burn,
yearning, to burst my bonds and sojourn
joined with you for some sweet spell . . .
in Court, and raise all kinds hell.

The music changes.

O Zeus who launchest the lightning,
metamorphose me to smoke.
Infuse me with Proxenides' bluster,*
or the Flabber-Gas of Aeschines, son of Bloat,
and float me away on a tissue of lies.
Lord, shed sudden grace on Thy servant,
the slave of his convictions.
Cast on me a blast of unleavened levin,
roast me in the ash, catch me to heaven,
and waft me to rest in tartar-sauce . . .
or, better, Sovereign,
make me the rock on which they count
the verdict. Thanks. Amen.

FIRST SEMICHORUS

A point of information,
strictly *entre nous*—
Who shut you up? Who threw the bolt?
Who, dammit, who?

PHILOKLEON

It was my son—Phobokleon. But shhh! Don't shout—that's him right there in front, asleep. So please, not so loud.

FIRST SEMICHORUS

What's behind this outrage?
Where do his motives lie?
We trust he adduced some flimsy excuse—
Why, dammit, why?

PHILOKLEON
He refuses to let me judge, or court any trouble. He claims he intends to lap me in luxury at home. And I say no.

FIRST SEMICHORUS
That Fibberkleon's elusive!
Obviously evasive!
He means to muzzle a patriot
who dares expose the truth about
the way our Navy's going to pot.*
The evidence—conclusive:
your son's a SUBVERSIVE!

FIRST KORYPHAIOS
No time to waste. You need a novel synthesis, a striking scheme to spring yourself without disturbing your offspring.

PHILOKLEON
Easy to say—but what? *You* try—I'm ready for anything. I'm wild to stroll along the docket, just me and my ballot.

FIRST KORYPHAIOS
You require scope. Scoop out a hole somewhere and slip through, muffled in rags, like Odysseus at Troy.

PHILOKLEON
Odysseus I tried
already. Not that hole. Besides, they've sealed the place—
no niche big enough for a gnat. Think of something else.

FIRST KORYPHAIOS
Remember our Navy days? When we took Naxos—and you took off without leave? You stuck some stolen spits in the wall and *ran* down.

PHILOKLEON
Oh, I remember, but how does that help? I'm forty years older. There's no resemblance.

THEN I was mighty—muscular—sly—
a matchless master at poaching.
All unperceived I could steal away . . .
besides, nobody was watching.
NOW I'm besieged by a whole damned army
loaded with ordnance, vigilant, vast.

Those two at the door are waiting to skewer me
like a common domestic pest.

AND the spits that I'd have to make do with
are the ones they'll run me through with!

SECOND SEMICHORUS

But now it's NOW, and it's morning!
This is an emergency!
Speed your planning! Improve the shining
hour, honey-bee!

PHILOKLEON

I'm afraid there's only one way open—to gnaw through the net.
—Pardon me, Artemis, goddess of traps! Don't be nettled.

SECOND SEMICHORUS

As Philokleon begins to chew the strands.

The man who squares his jaw is
the man who never succumbs.
Attack that mesh—forward, gnash!
Courage! Grind those gums!

PHILOKLEON

Well, it's done. I chewed it through.

The Chorus breaks into a cheer.

Stop that shouting!
Please proceed with caution—you'll wake up Phobokleon!

SECOND SEMICHORUS

Suspend your apprehension;
leave him to our discretion.
He'll cease his sacrilegious abuse
with his heart in his mouth!
With his heart in his shoes
he'll run for his life—and probably lose!
We'll stop his profanation
of Demeter's legislation!*

SECOND KORYPHAIOS

Now for a rope. Secure one end to the window, the other to you.
Then let yourself down. Slowly. Be brave; remember the motto:
Trust in Zeus, and take short views.

PHILOKLEON

Busy with the rope.

A teeny question:
If they should hook me on this line, and haul me back in—what then?

SECOND KORYPHAIOS

We'll call on our Courage, that old oaken Courage, and drive them away!
They won't pen *you* up again—no, sir! We'll think of something.

PHILOKLEON

Clambering into a rope seat and dangling just below the window.

All right. I place my life in your hands. If anything happens,
take me up, and mourn me, and bury me under the Bar.

SECOND KORYPHAIOS

Nothing is going to happen!
Of course, you might invoke
your ancestral gods before you slide. Why take chances?

PHILOKLEON

Dangling in prayer.

Lord of Lawsuits, Patron of Plaintiffs, Lykos my Master,*
whose eternal delights—even as mine—are the screams and wails
of convicted defendants; whose shrine is set,
the better to feast thine ears, at Court;
who choose, alone of the gods, to sit
on the losing side by the mourner's seat—
save thy neighbor, preserve him intact,
and nevermore, from this day hence,
will I piss on thy precinct or fart on thy fence.

He descends slowly on the rope, as quietly as he can. But his prayer has awakened Phobokleon.

PHOBOKLEON

From the roof, to Sosias.

Hey, wake up!

Both slaves wake.

SOSIAS

What's wrong?

PHOBOKLEON

A voice is whirring around,
I think. The old man didn't slip out another hole?

SOSIAS

Looking up.

God, no! He's tied himself to a rope and sliding down!

PHOBOKLEON

Looking straight down and seeing his father.

Again, you old cesspool? What do you think you're doing?
Get back up there!

Sosias pulls the blockade from the front door and runs in. Xanthias, still fuddled, stands confused until Phobokleon addresses him.

—Don't just stand there—
climb up outside
and hit him with the wreath!

XANTHIAS

What wreath?

PHOBOKLEON

The Thanksgiving wreath—
over the front door, stupid! If we deck his bow, maybe
he'll back his stern inside. But whatever you do, do it FAST!

He disappears into the house. Xanthias grabs the wreath from over the door and clambers up the net, hand over hand. When he comes even with Philokleon, he flails at him with the wreath. During the next speech, Sosias and Phobokleon appear at the window and haul the rope in slowly, and Xanthias keeps pace with the rising Philokleon, beating away.

PHILOKLEON

Sorely beset, to the audience.

A word to all this year's prospective plaintiffs—
HALP!
Hey, informers—Jekyll! Leech! You, Finque!
And all you parasites—Skimpole! Grafton!
Come on, fellows, you need me! Don't let them haul me back!

A little aid?

A little succor?

Last Chance—

Just as Phobokleon and Sosias pull him through the window.

HAAALP!

Xanthias follows him in, still flailing, and the four disappear inside the house. The Chorus bursts into action.

FIRST KORYPHAIOS

Throwing off his cloak.

The Wasps are ruffled! Our nest's been disturbed! No Delay!
Let's churn up our Double-Distilled, Triple-Action ANGER!

The members of the Chorus throw off their cloaks, exposing their stings, which they raise to the ready. The Little Boys collect the cloaks.

ENTIRE CHORUS

Raise the Sting and hold it high, Boys!*
Show them how we stand,
fierce to cut and thrust for Justice,
feared throughout the land!

FIRST KORYPHAIOS

To the Little Boys.

Drop those cloaks! Run and shout the news to Kleon!

The Little Boys drop the cloaks and exit at a run.

ENTIRE CHORUS

Fight and smite the foe of Athens!
Hit with all your hate!
Show your Fury! Save the Jury—
Bulwark of the State!

A locomotive cheer:

AËRATE HIM!
PERFORATE HIM!
THAT'S THE WAY TO WIN!
OPEN UP HIS HEART AND LET THE
SUN
SHINE
IN!

Phobokleon emerges from the house, followed by Xanthias, Sosias, and, in the clutches of the two slaves, Philokleon.

PHOBOKLEON
Gentlemen, gentlemen, please! Stop shouting and hear my case.

FIRST KORYPHAIOS
We'll shout if we want to! As loud as we want to!
—Won't we, men?

PHOBOKLEON
It won't make a bit of difference. I refuse to let him go.

FIRST KORYPHAIOS
What's that? You WON'T? You refuse to obey the Voice of the People?

PHOBOKLEON
Precisely.

FIRST KORYPHAIOS
Patent, plain, and obvious DICTATORSHIP!

To the audience.

O Athens, Pearl of Attica!
O Theoros, Peer of Debasement!
O all you spongers,
scroungers,
moochers,
chiselers,
fatcats—
in short, Everybody in Charge—
DID YOU HEAR WHAT HE SAID?

SOSIAS
Holy Herakles, they DO have stings! Don't you see them, Boss?

PHOBOKLEON
That's what finished Philippos, the sophist—they ran him through three suits in one afternoon. Completely gouged. Sad case.

FIRST KORYPHAIOS
And that's the way we'll finish YOU off!

To the Chorus, who complies with his orders.

COMPANY, TEN-*SHUN!*

RIGHT—*FACE!*

CLOSE—*RANKS!*

DRESS UP THAT LINE!

All right, men, let's put some spleen into it. Be Nasty!

Pointing at Phobokleon.

There's our objective! Make sure that he knows, in future, what sort of a swarm he roused!

PRESENT . . . *STINGS!*

The Stings, which have been sagging slightly, are snapped to the ready again.

READY, AIM. . . .

SOSIAS

God, this is awful—we're really going to FIGHT? *THEM?*
It scares me green just to see those prongs!

FIRST KORYPHAIOS

To Sosias.

Release that man!

I warn you, the time will come when you'll envy turtles their shells!

He waggles his Sting wickedly. Sosias tries to bolt, but is cuffed by Phobokleon, and continues, reluctantly, to hold Philokleon.

PHILOKLEON

Colleagues! Jurors! Talesmen! Angry Wasps!

COME ON!

To the First Semichorus.

Mount a savage sortie there and spear them in the rear!

To the Second Semichorus.

A frontal attack—lance their fingers! Stab their eyes!

Phobokleon leaves Philokleon with the slaves, runs to the front door, opens it, and yells inside.

PHOBOKLEON

Hey, Midas! Phrygian! Help—come here! You, too, Greedy!

The three slaves trundle forth. Phobokleon points at Philokleon.

Grab that man! And don't let go of him for anybody—
because if you do, it's solitary confinement! Bread and water!

To the Chorus, as the three slaves fill in around Xanthias and Sosias.

Keep up your blather—I know what it means. Look at my father!

He hurries into the house. The First Koryphaios continues to work on Sosias.

FIRST KORYPHAIOS

Let him go—unless you relish the prospect of being a scabbard!

SOSIAS

A *s-scabbard?*

FIRST KORYPHAIOS

Or maybe a quiver.

SOSIAS

A-quiver? God, I AM!

He attempts to bolt again, but is prevented by Xanthias and the other slaves. Philokleon tries another prayer.

PHILOKLEON

O Twi-formed Kekrops, Founder of Athens, hero-headed,
snake-shanked—Juror above, defendant below—
are you going to let an Old Athenian like me be mauled
by these FOREIGNERS? My foreigners? The ones I whipped
and whopped and taught to weep five quarts to the gallon—
HUH?

SECOND KORYPHAIOS

The proof is plain—old age is nothing but a skein of agony.
What miserable evidence—two slaves mauling their poor old master!
Have they forgotten the love he covered them with in the old days?
The sheepskin jackets? The lambskin vests? The dogskin caps?
The care he showered on their feet each winter? No, their feet
didn't freeze; their hearts did. Look in their eyes: no gratitude,
no respect for anything old—not even old shoes.

PHILOKLEON

To Sosias.

Hear that? I'm kind, I'm considerate—
NOW will you let me go,
you dirty sonofabitch? Don't you remember all those skins?

Or yours—when I caught you stealing grapes, and took you out
to the olive-tree, and flayed you like a Man—forgot that?
I took the hide off clean—slaveskin all over the place.
You were *famous*—the Talk of the Town for weeks! But gratitude?
Respect?
Not YOU!

With a nervous glance at the door.

Hurry up! He'll be back in a minute—LET ME GO!

Only Sosias is tempted, and the old man struggles fruitlessly. The Chorus advances slowly toward the slaves, who retreat, dragging Philokleon with them.

FIRST KORYPHAIOS

To Xanthias and Sosias, who are in the forefront of the group.

You can't delay your day of reckoning much longer, you two!
Then you'll know what manner of men WE are! Our hearts
are written on our faces—full of gall, and spleen, and law!

The Chorus presses on. The slaves and Philokleon back toward the front door. Just as they reach it, the door bursts open and Phobokleon bursts out, carrying a club and a lighted torch. He gives the club to Xanthias.

PHOBOKLEON

Hit them, Xanthias! Beat the Wasps away from the house!

XANTHIAS

I am, I AM!

PHOBOKLEON

Shoving the torch into Sosias' reluctant hands.

Smudge them out, Sosias! Smoke them off!

XANTHIAS

Swinging his club.

GIT! GO TO HELL!

PHOBOKLEON

Pushing Sosias.

SCAT! GET OUT OF HERE!

SOSIAS

Eyes closed, torch held stiffly before him.

Shoo—please?

PHOBOKLEON

That's it, Xanthias! Club them, boy!

To the nearly catatonic Sosias.

—Pour on the smoke!

The Wasps, merely very old men, are easily routed and retreat without much resistance to the side of the stage. The attack ceases. Phobokleon releases Sosias, who opens his eyes, takes in the situation, and swaggers over to the Chorus.

SOSIAS

Scared off, huh? Could have told you—you didn't have a chance.

The First Koryphaios brandishes his sting. Sosias races back to his own group.

PHOBOKLEON

Even *you* couldn't have driven them off so easily, Sosias,
if they'd been trained on different songs. Take the awful stuff
that Philokles writes. Why, they could strangle you with a single chord.

ENTIRE CHORUS

To the same tune as the fight song, but without the final locomotive.

Now the Poor can see their Peril,
feel its slippery grip,
know its stealthy aggrandizement:
DREAD DICTATORSHIP!

SECOND KORYPHAIOS

Pointing at Phobokleon.

There's Exhibit A: the arrogant Autocrat himself!

ENTIRE CHORUS

See him keep us from our City's
Laws so flagrantly!
No excuses can confuse us.
He wants TYRANNY!

PHOBOKLEON

To the Chorus.

Is there any way to stop these fights, and that awful screeching?
Can't we hold a parley and come to some compromise?

SECOND KORYPHAIOS

Parley? Compromise? With YOU—an Enemy of the People?

Just look at you: the Compleat Pro-Spartan Aristocrat.
Those crazy tassels on your clothes spell Lunatic Fringe. And that messy
beard declares you're a hero-worshipping mimic of Brasidas.*
Parley with a Spartan-lover? To put it Laconically,
NO!

PHOBOKLEON
I'm tempted to let Father go. I can't fight a war every morning.

SECOND KORYPHAIOS
You think you have troubles now? This is just the appetizers! (Please excuse our table-talk.) You don't hurt at all—not yet.
Just wait for the main course, down in Court, when the Public Counsel
carves you to bits with these charges. *Plus* a new one:
SUBVERSIVE!*

PHOBOKLEON
Will you kindly get the hell out of here? Or is there a law
that says we have to stand here trading blows all day?

SECOND KORYPHAIOS
Leave? Desert my duty? Not while I'm alive! Me leave
a man unguarded who wants to bring DICTATORSHIP back?

PHOBOKLEON
"Dictatorship" and "Subversive"—that covers every case
you judge, large or small. Everything you do, in fact:
the universe in two nouns. It's the same way all over town.
I hadn't heard the *word* "Dictator" for fifty years
in Athens, and suddenly it's cheaper than smelt. It clutters up
the Market-place, chokes the shops—you trip on it.
Example. You don't want sardines for supper; what you want
is a nice, fat, juicy sea-bass. So down to the Mart you go,
and BUY a nice, fat, juicy sea-bass. And the man next door,
—who, incidentally, just happens to sell sardines—starts up:
"Sea-bass, huh? That's real rich food—expensive, too.
TOO expensive for a real Athenian democrat. Hey, Mac—
why the bass? You want to bring DICTATORSHIP back?"
Or say you're having herring for lunch, and you want an onion,
a pretty, round onion, to keep it company. Have you ever
tried to buy that onion? You do, and the woman next door—
you know, the one who sells scallions—takes a squint, and:

"You think
that Athens pays taxes so you can have fancy food? Hey, Mac—
why the onion? You want to bring DICTATORSHIP back?"

SOSIAS

Boy, are you right—you can't even get out of line in a whorehouse!
Yesterday noon I told this girl to climb on top
and you'd think I'd tried to start a revolution!
"SUBVERSIVE!
There's only one way to do this," she says, "and that's flat!
You're trying to raise up Hippias' DICTATORSHIP!"
I ask you!

PHOBOKLEON

I know. That's what goes in Court. It's music to *them.*
Take my case. All I want to do is keep Father away
from this early-to-Court-and-early-to-lie-and-do-the-defendant-one-in-the-eye mode of existence; I want him to lead
a pleasant, luxurious, gentleman's life, like Morychos.
And what do they charge me with? Committing some heinous crime:
I'm a SUBVERSIVE; I'm plotting to restore DICTATORSHIP.

PHILOKLEON

By god, they're right, too! Can't you understand me, Son?
I don't WANT all this pie in the sky and pigeon's milk,
not me, not if I have to be barred, debarred, and disbarred
from the only life I know. And live like Morychos—why?
I'm not one of your goormays; I don't like eels, or rayfish.
What *I* like's a little lawsuit, chopped up fine
and stewed in its own juice. We call it a case-erole.

PHOBOKLEON

Habit, Father, sheer habit. A conditioned obsession—a deep one.
And yet, if you'll just keep quiet and listen to what I say,
I think that I can change your mind. I'll demonstrate
that your entire way of life is a Grand Mistake.

PHILOKLEON

I'm mistaken to JUDGE?

PHOBOKLEON

Worse. You're a butt, a laughingstock,
all unconscious, to men you nearly enshrine. In a word,
you're a SLAVE, and don't know it.

PHILOKLEON

Don't talk any slavery to ME—
I rule the WORLD!

PHOBOKLEON

Correction: you serve. Your rule's an illusion.
—All right, prove me wrong.
You "reap the fruits of Hellas"—
Demonstrate. Show us a fruit or two. Produce your profit.

PHILOKLEON

Will I ever!

Pointing to the Chorus.

I'll make a speech and let them arbitrate.

PHOBOKLEON

And so will I.

To the slaves.

All right, everyone, let him go.

The slaves obey and enter the house. Philokleon, free, yells after them.

PHILOKLEON

And bring me a sword!

To Phobokleon.

By god, if I lose a debate with YOU,
I'll stick a sword in the ground, point up, and fall on it,
face down, the way Ajax did when he lost to Odysseus.

Sosias returns with a sword, gives it to Phobokleon, and re-enters the house.

PHOBOKLEON

Handing the sword to Philokleon.

Pardon me,
but there's one little thing—the Oath.

PHILOKLEON

What Oath?

PHOBOKLEON

You should know more
about it than I do. The Oath where you specify the penalty you'll pay
if you fail to abide by the—how do you say it?—the disposition
of this debate.

PHILOKLEON

Oh, *that* Oath.

Sonorously.

I pledge myself to abide
by the just, impartial decision of this just, impartial Board
of Arbitration. If I should fail to do so, this be my punishment:
May I never, whenever the toasts go round, touch a drop—of my pay.

ENTIRE CHORUS

Arranged in judging position, it sings to Philokleon.

Defend the Old School's Honor!
Let none her Glory dim!
Be fresh in word and manner . . .

PHOBOKLEON

Breaking in on the Chorus, which holds on grimly to the "-er," he calls toward the house.

Bring me out a tablet and a stylus—and be quick about it!

Noticing the Chorus' held note.

A fine exhibition he'll make, with a song like *that* to inspire him.

ENTIRE CHORUS

Continuing the song, with a baleful wave at Phobokleon.

. . . but don't be fresh like *him!*
The verdict on your Great Debate
can overrule and abrogate
our Way of Life! The stakes are great.
If you incur the loss—
he's Boss!

PHOBOKLEON

Seated at a table, he receives the tablet and stylus from Xanthias.

That's fine. He'll talk at random; I'll write at memorandum.

PHILOKLEON

Nervously, to the Chorus.

You were saying—what happens to us if he wins the debate?

ENTIRE CHORUS

We'll be reviled and called effete!
We'll be repealed as obsolete!
They'll only use us to complete
the files in some parade—
unpaid!

FIRST KORYPHAIOS

To Philokleon.

And so, old friend, you who intend to debate and defend,
from stern to stem, the range of our rule, the utter extent
of our kingdom—courage! Extend your tongue to its utmost—
and utter!

PHILOKLEON

I spring from the post to establish our claim as Best of Breed.
No Crowned or Sceptred Potentate can surpass our power.
We're kings.
The proof is plain: what creature on earth can match the delight,
the luxury, power, respect, and glory that falls to the lot
of that little old man, the simple Athenian Juror?
None!
Example. I rise from my bed in the morning to find them waiting,
the Men of Importance and Size (some of them *six feet tall!*),
waiting for me, by the Bench. No sooner do I go inside
than a tender hand steals into mine, still warm from tapping
the Treasury. And then they beg, and bow, and wheedle, and whine.
"Father," they say (they call me Father), "pity me, Father.
You must have been a Quartermaster, or held a Public Trust.
You know what it is to feather your nest. Pity me, Father."
Do you think that a Very Important Person like that would know
that I was alive, if I hadn't acquitted him once before?

PHOBOKLEON

Yes, I'd better put that down. Let's see—
Beggars.

He writes the one word. Philokleon glares at him.

PHILOKLEON

Well, sir, I'm all begged up, my bad temper's wiped off clean;
I've made my promises of mercy—so I take my seat and proceed
to forget every one. It's not that I shut my ears to the pleas;
I listen to them all. Every rhetorical trick in the book
is unfolded, and, as for kinds of flattery—well, if I haven't
heard it in Court, it doesn't exist.
I'll be specific:
First, The Paupers. They plead—or scream—that they're poor, and so
Not Guilty. They heap their disasters so deep I almost believe them—
they sound as poor as I am.

Next the Story-Tellers, with Fairy-Tales,
or little quips from Aesop, or else, on occasion, a Joke.
If I shake with laughter, the theory runs, I'll shed my anger.
I don't.
When this fails, and we sit like rocks, they summon The Kids
(as they're called)—the little girls and boys, dragged up by the hand.
They bend them down and make them bleat—and me, I listen.
Then the father, trembling with grief or fear (or maybe religion)
entreats me, as though he were praying to a god, to spare his children—
by acquitting *him* on the charge of embezzling public funds.
"If you delight to hear the bleat of a poor little lamb,"
says he, "be moved by the plea of this little lost sheep—my son."
Of course, if our taste is for pig-meat, he begs us to pity his daughter.*
(And in this case, I admit, we unscrewed our anger a bit.)
Well, now, I ask you: doesn't this show our position, and power—
a contempt for wealth which makes mere money something to laugh at?

PHOBOKLEON
I'll get that down. Point Two: *The money is something to laugh at.*
—But as Ruler of Hellas (you said it, I didn't), just how do you profit?

PHILOKLEON
How? Why, son, we have Sex, the Drama, Music, Money . . .
You name it!
First, we're the body that examines prospective citizens,
puts handsome boys to a probing to see just how they'll fit in
to the life of the City. We're thorough.
Or the Arts: Suppose an actor—
say Oiagros—is accused. He knows his plea had better consist
of that beautiful soliloquy from the *Niobe,* recited for us alone;
unless he'd rather be convicted.
And Music? Ever see a flute-player
when he's won a case? Notice sometime. He waits around,
reed at the ready, till Court's adjourned, to pipe a march
when the Jury retires.
Next, Money: A man dies with only a daughter,
but designates a son-in-law and heir in his will, all signed and sealed.

What do we do in Probate? We break that will to bits,
and assign those bits, *and* the daughter, to the highest . . . well, *beseecher.*
It's safe and easy, since nobody audits *our* books—No Other
Public Office Can Make That Statement.

PHOBOKLEON

True. Congratulations—
on *that* alone. But the poor heiress! That's downright immoral—
breaking a young girl's will and tampering with her entailment.

PHILOKLEON

But better is Respect: When the Senate and Assembly have trouble impeaching,
they pass a decree and remand the rascals to us for trial.
And then it's Pure Pie—Praise from the Greats of Athenian politics—
that clever young lawyer Euathlos, or maybe the famous athlete
(he holds the record for the shield-put) Flee-onymos.* They cover us with Love,
and say they'll "Uphold the Humble" and "Sweat for the Salt of the Earth."
What's more, no speaker can *ever* ram a motion through Assembly
without *our* votes. So Court adjourns early—short day, full pay.
Why, even *Kleon* respects us. He barks and flattens the rest,
but doesn't even snap at our heels. He's Our Defender, in fact:
He throws his arms around us and shoos the flies away—

Violently to Phobokleon.

a damned sight more than you ever did for your own father!
Or take Theoros. He's *Important* . . .

You know Theoros?

*A negative silence from Phobokleon.**

Why, everyone knows Theoros! *He's* like Euphemios—
that *Big!*

You *do* know Euphemios?

Another negative silence.

Well, take Theoros—
Know what he does? He takes a sponge and shines our shoes!
A man like that! Yes, sir!

Well, take a good long look.
Those are the profits you pen me away from. Count those Blessings;
then figure out how to convince me that I'm a SLAVE or a SERVANT!

PHOBOKLEON

Aside.

Talk till you're sick—and you will be. I'll show you up, soon enough.
You and your Holy Assizes! Ass-holes of Athens, that's you.
And your mighty Orbit of Influence—the ring you leave in the bathtub.

PHILOKLEON

But I almost completely forgot my greatest joy as a Juror:
I get my pay and go home at night, and they all see me coming,
and give me a big hello—just because of that money. My daughter
washes me off, and massages my feet, and calls me "Popsy,"
bends down for a kiss—and fishes the money right out of my mouth.
And the little woman talks sweetly for once, and serves me cake,
that puffy sweet cake, and sits beside me. "Go on and eat,"
she says, "there's more—eat it all." Then my star's at its brightest.
I don't have to worry about supper, and keep looking over at you
and that grumbling, grousing steward, who lives in terror that he might
have to make me another cake.
I have no worries *at all,*
thanks to my Bulwark, my Armor against the Slings and Arrows
and so forth. Refuse me a drink if you choose, I always have with me
my faithful donkey full of wine—

He drags from the folds of his cloak an enormous wine-jar with two huge handles.

and I pour him myself.
And he opens his jaws, and brays at your bowls—

He drinks deeply from the jar, which gurgles loudly, then sets it down.

and farts like an army!
This is my job, my Empire—the Greatest Empire on earth!

He takes another drink.

On earth?—
Why isn't my Empire just as good as Zeus's?

What they say about Zeus,
they say about Me!
When we kick up a fuss
in fixing a fee,
the passers-by rush
and shout out, "Hey!
Thunder in the Jury—
Zeus Almighty!"

Faster yet; almost swelling into a god.

When I brandish the lightning
    and throw it,
the rich men are frightened,
    and show it—
they blubber! They shit, and
    don't know it!
    And they're so mighty,
    so hoity-toity!

Assuming a statuesque pose, pointing an imperious finger at Phobokleon, and going as fast as he can.

What's more, YOU'RE *scared*—
    you, too!
YOU fear me! By GOD
    you DO!
But I'M not afraid
    of YOU!

Completely overcome by his divine role.

    Puny, petty
    MORTALITY!

ENTIRE CHORUS

A more persuasive lecture
    these ears have never heard.
Such clarity! Such structure! . . .

PHILOKLEON

Relaxing into a strut, he interrupts the Chorus.

Yup. He must have thought he'd clip my vines by default;
he certainly knows well enough that *I* don't lose debates.

ENTIRE CHORUS

    . . . Such Wizardry of the Word!
His speech sustained my self-esteem
and summoned me, in dream, to seem
Grand Juror in the Court Supreme,
    to hear the Happy Isles'
        retrials!

Phobokleon rises.

PHILOKLEON

Look at him shift his ground and fidget—no self-control!
—Before tonight, I'll make you look like a flogged dog, boy!

ENTIRE CHORUS

To Phobokleon.

No vain Chicane, no sly Finesse
can shake the Faith that I profess!
I only guarantee success
to one Device, i.e.—
be ME!

SECOND KORYPHAIOS

Wherefore, unless you really have something to say, my advice
to you is this: It's time to look around for a millstone,
sharp, fresh-hewn. Perhaps *it* can crush the edge of my temper.

PHOBOKLEON

Taking his place and addressing the Chorus.

To cure a disease so long engrained in the Body Politic
demands far more than the rude and feeble wit of a mere
Comic Poet. I begin, therefore, with a prayer from Homer:
Scion of Kronos, Zeus our father . . .

PHILOKLEON

Don't "father" me!
You show me how I'm a SLAVE, right quick, or I'll murder you!
God, what a thought! Murderers don't get fed at the Feasts!

PHOBOKLEON

Very well, *Daddy,* smooth your brow a little and listen.
First, some simple arithmetic.—No, not with pebbles;
use your fingers.
Figure up the total of all the tribute
that Athens receives from the Federated States, and add to this
the direct taxes *plus* all those little one-per-cents,
court-costs, confiscations, mine-franchises, rents,
sales-tax, licenses, duties, tariffs, wharfage *and* tonnage,
and we get a sum of . . . roughly, twenty thousand talents.
Now deduct from this the annual pay of all the Jurors,
six thousand of you—at least, that's all we have for the moment—
giving us a total salary (let's see: six thousand Jurors,
three obols a day, eighteen days a month, times ten,
divide by six, divide by a hundred, divide by sixty)—
yearly, the Jurors cost Athens one hundred and fifty talents.

PHILOKLEON

Out of twenty thousand? We don't even get *ten per cent?*

PHOBOKLEON
Why, no. Not at all.

PHILOKLEON
But where does the rest of the money go?

PHOBOKLEON
Where? To the men with the mottoes, who will always "Uphold the Herd"
and "Sweat for the Salt of the Earth." So now you're held up and sweated,
and it's all your doing. *You* let them slather you in slogans, and *you*
elected them. To rule, of course, *you.* But not only you:
They petrify the Federated States with other slogans—e.g.,
"PAY THE TRIBUTE OR I ROLL THE THUNDER AND COLLAPSE THE CITY!"—
and proceed to squeeze fat bribes (fifty talents at a crash) for themselves;
while you, you're content to nibble the edges of your Empire's garbage.
The impression this makes on our Allies is not too hard to imagine.
They see you, the scum of Athens, weazening away on a diet
of ballot-box scraps, topped off, for dessert, with a succulent nothing,
and conclude, quite naturally, that you're as important as a fiddler's franchise.
So, without more ado, they turn to your leaders—and the stream begins.
They literally lave them in luxury: pillows, and dishes of fish,
honey, sesame, flagons of wine, firkins of cheeses,
cups and goblets, garlands and chaplets, clothing and carpets,
Health, Wealth, Long Life, Prosperity, and Such.
While you—
the Ruler, the Founder, the Grand Panjandrum who shaped this Empire
with the strokes of your oar, on Land and Sea—from your vast domain
you derive not even one head of garlic to season your smelts!

PHILOKLEON
Well, that's true enough. I had to send out to a friend for three cloves
last night . . . but *this* is SLAVERY? Get to the point—you're killing me!

PHOBOKLEON

I submit this as Slavery in its most acute form: when men like those,
ringed by their toadies and jackals, can roll in public gold,
but you are, perforce, overjoyed if they dribble you three little obols!
What a fine reward for the toil and agony that won our wars!
Not precisely a reward, of course: you *work*. By the numbers, where
and when they tell you. And that's what sticks in my gorge,
when a fancy young pansy like Chaireas' brat (not even a citizen!)
waggles up to you, legs well apart, with that fairy air,
and orders you to be in Court early tomorrow:
"If a *single* one
comes after they blow the signal, he simply *won't* get *paid!*"
But Time doesn't matter to *him;* he's a Public Prosecutor and draws,
come early, come late, *six* obols. Plus supplementary bribes from defendants.
These he splits with Defendant's Counsel—an intimate of his circle.
Then these strange bedfellows arrange the case, decide the outcome,
rough out a script, and fall to.
You'd think they were handling a saw.
One pushes, one pulls—and, right in the middle, there's you. Watching.
For your pay, as it happens; so the whole sordid mess slips by you.

PHILOKLEON

That's what they do? To *me?* Do you mean it? Son, you're rocking
the bottom of my being—tugging at my reason—what ARE you doing?

PHOBOKLEON

Consider this rationally. You, and everyone else, could be *Rich*—
if you didn't let these Friends of the People keep you caged.
You *do* rule the world, or most of the world, from the Black Sea to Sardinia,
and what's your Profit?
Your pitiful pay, doled out in dabs—
the exact amounts to keep you teetering on the edge of starvation.
They mean you to stay poor, don't you see? Their motive is obvious:
Hunger knows no friend but its Feeder.
And so, whenever
your Tamers are threatened, they cluck their tongues, and flick your leash,
and you leap, ravening, on their enemies and tear them to bits.

But if these men *did* have the public welfare at heart,
it would be child's play to attain. Just take a look at the books:
At present, one thousand cities are paying tribute to Athens.*
Assign them each the board of only twenty Athenians—
and twenty thousand citizens would swim in savory stew,
and wreaths, and crowns, and cream, and Grade-A Milk and Honey,
tasting their fitting prize for saving Hellas at Marathon.
But, as things are now, you act like migrant olive-pickers:
no matter where he leads you, you follow the man with the obols.

PHILOKLEON

What's come over me *now?* I can feel my hand getting numb . . .
and the sword—can't hold it any longer. I'm soft as a grape.

PHOBOKLEON

Whenever you frighten your Masters, they say you can have Euboia,*
and fifty bushels of wheat apiece—
and you never get any.
No, I'm wrong: not too long ago, they gave you five bushels:
But you barely got *that,* of course—they accused you of being an alien—
they trickled it out by the quart—and it wasn't wheat—
it was barley.

Which is why I've kept you from the Courtroom premises.
You can't subsist on hollow promises,
on imitation ersatz substitutes,
steamed in scorn by chauvinist chefs.
You need Nourishment; I'm frantic to feed you;
Unlimited Menu—with a single proviso:
the larder and cellar are stuffed and unlatched,
so absolutely no more three-obol drafts
of the Milk of the City Cashier.

SECOND KORYPHAIOS

Who said, *Don't judge till you've heard both sides*—remember? Regardless,
he had something there.

The Chorus huddles, then the First Koryphaios turns to Phobokleon.

FIRST KORYPHAIOS

This Body's thoroughly considered decision,
Sir, is that YOU WIN, by considerably more than a mile.
In token whereof, we unstring our rods of anger and office
and dip them to you.
—By the Numbers, Men: One, Two,
DROOP!

The Stings, which have been at the ready, fall at the command.

SECOND KORYPHAIOS

Now a word to you, dear friend of our youth, comrade in our creed:

SECOND SEMICHORUS

Picking up the cue and singing to Philokleon.

Give in to his Logic, yield to his Proofs,
give in to his object—stop being obtuse!
I wish *I* had a relative to tell me what to do
so clearly and precisely, but the Lucky Man is YOU!

At your elbow there's a god;
he's giving you a hand.
Take his favors. Don't be awed—
accept them while you can!

PHOBOKLEON

I promise all comforts prescribed for his years:
gruel for his gums; chiffon; warm furs
to keep out the cold; a whore to indulge
in comprehensive below-the-belt massage.
But look—not a word; not even a wheeze:
I don't expect thanks, but I'm not exactly pleased.

FIRST SEMICHORUS

Singing to Phobokleon.

He's come to his senses, returned to himself,
he's come to repentance—he's going to get well!
He rues his rash litigiousness, his passion for so long.
Be patient, please. He's just found out his every act was wrong!

For the future, you're his norm:
he'll heed your eloquence;
he'll change his life, revise, reform—
he *may* acquire some sense!

PHILOKLEON

OH, WOE, WOE, WOE, etcetera!

PHOBOKLEON

At last!—What's all the shouting for?

PHILOKLEON

In a Euripidean transport of grief.

Press not on me these paltry promises!
Lost are my loved ones! Reft am I left!
No more to tread those precious premises,
to hang on the Herald's accents soft:
"WE LACK ONE VOTE! WE'RE ONE VOTE SHORT!
WHO IS IT? DON'T NOBODY LEAVE THIS COURT!
STAND UP!"—and proudly to rise alone
and stride to the urns and cast the last stone!
—PRESS ON, O SOUL! ALL SPEED, O SOUL!
MAKE HASTE, O—
(Where'd I put that soul?)
—HITHER, SHADOWY ONE!
—And Kleon
better not let me catch him stealing
down in Court!
He better not!
He. . . .

The reversal is too much. He stands mute, confused, bewildered.

PHOBOKLEON

Enough of this, Father. For heaven's sake, give in!

PHILOKLEON

I'll give in, boy. Anything you ask. Except—
don't ask me to renounce that *one* thing . . .

PHOBOKLEON

What one thing?

PHILOKLEON

My jury career. Before I give in on *that,*
they'll render the final verdict on me in Hades.

PHOBOKLEON
I know it's your greatest delight, and I won't stop you.
But don't go down to Court any more. What you need
is a change of venue. So stay right here, in the privacy
of your own home, and judge the servants.

PHILOKLEON
Judge the Servants,
boy? On what charge?

PHOBOKLEON
The charge doesn't change; just the Court.
For example, a simple misdemeanor: The maid "forgets"
to lock the door—she *says. We* prove Intent;
it's an open and shut case. So what do you do? You stick her—
with a smallish fine. One drachma. You've done it a thousand
times in Court. And this is Law at Leisure,
tailored to suit you, the easy, *rational* way.
If the day dawns bright, be a Solar Solon. Just move
the Court out into the sun. But suppose it snows.
Why freeze? There's Fireside Fining! Or, if it rains,
bring in your verdict—bring it inside, and be comfortable!
And sleep till noon, if you want; *then* open the session.
No official can turn you away for coming late
to your private jury box!

PHILOKLEON
Now, *that* sounds nice.

PHOBOKLEON
But that's not all—no, *Sir!*
Remember those endless
speeches when you were starving, eating your heart out
for a big, fat bite of Defendant, done to a turn?
Well, that's all over. Mix Litigation with your Lunch!

PHILOKLEON
Can I judge my best if I'm chomping on my food?

PHOBOKLEON
Better than your best! Your efficiency will double—triple!
It's a proven fact: in order to digest the evidence,
a jury needs to RUMINATE!

PHILOKLEON

You're getting there, Son.

I'm wavering. But there's one little point you haven't mentioned.
Who's going to pay me?

PHOBOKLEON

I'll pay you.

PHILOKLEON

Well, that's just grand.

I'll draw all my pay to myself. Won't have to share it.
I've been burned on that.

The other day Lysistratos,
that practical joker, drew a drachma, the pay
for him and me, and got it changed at the fish-market.
Three obols for him, three for me. So I popped mine in
my mouth to take home, and—ugh! That taste! That smell!
I spat them out. He'd given me three mackerel scales!
That jokester! I started to haul him to Court, of course.

PHOBOKLEON

What was his reaction to that?

PHILOKLEON

Him? Oh, he said

that I had the belly of a billy-goat. "You're pretty quick
at digesting good, hard cash." That's what he said.

PHOBOKLEON

But no more of that for *you!* Another advantage
of the New Home Jury System!

PHILOKLEON

And no small one, either.

He ponders briefly.

Son, you've won your case; you can sign me up!
Let's get to the judging!

PHOBOKLEON

Wait right here. Don't move.

I'll bring out all the necessary equipment.

He enters the house.

PHILOKLEON

I can't believe my eyes. I heard a prophecy
once which said it was only a matter of time
before every Athenian judged cases right at home,
and built a little courthouse on his front porch,
right next to the shrine to Hekate. And it's coming true!

PHOBOKLEON

Returning at the head of a column of slaves who carry various improbable objects, he waves expansively at them.

And here we are. What do you say to *that?*
My original estimate has been greatly amplified.
For example, this.

He holds up an enormous jug.

PHILOKLEON

What's that?

PHOBOKLEON

A chamber pot.
Put the case that you're passing judgment and need
to pass water. This hangs right at hand. That prong
should hold it nicely.

PHILOKLEON

Son, that shows some sense!
And it's mighty thoughtful, too. Just the thing
for an old sea-dog like me. I'll have safe harbor
for a floating kidney.

PHOBOKLEON

Bringing a brazier and a bowl.

And here's a fire, and a bowl
of lentil soup. If you're hungry, warm it and eat.

PHILOKLEON

Now, that's ingenious! With colic or fever, I'll stay in,
and eat my soup, and still collect my fee!

Phobokleon advances with a rooster in a cage.

But why the rooster?

PHOBOKLEON

We provide for every contingency:
You know how defendants' speeches make you doze—
well, this cock crows you awake in time for conviction!

PHILOKLEON

All this is wonderful, son, but I miss one thing.

PHOBOKLEON

Name it.

PHILOKLEON

Do you think you could have them bring me
the shrine to the Juror's Protector—Lykos? I'd like it.

PHOBOKLEON

Caught flat-footed.

Why, certainly. It's—it's here already.

PHILOKLEON

Peering around.

Where?

PHOBOKLEON

*Desperate, then suddenly pointing at the huge chamber pot.**

Here's the hero.

PHILOKLEON

That's Lykos?

PHOBOKLEON

Certainly.
You pour libations at a shrine, don't you? Well?

PHILOKLEON

Dubiously, to the chamber pot.

Master, please pardon me—but you were pretty hard
to recognize.

PHOBOKLEON

I don't see why. He seems as big
as Kleonymos.

PHILOKLEON

Looking inside the chamber pot.

You're right—another hollow hero.

PHOBOKLEON

The quicker you sit down, the quicker I'll call
the first case.

PHILOKLEON

Taking a seat.

Son, I was sitting before you were born.
Call away!

PHOBOKLEON

In a worried aside.

Let's see. What case to introduce first?
Just who in this house has done anything wrong?
Oh, well—

Raising his voice to an official bellow:

CALL THRATTA, THE MAID, FOR BURNING UP—

PHILOKLEON

Hold it, son!
You'll be the death of me! Imagine calling a case
in a Court without a Bar!

PHOBOKLEON

A Bar?

PHILOKLEON

That fence
between the jury and everyone else. Why, that's
the holiest thing in Court. You want bad luck?

PHOBOKLEON

We don't *have* a Bar.

PHILOKLEON

Well, I'll run inside and get one.
I can rustle one up right away—need a Bar. Watch!

He dashes into the house.

PHOBOKLEON

What next, I wonder? Habit's an awful thing.

Xanthias runs out of the house, yelling over his shoulder.

XANTHIAS

Go to hell!

Muttering.

Try to feed a dog like that!

PHOBOKLEON

What's the matter?

XANTHIAS

What else *could* be the matter?
That grabby dog Chowhound,* of course! Jumped into the pantry,
clamped onto a rich Sicilian cheese and gulped
the whole thing down!

PHOBOKLEON

That's *it!*

XANTHIAS

What's *what?*

PHOBOKLEON

The *crime*—
the first case I'll introduce to father for judgment.
You stay here and prosecute.

XANTHIAS

Not on your life,
not me!
But the other dog there says *he'll* prosecute,
if someone files a charge.

PHOBOKLEON

Excellent! Fine!
Go bring them both out here.

XANTHIAS

Just as you say, Sir.

He exits into the house. After a short pause, Philokleon emerges from the house, carrying a section of fence.

PHOBOKLEON
What in the world is *that?*

PHILOKLEON
The pigpen. Our Bar.

PHOBOKLEON
You mean the pen for the pigs we sacrifice to Hestia?

PHILOKLEON
Yup.

PHOBOKLEON
But that's sacrilege!

PHILOKLEON
Not sacrilege—sacri*fice.*
Lets the defendant know where he stands. Be fair,
that's what I say.
But bring on that first case—
I've got that old conviction-itch.

PHOBOKLEON
One moment.
We need the docket and the indictments.

He enters the house.

PHILOKLEON
I tell you, boy,
you're grinding me down. Delays, delays, delays—
you're killing me!

He shows the wax tablet he uses to pass sentence.

I only want to plow
a nice long furrow in my little field here.

PHOBOKLEON
Returning with some scrolls.
Here we are.

PHILOKLEON

Then call that first case!

PHOBOKLEON

Pretending to peruse the scrolls.

Let's see;

who's first . . .

PHILOKLEON

Tarnation!

PHOBOKLEON

What's wrong?

PHILOKLEON

I forgot the urns—

the Jury's ballot boxes! Makes me sick!

He rises.

PHOBOKLEON

Hey, there! Where are you going?

PHILOKLEON

To get the *urns!*

PHOBOKLEON

Sit down; I saw to that. We'll use these pots.

He places two small pots on the table.

PHILOKLEON

That's pretty—real pretty. We've got everything,
all we need. Except—

where's the water-clock?

He rises. Phobokleon pushes him down and points at the chamber pot again.

PHOBOKLEON

There.

PHILOKLEON

That? A water-clock?

PHOBOKLEON

What else could it be?

PHILOKLEON

Dubiously.

Er—sure.

He shrugs and surveys the scene happily.

Well, nothing's missing. You know the Court like a native.

PHOBOKLEON

Calling into the house.

Bring out the myrtle, the incense, the holy fire!
And hurry! Court can't be convened before
we invoke the gods and beg them for their blessings.

Slaves from the house bring the desired articles.

FIRST KORYPHAIOS

To Philokleon and Phobokleon.

From war and trouble
you've made a noble
metamorphosis.
And so, to your vows
we add our prayers
for your success.

To the Chorus.

Now let holy silence
preface our petitions.

ENTIRE CHORUS

Pythian God
Apollo, heed
our hymn and bless our word.
Attune the plan
of this young man
to *our* existence, Lord.
And may it bring
our wandering
to rest in clear accord.
Hail, Paian—Healer!

PHOBOKLEON

Mighty Apollo, God of the Ways, Watcher at the Gate,
receive this rite, newly minted, fresh for my father.
Soften and supple the stiff, the unbending oak in his soul;
honey and mellow his temper's tartness, the must of his heart.

Sweeten him, Lord, to the human race,
prone to pity, tending to tears,
tears for the suppliant,
tears for the victim—
none for the plaintiff—
his bitterness bottled,
his anger unnettled.

ENTIRE CHORUS

The canons you
set forth, so new,
provide for us a key.
Our descant prayers
we raise to yours
in perfect harmony.
This note of grace
from youth to age
is no set cadency.
Hail, Paian—Healer!

The prayer over, the Chorus retires to the wings and Xanthias brings from the house two dogs, Chowhound (the defendant) and Fleahound (the plaintiff). Phobokleon, who acts the parts of various court officials during the succeeding scene, addresses the Jury—Philokleon—now in the manner of a herald.

PHOBOKLEON

OYEZ! ALL JURORS IN THEIR SEATS! POSITIVELY NO ADMITTANCE TO THE BOX AFTER THE COMMENCEMENT OF DEBATE!

PHILOKLEON

Settling himself.

Who's the defendant?

PHOBOKLEON

Pointing at Chowhound.

He is.

PHILOKLEON

Oh, what I've got
in store for him—Unanimous Conviction!

PHOBOKLEON

ATTENTION!

THE INDICTMENT: THE CASE OF FLEAHOUND, OF KYDATHENEA,
VS. CHOWHOUND, OF AIXONE! THE CHARGE: UNLAWFUL
POSSESSION AND SELFISH DESTRUCTION OF ONE SICILIAN
CHEESE! PROPOSED PENALTY: IMPOUNDMENT, THIRTY
LEASHES, AND PERMANENT CONFINEMENT IN A WOODEN COLLAR!

PHILOKLEON

A stock penalty. They're getting soft. When *I*
pass sentence on him, by god, he'll die like a dog!

PHOBOKLEON

THE DEFENDANT CHOWHOUND WILL ADVANCE TO THE BAR OF JUSTICE!

PHILOKLEON

As the terrified dog shambles up to the railing in front of him.

Criminal Type. I can spot them every time:
Pointy ears, eyes set close together, weak chin,
wet nose . . .

Chowhound gives a dog's yawn.

There! See that? He's showing his teeth!
Trying to Intimidate the Jury, eh? I'll fix him!
—But where's the plaintiff? Where's this Fleahound fellow?

FLEAHOUND

GRRRRROWF!

PHOBOKLEON

Weakly.

He's here. Another Chowhound, that's what he is.

PHILOKLEON

Now, wait. You must admit he's a powerful barker . . .

PHOBOKLEON

. . . and licker of pots. And boots.

—ORDER IN THE COURT!
PLAINTIFF, MOUNT THE STAND AND BRING YOUR CHARGE!

Fleahound mounts a bench. Philokleon turns to the brazier where the soup is heating, and pours out a bowlful.

PHILOKLEON
This seems a good time to sustain my judgment with soup.

FLEAHOUND
In a roar, the volume varying, seemingly at random, from very loud to much louder.
Gentlemen of the JURY! You have already HEARD the writ
I WROTE, and there's no point in reading IT again!
That mealy-mouthed MONGREL there is ACCUSED
of High CRIMES and MISDEMEANORS—i.e., he cheated
ME! and all the yo-heave-HO boys in our NAVY!
Just what did this PUTRID pooch do? He BOLTED away
into a corner, a DARK corner! And there
he GUZZLED up a WHOLE CHEESE—
SICILICED it to bits!

PHILOKLEON
Yup. True enough. That stinker belched just now,
and I nearly got choked by the smell of cheese! GUILTY—
out of his own mouth.

FLEAHOUND
And *I* DIDN'T get a BITE!
Look here—WHO'S going to help you OUT—WHO'S
going to look AFTER you, if people start to STOP
kicking in—I MEAN, throwing a SCRAP
or two to ME, your faithful HOUND—Your BODYGUARD?

PHILOKLEON
Indignant.
And he didn't give any to *me,* the Body Politic!
Oh, but he's a sly one—sharp—he bites—
just like this—ouch!—soup. Dammit, it's hot!

PHOBOKLEON
Father, for heaven's sake! You can't condemn him
before you've heard both sides!

PHILOKLEON

Oh, come, now—look

at the facts. The case is clear.

With a wave at Fleahound.

It barks for itself.

FLEAHOUND

You CAN'T acquit him—of ALL the dogs in the WORLD,
that man's the SELFISHEST greedyguts there IS!
Know what he DID to that Sicilian HOARD?
He sailed AROUND the plate—
he STRIPPED the rind
off all the CHOICEST sections, and wolfed it DOWN!
All that was LEFT was the HOLES!

PHILOKLEON

Holding up a flap of his motheaten cloak.

And I got those.

FLEAHOUND

One more REASON to PUNISH him . . .

PHOBOKLEON

. . . is because
one trough isn't big enough to feed two thieves?

FLEAHOUND

. . . is THIS—to serve your FAITHFUL HOUND! Don't let
my BARKING go in vain! If he goes FREE,
I'LL NEVER BARK *AGAIN!*

PHILOKLEON

Bravo! Bravo!

Fleahound bows and steps down.

Now *that's* an accusation—crimes and more crimes!

Pointing to Chowhound.

That man's
solid larceny!

To the rooster.

You agree, old cock?
By god,
he winked!
—Bailiff! Where's the Bailiff?

PHOBOKLEON

I'm here.

PHILOKLEON

Well, pass me the pot!

PHOBOKLEON

Get it yourself. I'm also
Herald, and it's time for me to call the witnesses.

Philokleon rises and avails himself of the chamber pot.

I CALL THE WITNESSES FOR THE DEFENDANT CHOWHOUND.

As he summons them, a host of kitchen implements emerge from the house and take up positions before him.

BOWL!
GRINDER!
CHEESE-GRATER!
GRILL!
STEW-POT!
AND ALL THE OTHER UTENSILS UNDER SUBPOENA!
—Haven't you finished pissing yet?
BE SEATED!

PHILOKLEON

Don't need to, son—but I know someone who *will:*

He leers savagely at Chowhound, who cringes.

Oh, am I going to scare the shit out of him!

PHOBOKLEON

Don't be such a compulsive grouch. Whenever
you see a defendant, it's always dog-eat-dog.
—THE DEFENDANT WILL MOUNT THE STAND AND MAKE HIS PLEA!

Chowhound, in terror, climbs on the bench and trembles, unable to utter a sound.

Well, say something! Speak *up,* dog! Make your plea!

PHILOKLEON

I don't think there's a single thing he *can* say.

PHOBOKLEON

No, you're wrong. I know the trouble—he's sick.
I saw it happen to old Thoukydides once*
when he was on trial:
Litigation Lockjaw.
It comes on suddenly. No immediate cure.

To Chowhound.

All right, down, out of my way.
I'll defend you.

Chowhound leaves the bench; Phobokleon mounts it and addresses Philokleon.

Gentlemen of the Jury:
Give a dog a bad name,
and his defense in a Court of Law becomes difficult.
But I shall make the attempt—make it because
he is A Good Dog, and chases away the wolves.

PHILOKLEON

He's a thief, too—and worse than that, a SUBVERSIVE!

PHOBOKLEON

I object. Of all today's dogs, this is Best in Show.
The perfect type to tend a huge and brainless
flock of sheep.

PHILOKLEON

What profit is that?—HE EATS
THE CHEESE!

PHOBOKLEON

What profit? List his points: he fights
your battles, guards your premises—what profit?

PHILOKLEON

HE EATS
THE CHEESE!

PHOBOKLEON

Oh, yes, the cheese.
So he steals a little—
and why? Because he's rough and tough—and that's
the thing we need, in a dog or a general.
Pardon
his lack of polish; he never studied the harp.

PHILOKLEON

Holding up a scroll.

I wish he'd never learned to write. Or hide things.
He buried that cheese somewhere in his Statement to the Court.

PHOBOKLEON

Stepping down.

Please try to be fair and hear my witness out.
—CHEESE-GRATER, MOUNT THE STAND!
Now then, speak up.
When Chowhound is alleged to have seized the Sicilian cheese,
you held the post of steward?

The Cheese-Grater nods.

Now then, answer clearly:
Did you portion out your receipts to these soldiers here?

He gestures at the other utensils. The Cheese-Grater nods. Phobokleon addresses Philokleon.

—He affirms that the soldiers received the regular grate.

PHILOKLEON

I say he's lying—his story's full of holes!

PHOBOKLEON

Oh, Sir, I implore your compassion. Pity the underprivileged.
Behold the luckless Chowhound! His only sustenance
the scrapings of tables, the heads of fish!

Chowhound fidgets madly.

Condemned
to a restless existence—a rover with no place for his head!

With a wave at Fleahound.

Compare this sleek, well-kenneled cur. What profit?
His profit. A watchdog—an *inside* watchdog, who snarls
for his cut when anyone enters. And gets it—or bites.

PHILOKLEON

But what's bitten ME? I'm sick—I'm going all soft
inside! I can feel it slithering, winding over me—
the Juror's fatal disease—*Creeping Persuasion!*

PHOBOKLEON

Gentlemen of the Jury, O Father, heed now my entreaty.
Harden not your hearts, but melt it in mercy!*
Deign not to demolish this dog!
—Where are the children?

Xanthias herds a group of crying puppies out of the house.

MOUNT THE STAND, O POOR, O PITIFUL PUPS!

The puppies climb the bench beside Phobokleon, who cuddles them.

You sorry, stricken whelps of a helpless hero,
Whine!
Whimper!
Weep!
Beseech the Court
to melt in Simple Humanity for your miserable sire!

The air is rent with hideous doggy howls. Philokleon is reduced to tears.

PHILOKLEON

Stop! I can't stand it! Step down! STEP DOWN!

PHOBOKLEON

I shall
step down, though I know that Jurors' Trap, that Quasi-Legal
Fiction. You let the defendant think he's won
by shouting "Step Down!" and down he steps, breaks off
his defense—whereupon you convict him. Nevertheless,
I shall step down . . .

PHILOKLEON

Recovering his spleen at the last moment.

. . . STRAIGHT
TO
HELL!

Disgustedly throwing down his soup-bowl.

This eating—
It's no good, that's all. Just now I melted every grain
of Sense I own in tears—and why? Because
I was full of hot soup, that's why!

PHOBOKLEON

You mean he's *convicted?*

PHILOKLEON

It's difficult to tell at this point. The votes aren't in.

PHOBOKLEON

Father, dear Father, turn to Finer Things!

To kindness, and justice! Take this pebble and close
your eyes for the painful task, the work of a moment.
Speed to the Second Urn and *acquit* him, Father!

PHILOKLEON

No, son, those Finer Things aren't for me. Pardon
my lack of polish; I never studied the harp.

He starts for the table with the voting urns.
Phobokleon intercepts him and grabs his arm.

PHOBOKLEON

I'll take you over, Father; I know a shortcut.

He leads Philokleon to the table by a route which
includes a number of dizzy twirls, so that when his
father arrives before the table, he is quite confused.

PHILOKLEON

Pointing to the Second Urn. The markers of the
Urns, if any, are turned away from him.

Is this the First Urn—the one for "GUILTY"?

PHOBOKLEON

That's it.

PHILOKLEON

Dropping his voting-pebble in the Second Urn.

Then there's my vote!

PHOBOKLEON

Aside.

He took the bait! In spite
of himself, he voted to acquit!
—I'll tally the votes.

PHILOKLEON

Impatiently.

Well, what's the verdict?

PHOBOKLEON

Time will tell. Be patient.

He empties out the Urns, one after the other,
very deliberately.

—THE DEFENDANT CHOWHOUND IS FOUND TO BE *NOT GUILTY!*

Philokleon falls senseless to the ground.

Father, Father, what's wrong?

Oh, *dear!*

WATER!

Xanthias dashes up with a jug of water and empties it over Philokleon.

Excelsior, Father!

PHILOKLEON

Struggling up feebly on one elbow.

Don't play tricks on me, Son.
Was he really, truly acquitted?

PHOBOKLEON

I swear it.

PHILOKLEON

Falling back.

I'm extinct.

PHOBOKLEON

Don't brood—put it out of your mind. Here now, stand up.

He helps Philokleon rise and supports him.

PHILOKLEON

But how can I live with what I've done? How
can I bear that dreadful load on my conscience? How?
I ACQUITTED A DEFENDANT! What evil fate will befall me?

Raising his arms to heaven.

O gods on high, adored and honored, absolve your
servant, a sinner in spite of himself! My nature
is not so heinous as to plot a deed like that!

PHOBOKLEON

Of course it isn't. Away with these worries, Father.
Place yourself in my hands. My sole concern
will be your care and comfort. The two of us
will go *everywhere* together, sampling all
the sophisticated, genteel joys that Athenian society
offers—dinners, banquets, parties, and the theater.
The balance of your days will pass in utter bliss,
and never again will you play the demagogues' dupe.
Let's go inside.

PHILOKLEON

A broken man.

All right, Son, if you say so.

They enter the house, Philokleon guided tenderly by his son, followed by the puppies, the utensils, the dogs, and the slaves.

FIRST KORYPHAIOS

Hail and farewell, friends!
May fortune attend your
every venture!

Turning to the audience.

Meanwhile, to you Numberless Millions,
I offer a message of caution:
PROTECT YOUR GOOD NAME.
The ensuing remarks contain
pith and profit in plenty;
and any self-respecting
audience, caring at all
to avoid the general
appellation of IGNORAMUS
—and worse—really must
be improved thereby.
Verbum sap., say I.

Stepping forward.

People of Athens, prove your vaunted taste for Truth
and attend the Complaint which the Poet brings against the spectators.
WANTON INJURY, WITHOUT PROVOCATION, AGAINST A BENEFACTOR—
so runs the charge brought by Our Bard.
He was ever your Savior,
from his first, incognito essays at the stage—when he took a leaf
from the book of that supple, sage ventriloquist-prophet EURYKLES,
and cast his very self and voice into others' mouths*
to pour forth a purest stream of comedy, funny and ribald—
down to the day when he threw off the mask and ran his own risks,
charioteer for his own, his private stable of Muses.
Through all that time your safety and comfort was his only concern.
And then, when you raised him, and prized and praised him as none before him,
did conceit inflate and balloon his brain? Perhaps he perverted
his talents and titles, scouring the schools for talented perverts
(like certain comedians who shall be nameless*)?

The answer is NO!
What's more, if a thwarted pederast pressed him to slander a boy-love
back into bed, he refused. His Muses are public servants,
not private pimps; his sense of fitness knows Right from Wrong.

—Next, his aims are high. When he took to the stage, he attacked no MEN,
but with Herakles' courage and rage he loaded his Chorus for MONSTER
and marched on the mighty, assailing all manner of Gogs, Magogs,
and Demagogues. From his first performance,* he dared to measure his strength
with that rankest of reptiles, the Brown-Tailed, Saw-Toothed KLEONOSAURUS REX.
Its eyes flashed fire with a whorehouse glare, while in its hair
in a writhing mass, a hundred heads of lousy leeches
circled and weaved—and kissed its foul ass. It screamed in the voice
of a roaring river in labor, and bore the stink of a seal,
the greasy balls of a female troll, the rump of a camel.
But before this sight, did our dauntless poet take fright—or a bribe?
No, friends, not a bit. For you he warred then—for you he wars now.

Again, last year he turned his sights on those vampire demons
of chills and fever who stole by night to strangle fathers
and suck the breath from fathers' fathers; who then lay down
in their beds to plot and paste together a cruel collage
of suit and summons, writ and witness, against the harmless.
He attacked these informers* with such success that many leaped,
scared out of their wits and beds, to complain to the courts that they,
as alien goblins, were suffering torture commonly reserved
for full-fledged citizens.

In short, you'd found a Champion to cleanse
and purge your city of evil—

Wherefore (and here's the core
of the Complaint) last year, when your Savior sowed New Ideas by the sackful,
your heads were so hard that you ruined his crop. Nothing came up.
You betrayed him, and gave, in your idiot folly, LAST PRIZE to *THE CLOUDS!*—
to the best of all comedies ever performed (a firmstanding fact,
which Our Author repeatedly urges the god Dionysos to witness).
This award confers dishonor on YOU, for slow-witted dullness.

ARISTOPHANES suffers no slur from those with a *right* to opinions:
he wrecked his hopes—
but only because he was passing his rivals.
Hence, for the future,
you witless wonders,
when poets you find
with freshness of mind
who exhibit intentions
toward novel invention
of thought or expression,
cherish them, nourish them,
cull their conceptions
and carefully place
them in chests with sachets—
and through the next year
the clothes that you wear
will give off an air
of ineluctable savior-faire.

FIRST SEMICHORUS

Long ago—
We were mighty in the dance,
we were mighty at advance,
and our mightiness resided in the sting we bear;
but our power didn't last,
and our lustihood is past,
and whiter than the swan fade the flowers of our hair.

From these remnants we must recover
some spark, some trace of youthful vigor.
And my old age
is more than a match
—at least, in my estimation—
for the pansy poses, girlish curls,
and happy homosexual whirls
of the younger de-generation!

FIRST KORYPHAIOS

And now, to you in the audience who swell with confusion, curiosity
pricked by these spiky stings, intellects squeezed by our wasp waists,
a palliative explanation: the cause of our costume in a very few words,
words carefully chosen so as not to puzzle the dullards among you.

We, then, whom you behold so sharply appointed, are *Attic*
(and thence contentious)—the only authentic race of Attica,
tracing our lineage to those sprung from the soil by spontaneous generation.
For virulent virility, we remain unmatched. At Pest Removal,
the City has not known our peer in sheer belligerence, as witness
the coming of the Persians.*

Their aim was simple—to drive us from our hives.
And they put the entire City to the torch to supply the smoke.
Straightway, forth we swarmed, our bravery bolstered with gall.
We took our stand with shield and spear in single combat,
and ground our jaws with ire as they blotted out the sun with arrows.
But the owl of omen flew over our ranks before the attack,
and when evening blotted the sun in truth, the Persians bolted,
routed. We raced behind and riddled their Oriental rears,
while their jaws and brows ballooned, harpooned by our Sting.

Wherefore,
since men are known by their attributes, throughout barbarian lands
we are famed as the manliest race alive: the ATTIC WASP.

SECOND SEMICHORUS

Then it was—
I inspired so much dread
that I never was afraid;
when I sailed against the foe I made him kneel or flee;
for my mind was free and clear
of these new civilian fears:
"Can I make a good rebuttal?"
"Who'll inform on me?"

The only conviction that ever we bore
assigned the verdict to the fastest oar.
And that we plied;
but now must plead
Guilty in the First Degree
to pillaging the Persians' power
of gold, and thus providing for
our young delinquents' larceny.

SECOND KORYPHAIOS

Observe us, and you will find complete correlation between
our habits, manners, ways of life, and those of Wasps.

Imprimis: The world holds no other creature which, when ruffled,
can hope to approach us in presence of rancor or absence of temper.
And all our other activities are equally nasty and waspish.
Clumped together in swarms we sit in our *hives,* you might say—
the Archon's Court, the Eleven's Court, the converted Odeion*—
and render judgment.
We're packed in solidly, squeezed against
the walls, bent double right down to the ground, not able to move.
Compare the wasp-grubs, sealed in cells.
We're industrious, too.
To win subsistence by stinging *everyone* without distinction
is Very Hard Work—and that's the way we earn our living.
There, too, comes trouble: we have our drones, who laze among us
but have no stings, and yet, in their pointless existence, devour
the fruit of our labors without a hint of motion or effort,
not even a bit of bitterness.
But our greatest vexation is to view
our salary swilled by a NON-VETERAN slacker, whose hand never knew
oar, nor lance, nor blister upraised in his Country's defense.
Hence, my decision:
In future, no citizen without a sting
may draw the Juror's three obols. Briefly:
No prick, no pay.

The Chorus retires. Philokleon stumps from the house in vexation, clutching his threadbare cloak with the tenacity of a drowning man. He is followed by the equally tenacious Phobokleon, who carries a new cloak of Persian make, very shaggy, which he is intent upon exchanging for his father's old one.

PHILOKLEON
Pressing his cloak desperately to his bosom.
If you take me out of this cloak, it'll be feet first!
We were in the service together—it saved my life!
There we were, shoulder to shoulder, standing off
the first attack of the winter—I might have frozen!

PHOBOKLEON
I don't think you appreciate nice treatment, Father.

PHILOKLEON
Why should I? Just costs me money.

Take eating—
I filled up on herring yesterday, and so it cost me
three obols—a whole day's pay—to get *this* cloak cleaned!

PHOBOKLEON
I'm afraid you don't have much choice.
You know the agreement.
You've made me your legal guardian, once and for all.

PHILOKLEON
Sulkily.
Oh, all right. What do you want me to do?

PHOBOKLEON
Simple. Take off that worn, sleazy old cloak,
and put on this bright, spanking new robe here.
Be the smart, natty man of the world you really are.

He removes the old cloak from his father, who, though resigned, is none too co-operative. The process is thus rendered rather more difficult than it should be.

PHILOKLEON
Emerging at length from his cloak.
What's the point in having children, anyway?
I fathered him, and now he smothers me.

PHOBOKLEON
Proffering the robe.
Less chatter and more action—put this on!

PHILOKLEON
Son, will you tell me what the hell this *is?*

PHOBOKLEON
It's Persian—they call it a burnoose.

PHILOKLEON
Burn whose?

PHOBOKLEON
Or else an astrakhan.

PHILOKLEON
I thought it was a scatter rug.

PHOBOKLEON
Understandable—you've never been to Sardis
on one of those embassies. If you had, you'd know
what it is.
But now you don't.

PHILOKLEON
You're right enough there—
It looks to me like Morychos' overcoat—
with Morychos
still inside it.

PHOBOKLEON
It's *Persian,* I tell you—woven
in Ekbatan. It's an *astrakhan!*

PHILOKLEON
ASS-trakhan?
Those tricky Persians'll fleece anything that walks.

PHOBOKLEON
Oh, stop it, father. This is a Persian burnoose,
woven in Ekbatan at absolutely ruinous expense.
One of these consumes sixty pounds of wool.

PHILOKLEON
Hungriest looking cloak I ever saw.

PHOBOKLEON
PLEASE STAND STILL AND PUT THIS ON!

PHILOKLEON
Accepting reluctantly and sniffing.
Pew!—
You're right, it's astrakhan.
He starts to slip it on.
Burnoose, too—
God, it's hot in there!
He takes it off.

PHOBOKLEON
PUT THAT THING ON!

PHILOKLEON

I won't. Son, if you feel like this, why not
stick me in the oven right away? It's quicker.

PHOBOKLEON

Very well, *I'll* put it on you.

He envelops Philokleon in the shaggy robe, then notices the old cloak lying on the ground. All his frustration emerges in a violent kick at it, accompanied by an address.

Get out of here!

PHILOKLEON

Faintly, from the depths.

Anyway, keep a fork handy.

PHOBOKLEON

Why a fork?

PHILOKLEON

To fish me out of here before I melt.

PHOBOKLEON

Surveying.

Let's see—what next? Those shoes are a disgrace.
Here, take them off. Put on these Spartan slippers.

PHILOKLEON

Spartan slippers?
That's enemy produce—contraband!
They're hostile. They'll corrupt my sole.
I refuse.

PHOBOKLEON

Kneeling to fit the first slipper on.

Come on, father—quick march, off to Sparta.
Put your foot in it.

PHILOKLEON

What you're doing is a disgrace—
making me step on Spartan soil. I feel
as though half of me were deserting to the enemy.

PHOBOKLEON

And the other foot.

PHILOKLEON

Nope—not that one. The big toe
hates Spartans—gets inflamed every time I turn south.

PHOBOKLEON

Sorry, this is the way things are.

PHILOKLEON

Now completely covered, except for his head, from which he wipes the sweat.

Nothing
is worse than growing old—can't do this,
can't do that. Now I can't even catch cold.

PHOBOKLEON

Will you let me get this slipper on?
There we are.
Now, walk as though you had money. You know, a little
insolence, a little lecherousness. Wiggle a little!

PHILOKLEON

Rich, eh?

He tries a tentative strut.

Like this? Watch me walk, and tell me
which rich man you think I look like.

He swaggers.

PHOBOKLEON

Hmmm.
Hard to say. Rather like a pimple with a bandage on.

PHILOKLEON

What's that, son? Like a pimp? But *which* rich man?
Doesn't matter—I know just the thing—
a bump, and a grind, and a couple of shakes of the tail.

PHOBOKLEON

Fine, just fine. Now, then, to Conversation.
Will you be able to hold your own in weighty
discourse with clever, witty, learned men?

PHILOKLEON

Nobody better.

PHOBOKLEON

Doubtfully.

Well, what would you say? Do you have
an anecdote, maybe?

PHILOKLEON

I've got millions.

PHOBOKLEON

For example?

PHILOKLEON

Well, first there's how they snared the ogress Lamia
and she farted loose; and then there's the one about Little
Kardopion, taking his mother by the . . .

PHOBOKLEON

No!
Not that! No fairy tales! You'll have to be realistic:
Everyday stories about everyday human beings—
domestic anecdotes—things around the house.

PHILOKLEON

Things around the house? Oh, I get you now.
Like this:
Once upon a time a cat and a mouse . . .

PHOBOKLEON

OF ALL THE GAUCHE, UNLETTERED IDIOTS!—and I quote
(Theogenes said it to another collector of crap!):
Are you going to talk about cats and mice in *Society?*

PHILOKLEON

Sulkily.

What *am* I supposed to tell them?

PHOBOKLEON

Important things—
stories that confer some dignity, fix some *fashion*
on you as narrator. For instance, tell them how
you were Athens' representative at a festival—you,
and Androkles, and Kleisthenes.

PHILOKLEON

Kleisthenes? I thought you said
no fairy tales. And anyway, I never represented
Athens—except at Paros. Got two obols a day
for that—the same as all the other privates.

PHOBOKLEON

Er—yes. Well, no matter: You've been to Olympia.
Remember? Ah, what a story! You saw Ephoudion,
old and grizzled as he was, hold his own against
young Askondas, wrestling catch-as-catch-can.
Ah, that was a battle, now! Age against youth—
the stag at bay! Tell them of Ephoudion's might—
how, for all his gray hairs, his chest was a brass-bound
barrel, his hands were hammers, his sides were steel,
his breast was bronze, his—

PHILOKLEON

Stop it, son—that's foolish.
He couldn't fight—he couldn't even move.

PHOBOKLEON

Deflated.

Well, that's the clever set's conversation.
We'd better
try something else. Let's have a suggestion from you.
Now, if you're drinking and making society small talk,
what would you tell your hosts was the most manly deed
you performed in those far-off days of your youth?

PHILOKLEON

Most manly?
Most grown-up? Oh, sure—I stole Ergasion's vine-poles.

PHOBOKLEON

Vine-poles? No, no, NO! Didn't you ever
chase a boar, or at least a rabbit, or run
in a relay? What's your most heroic accomplishment?

PHILOKLEON

Heroic? I took a dare once—you know Phaÿllos?

PHOBOKLEON
The Olympic runner?

PHILOKLEON
That's the one. I took after him—
And I caught him. A close race. Beat him by just two votes—
libel suit. But I was in condition, then.

PHOBOKLEON
Enough!
Let's accomplish what we can. Lie down,
and learn to be convivial, fit for civilized intercourse.

PHILOKLEON
All ears.
How do I lie down for *that?* Hurry up!

PHOBOKLEON
With grace.

PHILOKLEON
Hurling himself onto his back, and assuming, roughly, the fetal position.
This what you want?

PHOBOKLEON
Definitely, irrevocably, NO.

PHILOKLEON
Well, then, *how?*

PHOBOKLEON
Manfully.
First, extend the knees.
That's it.
Now, slide the body in supple, liquid curves—
the ones they teach in school—over the tapestries.
Philokleon looks dubiously at his astrakhan. He becomes more and more confused as Phobokleon sweeps on.
Take up a piece of plate and praise it to the skies.
Inspect the ceiling. Marvel at the richly woven
hangings in the hall.

As if to a Waiter.

Water for our hands—over here!
Bring in the tables! And now we dine.

He mimes eating.

And now
the finger-bowls.

He mimes washing.

And now we pour libations.

He mimes pouring and drinking.

PHILOKLEON
That's a dream of a dinner, son—and just as filling.

PHOBOKLEON

Not to be stopped.

The flute-girl gives us a note. Our fellow-guests
are here—Theoros, Aischines, Phanos, and Kleon,
and there's somebody else right by him. Who is it?

He squints and cranes, imitated by Philokleon, who is still confused.

Oh,
it's Akestor's son.—When you're in *this* sort of company,
father, you have to know your drinking songs.

PHILOKLEON
Oh, I do.

PHOBOKLEON
When the man before you sings a line,
do you know how to top it?

PHILOKLEON
Perfectly.

PHOBOKLEON
Really?

PHILOKLEON
I'm even better than the yodelers up in the hills.

PHOBOKLEON
Well, we'll soon find out. Now, I'll be Kleon,
and I'll start off the "Harmodios." You try to top it.

Sings.

Never again will Athens find . . .

PHILOKLEON

Sings.

. . .a thief like you; *you've stolen her blind.*

PHOBOKLEON

You can't sing *that!* They'd howl you into your grave!
I can hear Kleon now:
"I'LL EXTERMINATE YOU!
EXTIRPATE YOU! EXCISE YOU FROM THE COUNTRY!"

PHILOKLEON

Excellent! Let him threaten—I'll sing another:

O Captain! my Captain! you've sold the bloody sail,
and hocked the mast, and pawned the poop, and traded the after-rail.
The Ship of State is still afloat, but trembles on the brink:
Sit down! Stop throwing your weight around! Do you want the boat to SINK?

PHOBOKLEON

Adequate, adequate.
But there's Theoros now, lying
at Kleon's feet. He strokes his hand, and sings:

"Admetos friended Herakles:
his profit was exceeding.
So learn from stories such as these:
be friends with men of breeding."

Do you have a song for that?

PHILOKLEON

A *lyric,* no less:
I'll never be ready
to play the toady
or wear the shackle
of the two-faced jackal.

PHOBOKLEON
Now then, after him, Aischines takes it up.
He's a man of colossal culture, mighty in music—
by his own admission. His song, of course, concerns *him:*

"Up North, in a song-competition,
I tied with a woman musician.
What money we grossed!
We're Thessaly's toast. . . ."

PHILOKLEON
We boasted it into submission.

PHOBOKLEON
Well, you *do* understand the way to sing. That's something.
So, now for dinner at Philoktemon's. Which means we'd better
take food.

Turning to the house.

Hey, boy!

Sosias appears at the door.

Pack lunch for the two of us.

Sosias retires into the house.

PHILOKLEON
Lunch?

PHOBOKLEON
Certainly. Philoktemon never serves *food*—it's a *party!*
For once, we're going to get drunk.

PHILOKLEON
No, son—not that!
Nothing good ever came out of bottles. Just trouble—
Breaking and Entering, Theft, Assault and Battery—
then the morning after, the hangover, those fines to pay . . .
Your wine's a mocker, and mighty expensive, too.

PHOBOKLEON
But not in Society, Father; not with Gentlemen!
Finesse is the word in these circles. You make a gaffe—
a lawsuit? No, it's a simple social lapse,
quickly soothed and smoothed by the intercession of friends;
Conversation leads to Reconciliation.

Or *you* release the tension, with a funny fable
from Aesop, or a Sybaris-story*—a people-fable.
Learn one at the banquet. Then, if something goes wrong,
you tell it, convert the crisis into a joke,
and your accuser will laugh urbanely, release you,
and return to the happy eddy of High Society.

PHILOKLEON

That so? I'd better learn a lot of those fables.
Crime without Punishment. What'll they think of next?

PHOBOKLEON

So it's off to Society! Way for Men of Fashion!

Father and son set off eagerly and exit right, followed shortly from the house by Sosias, who carries a heavy lunchbasket.

FIRST SEMICHORUS*

I thought I was The Champion,
at dining-out The Best.
I never dreamed that mincing fop,
AMYNIAS, could wrest
away my Prize for Guestmanship;
he somehow didn't seem equipped,
because he doesn't EAT,
not Amynias.

His manners were disgraceful.
Leogoras, the glutton,
invited him to gorge himself
from muffins down to mutton,
and you know what that shittard *did?*
He came—but *wouldn't eat!* Instead,
he fiddled with a quince—
that Amynias!

He differed from his goodly host—
the fundamental gaffe!
But now he's done a sharp reverse
and made me eat my laugh.
He went upon an embassy
to check on things in Thessaly
and carried off my crown,
did Amynias!

Up North, he didn't grace the Rich
and Mighty with his presence;
he ate and drank exclusively
with greasy, stinking peasants
who served him NOTHING!
What a coup!
I take my napkin off to you,
you greasy, stinking, starveling
Slob, Amynias!

FIRST KORYPHAIOS
Is Automenes in the audience?
Congratulations, sir—
you've been chosen FATHER OF THE YEAR!
Take a bow, sir!—
Three fine sons, unsurpassed in their service to ART!
We all know and love Son #1, Arignotos the Harper—
a harper's harper, I might say—unmatched in music.
And Son #2, Automenes Jr., the eminent Actor—
well, gentlemen, words fail me—what indescribable skill!
But it's Son #3, Ariphrades, who staggers the senses—
what an endowment of Natural Talent! Would you believe it,
gentlemen, that slip of a boy, completely untaught (his father
swears he never took a lesson in his life), devised,
by his own unaided wits, a method of Oral Expression
which enables him daily to visit the tightest spots in the city
and come off top dog through the use of his golden tongue?
Best Wishes,
Automenes, Father of Three:
a HARPER,
an ACTOR,
a PERVERT!

SECOND SEMICHORUS*
. . . .

SECOND KORYPHAIOS
To rectify the record:
Rumor has it that I, the author,*
have kissed and made up with Kleon. It alleges that he scratched and badgered
until I buried the hatchet.
A canard. Here are the facts:

I found I was fighting alone.
When the Tanner dragged me to court,
I expected popular support from the folks who flocked to the case.
And what did I get? Laughs.
He peeled my skin off in strips;
I howled—and the spectators roared.
Dimly, I saw that my backing
was only a comedian's claque, political voyeurs assembled
to see me prodded until I produced some tasty billingsgate.
Faced with such odds, I changed my tactics—played the ape,
flattered Kleon a bit.
But what does he think today,
now that this docile doormat is pulling the rug from under him?

Sosias, battered, bloody, bruised, and torn, reels in from the right, watched with amazement and consternation by the Chorus. With a great deal of agony, he manages to stagger to center stage, where he suddenly straightens up, advances, and speaks in a relatively untortured tone.

SOSIAS
I should like to take the present opportunity
to congratulate all you turtles, wherever you are.
Oh, happy creatures cradled in horny carapaces,
triply serene in solid siding on your ribs,
what a consummate genius was yours, to roof
your backs with tile, shelter from blows!—Whereas,
I'M BLACK AND BLUE! MY RIBS ARE CLUBBED ALL TO HELL!

FIRST KORYPHAIOS
What's the trouble, boy? (Since common usage
decrees that "boy" refers to one who suffers
beatings, be he old or young.*)—But what's the trouble?

SOSIAS
The trouble's that old disaster Philokleon—what else?
Nobody could possibly get that drunk; but *he* managed.
He beat the cream of Athenian alcoholism—easy!
What a party! Every local lush, lecher,
loud-mouth, pervert, bully-ragger—they were all there:
Hippyllos, Antiphon, Lykon, Lysistratos, Theophrastos,
that slimy dancer Phrynichos* and his pansy friends.

But Philokleon won the Degeneracy Prize hands down,
going away. And quickly, too. He filled himself up
and went completely wild, treating us all
to an exhibition of kicks, jumps, brays, farts—
an ass at a banquet of barley. Then he beat the hell
out of me: "BOY!" he'd shout—WHOP!
"BOY!"
WHOP!
Then Lysistratos saw him, and sharpened up his tongue:
"Hey, old man," he said, "what are you? A new way
to spice up leftovers? No, you look more like a jackass
loose in the pea-patch." But Philokleon brayed right back.
He compared Lysistratos—now, let me get this straight—
to a locust—who'd lost—the fig leaves—off his old overcoat—
". . . just like that playwright Sthenelos sheared of his props!"
No one knew what he meant, but they clapped like mad—
except Theophrastos. He's a wit. He sneered.
The old man charged right up. "What call have *you* got,"
he bawled, "to be so snotty and hoity-toity?
You suck the socks of every rich man in town!"
Then he got sort of insulting. He went right down
the guest-list, calling names like a mule-skinner,
all the time babbling these . . . *fables,* he called them. Just words—
no plot, no point, no place in the conversation.
Finally, when he's absolutely stinking, he leaves,
reels off for home—and clobbers everyone he meets
with his torch. And what's even worse than that . . .

Shouts, thumps, and crashes from offstage right.

Oh-oh!
That's him—I know that stagger by ear. Goodbye.
Beatings are one thing I do very well without.

He limps quickly and painfully into the house. After a short pause, a curious procession enters from the right. It is led by Philokleon, raving drunk —a condition in which he remains for the rest of the play. He carries a torch in one hand and clutches at a stark naked flute-girl, whom he has stolen from the party, with the other. They are followed, at a very slight distance, by an irate band of banquet-guests, small tradesmen, etc., whom Philokleon has managed to outrage in one way or another during the course of the evening. He keeps this group at bay by brandishing his torch at it occasionally.

PHILOKLEON

Singing a drunken variation on a wedding march.

Take up the torch! Hic!
Here comesh the bride!
Some—body behind me
will have his hide fried!
Here comesh the bride!
Hold high the torch! Hic!

He waves the torch at the followers.

Haul your asses out of here
or I'll scorch you in the crotch! Hic!

He makes a sudden lunge. The crowd shrinks back.
He turns. The crowd presses nervously toward him.
One guest from the banquet advances.

GUEST

You're not going to get away with this! You'll pay!
Tomorrow! And being a minor is no damn excuse!
Breaking and Entering! Theft! Assault and Battery!
We'll all come down together and SUBPOENA you!

PHILOKLEON

A real SUBPOENA—for ME?
Gee!

Shaking his torch.

Thash ancient history—
don't let me
hear any more
about COURTS!

He jabs at the crowd with the torch.

Parry!
Thrust!

He moves back and squeezes the flute-girl experimentally.

Here's the stuff!

He squeezes again.

Moshtes' an' beshtes'—

He gives a third, magnificent squeeze, and addresses the heavens.

SCREW JUSTICE!!!

Turning to the crowd again.

Git! Where's that lawyer?

The guest who brought the accusation hurriedly buries himself in the crowd.

Everybody out of here!

He swings the torch wildly. The crowd stampedes back the way it has come and exits. Philokleon watches with alcoholic satisfaction, then turns to the flute-girl and motions her to the front door. He gazes at the upper window.

All right, honey-bee, first thing to do is get in.
You mount—upsy daisy!

He looks at the window again.

'Shtoo high—need a rope.

Shows his phallus.

Here'sh one—grab this.
Careful—that rope'sh pretty rotten—
but a little friction—hic!—won't hurt it any.
C'mon, you little cockchafer, chafe away!

The flute-girl shakes her head.

Now look, is this gratitude? You know those guests
were just about to make you open up and play
that Lesbian lay—but I put the snatch on you.
You could do's mush for me. Or lend me a hand—

The flute-girl is unmoved. He tries the sulks.

But hell, you won't—won't even try. I know you:
you're juss a tease—you'll make thish come unshcrewed.
Thash what you did to everyone elsh. —Look,
I'll tell you what. You be nice t' me *now*—
real nice—you know—and when that son of mine dies,
I'll buy your contract, all legal—and you can be
my concubine. How's that, you queen of a quim? All right?
Don't worry; I've got money, but it's all in trusht—
I'm not of age: can't touch an obol—just yet.
How's about it?*

The flute-girl smiles, nods, and sidles up to him. He puts an arm around her, suddenly withdraws it, then replaces it cautiously, looking around warily.

We'll have to be careful—I'm WATCHED!
It's that moss-backed son—won't let me out of his sight.
Oooh, he's mean! And stingy?—Did you ever eat *half*
of a caraway seed? That's what he serves *me!*
Anyway, he's afraid I'll get corrupted or something.
I'm an only father, you know.
—Oh-oh! Here he comes,
fast. I get the feeling we're the target.
Here! Quick—hold this torch and make like a statue.

He needs a hazing, and I'm just the boy to do it.
I'll use the trick he tried on me before
my initiation. Be a brother to your son, as the saying goes.

He hands the torch to the flute-girl, who freezes into an appropriate attitude. He then adjusts his mantle and assumes an innocent expression just in time to greet Phobokleon as he rushes in from the right.

PHOBOKLEON

Angry both at the theft of a flute-girl and at the failure of a theory of father-raising.

There you are, you Senile Delinquent! You old
Bandersnatch! The Great Lover himself—too limp
for Rigor Mortis! You won't get away with this!

PHILOKLEON

Hungry, son? Do you want a nice fried lawsuit
with plenty of sauce?

PHOBOKLEON

This is terrible, Father!
Fun's fun—but you can't steal the flutist from a feast!

PHILOKLEON

Flutist? What flutist? You're babbling, boy. Looks like
you fell right off your pedestal and cracked your head.

PHOBOKLEON

Pointing at the flute-girl.

You know perfectly well what flutist—THAT ONE!

PHILOKLEON

That's no flutist, son. It's a public fixture.

PHOBOKLEON

A fixture?

PHILOKLEON

A torch. They burn them to the gods.

He knocks Phobokleon's hands away from the girl.

Be reverent, son.

PHOBOKLEON

A *torch?*

PHILOKLEON

Yup. New model—
see the handy-dandy slit? Fits anywhere.

PHOBOKLEON

What are these?

PHILOKLEON

Additional handles—reduce fatigue.

PHOBOKLEON

What's this black patch in the middle?

PHILOKLEON

That patch? Pitch.
Get one of these torches hot and out it comes.

PHOBOKLEON

What's this back here? An ass if I ever saw one!

PHILOKLEON

That's a knot in the wood. Interesting formation.

PHOBOKLEON

A knot? What are you talking about?

To the flute-girl.

—Come here, you!

He starts to drag her off right.

PHILOKLEON

Grabbing the flute-girl and tugging.

Hey, son, what are you up to?

PHOBOKLEON

More than you are.
I'm taking this girl away from you and back
to the banquet. Face facts, Father: You're worn out,
used up, rotten. *You* can't do a thing!

PHILOKLEON

Now, wait a minute. You listen to me!

Phobokleon, surprised, stops.

Once
I represented Athens at the Olympics,
and there I saw Ephoudion, old and grizzled,
fight young Askondas and hold his own—and more!
That old fellow lifted up his fist—like this—

He raises his right hand high.

and brought it down hard—like this—

He strikes Phobokleon a terrific blow on top of the head, and knocks him down.

and felled the whelp—
like that!

He quickly ushers the flute-girl into the house, shouting over his shoulder.

Watch out—next time you get a black eye!*

PHOBOKLEON

Staggering to his feet as his father returns.

By god—he finally learned the Olympia bit!

Myrtia, a proprietress of a bakery-shop, enters holding an empty breadbasket in one hand and dragging Chairephon, a tall, cadaverous man who is to be her witness, by the other. She has to keep chivvying Chairephon, who is rather unhappy about the whole affair.

MYRTIA

To Chairephon.

Come ON! Stand right here, please!
HERE, idiot!
There he is! There's the man who ruined me!

Phobokleon starts suddenly, and looks wonderingly at Philokleon.

He beat me up with his torch,

She brandishes the basket.

and knocked *this* over—
squashed the bread—ten obols—and the cover—four more.

PHOBOKLEON

Aside, to Philokleon.

Do you see what you've done—you and your wine?
All the troubles and lawsuits back again!

PHILOKLEON

Why, no, son. All we need is an anecdote—

Conversation leads to Reconciliation.
You just watch me reconcile this old bag here.

MYRTIA
Oh, you'll pay, you will! You won't get off so easy!
No, sir, no one can ruin the stock of Myrtia,
daughter and successor of Ankylion and Sostrate—
an old, established firm—and not suffer!

PHILOKLEON
Listen to me, woman. I want to tell you
a pretty little fable.

MYRTIA
Not me, you don't!

PHILOKLEON
Aesop was coming home from dinner one evening
when he was barked at by a shaggy, drunken bitch.
He moves closer to Myrtia. She recoils.
And Aesop said,
Yelling in Myrtia's ear.
"YOU BITCH, YOU BITCH, YOU BITCH!
It'd be a good idea for you to trade
that nasty tongue in on some grain—YOU BITCH!"

MYRTIA
Slander, too? Well! I don't know what your name is,
but I'll summon you before the Board of Trade
to face the charge of Damaging Merchandise. And here's—
Tugging at Chairephon.
and here's my witness—
Tugging again, this time with success.
(come ON!)—
Chairephon!

PHILOKLEON
You don't mean that. Here's another; see how it strikes you.
The poet Lasos was competing with Simonides once.
Know what he said? He said: "I couldn't care less."

MYRTIA
Oh, he did, did he!

PHILOKLEON

And here's old Chairephon. Hi, there!

Chairephon cowers behind Myrtia.

Pasty-Face a witness for Rose-Red here—

He indicates Myrtia, who is crimson with fury.

that's quite a match. You look like Ino, hanging
by the feet. Of Euripides. Begging him not to cast her
in one of his plays.

Myrtia grabs Chairephon and stalks off without a word. Philokleon, beatific, watches them leave, then turns back to the house. Phobokleon continues watching for a moment.

PHOBOKLEON

Here comes somebody else.
Looks like another subpoena; he's brought his witness.

Beaten and bruised, there enters haltingly a Man who looks like Euripides. He is followed by a Witness, who carries stylus and tablet.*

THE MAN WHO LOOKS LIKE EURIPIDES

AGONY! MALAISE! ALACKADAISY!

Grisard, attend:

I'll criminate thee with ATROCITY!

PHOBOKLEON

Atrocity? Oh, *no!*

See here, Sir—set whatever penalty you wish,
and I'll pay it for him, and thank you in the bargain.

PHILOKLEON

It's my place, son. I'm overjoyed to make restitution.
He's right—I admit Assault and Battery.

To the Man Who Looks Like Euripides, sweetly.

—Sir,

please step over here.

The Man Who Looks Like Euripides complies, groaning. The Witness follows.

I desire to be your friend
in perpetuity. Can't we settle this out of Court?
Will you allow me to fix the amount of the fine
I'll have to pay, or would *you* prefer to set it?

THE MAN WHO LOOKS LIKE EURIPIDES

Pronounce the escheat. Fain would I eschew
dispute and suit.
—OOOO!

PHILOKLEON

A man of Sybaris
fell out of a chariot once and smashed his skull
to smithereens; he was no horseman. A friend of his
came up and said, "The cobbler should stick to his last."
In your case, friend, it means you should hobble off fast
to the Free Clinic.

He knocks the tablet out of the Witness's hands, breaking it. Phobokleon buries his head in his hands.

PHOBOKLEON

If you have one virtue, it's consistency.

THE MAN WHO LOOKS LIKE EURIPIDES

To his Witness, who stands stupidly holding his stylus.

Impress in mind's inmost recess these insults!

He starts to leave.

PHILOKLEON

Don't run off. Listen: In Sybaris once, a woman
smashed a hedgehog.*

THE MAN WHO LOOKS LIKE EURIPIDES

To his Witness.

Attest that witless thrust!

PHILOKLEON

Just what the hedgehog did—it called a witness.
And the woman of Sybaris said, "You'd show more sense,
if you forgot this witness-business entirely,
and ran as quick as you could to buy a bandage."

THE MAN WHO LOOKS LIKE EURIPIDES

Indulge thy raging, till thou'rt led to judging!
OUCH!

He limps off, groaning, followed by the Witness. As Philokleon watches in satisfaction, Phobokleon sneaks softly behind him.

PHOBOKLEON

In a low voice which is not heard by Philokleon.

You simply can't stay here any longer.
I'll just lift you up and. . . .

He scoops the old man up in his arms.

PHILOKLEON

What are you doing?

PHOBOKLEON

Me?
I'm carrying you inside. If I leave you here,
every witness in town will be used up in half an hour.

He strides for the door, lugging his father.

PHILOKLEON

Once Aesop was accused . . .

PHOBOKLEON

I couldn't care less!

PHILOKLEON

. . . by the people of Delphi. They said he'd stolen a vase
that belonged to Apollo. But he told them the story
about the beetle.
Once upon a time, a beetle. . . .

PHOBOKLEON

Reaching the door at last.

I'll put an end to you *and* your beetles, by God!

The house-door closes behind them. Philokleon can still be heard babbling his fable.

FIRST SEMICHORUS

I envy Philokleon's luck,
so happily arranged.
His rough, and rude, and often crude
mode of life has changed.

[*Crashes and yells from the house.**]

He's learned the theory, has it pat;
now comes the execution.
He turns to Ease and Luxuries—
a Total Revolution!

[*The flute-girl appears at the upper window, screams, and disappears.*]

But will he really wish to shift
from Habit's well-worn routes?
Dame Nature's hard to disregard—
will he join in New Pursuits?

[*The door of the house bursts open, and out flies the flute-girl, chased by Philokleon. He pursues her around the stage.*]

Others change, for New Ideas
accomplish more than kicks.
With a gentle jog, the Oldest Dog
will gladly learn New Tricks!

[*Phobokleon and the slaves (Xanthias excepted) hurry from the house and chase Philokleon. The flute-girl escapes, but back into the house. Phobokleon and the slaves catch Philokleon and re-enter, carrying him.*]

SECOND SEMICHORUS

All men of sensibility
will join me, I feel sure,
as now I raise a song of praise
to the Author of this Cure.

[*More crashes and yells from the house.*]

All Hail to Philokleon's son!
Exalt him to the skies!
Did ever lad so love his dad?
Was ever boy so wise?

[*The flute-girl, screaming again, appears at the upper window. She is in the clutches of Philokleon, who is in turn being beaten by Phobokleon with the torch. The tableau disappears suddenly.*]

What manners! What demeanor! What
behavior in a boy!
What soft address! What gentleness!
It made me melt with joy!

[*The door bursts open, and the trio emerges: The flute-girl, chased by Philokleon, chased by Phobokleon with the torch.*]

And in debate, this paragon
inspired his parent's notions
to Things Above, by Filial Love—
the noblest of emotions!

ENTIRE CHORUS

ALL HAIL, PHOBOKLEON!

[Philokleon catches the flute-girl. Phobokleon trips and drops the torch. Philokleon scoops it up, throws the flute-girl over his shoulder, and beats his howling son before him into the house.]

Xanthias emerges from the house, shaking his head.

XANTHIAS

Dionysos, what a mess! Some god's been playing stagehand,
meddling with the set. The house is an absolute snarl.
It's the old man. After all these years, he took
a drink, and heard one note from the flute—and bang!
the combination sent him right out of his head.
To his feet.
He's mad, but now he's mad for dancing. Been at it
all night long. No end in sight. Except his.
By now, he's worked through all those antique dances
that Thespis taught his choruses a century ago,
and claims he's ready for the Modern School. Performers
in tragedies today, like Phrynichos and all his ilk,
are feeble old fogies, he says: they can't match *him!*
He's even threatened to come out here in a while
and show the young men up by dancing them down
at all their own steps.* Talk about the light fantastic!

He sits down, leaning against the door.

PHILOKLEON

From behind the door, declaiming Euripidean fustian.

Who couches before the courtyard portals?

The door rattles. Xanthias jumps away.

XANTHIAS

To the audience.

You're about to witness an outbreak of plague.

*He runs off.**

PHILOKLEON

Ho, there! Unshoot the bolts!

The door bursts open, and Philokleon jigs forth. He is rehearsing the violent movements of a grotesquely acrobatic dance. After him, sad and defeated, comes Phobokleon.

'Tis time!

The gambado commences!

PHOBOKLEON

Wearily.

And sanity ends.

PHILOKLEON

Let's see. How does Phrynichos do it?

Suiting action to words, as far as possible.

He begins with a flourish, a sudden convulsive
contortion of the ribs! A blare from the nostrils!
A ruffle and scrunch of splintered vertebrae!

PHOBOKLEON

How are you treating it? Hellebore? Hemlock?

PHILOKLEON

He coils in a crouch like an angry cock . . .

PHOBOKLEON

If that doesn't work, we could stone you, of course.

PHILOKLEON

. . . then lashes a kick that scrapes the stars!

PHOBOKLEON

And his ass gapes wide to the spectators' stares.

PHILOKLEON

You'd better watch out for yourself!

He revolves and jumps more and more wildly. Phobokleon moves out of the way.

And now
the final pirouette, the supple, unsocketed
whizzing and whirring of a dislocated femur!

He spins and kicks more frantically, coming to a stop before Phobokleon.

Pretty good, huh?

PHOBOKLEON

Positively NO! Utter Delirium!

PHILOKLEON

Paying no attention, he advances to the audience.

An Announcement:
To All Performers from the Tragic Stage
Who Make Any Pretense to Excellence in the Dance, I Fling
a Blanket Challenge: COME UP AND COMPETE WITH *ME!*

Silence.

—Anybody? Nobody?

PHOBOKLEON

Here comes one—but that's all.

A small dancer, dressed as a crab, scurries on stage.

PHILOKLEON

What happened to *him?*

PHOBOKLEON

Heredity. He's the son of Karkinos*
the dancer—you know what a crusty old crab *he* is.

PHILOKLEON

That's no competition. A downbeat or two from me,
and he's done. Cooked. Dished. He'll make a nice mouthful,
the way he makes hash of the rhythm.

A second crab-clad dancer scurries up.

PHOBOKLEON

I wouldn't have your luck.
What bait are you using? You caught another crab—
his brother.

PHILOKLEON

I didn't mean for this to be a dinner-dance.
I wanted a ballet.

PHOBOKLEON

Looking off.

You've got a buffet—three crabs.

PHILOKLEON

Three?

PHOBOKLEON

Well, here comes another son of Karkinos.

A very tiny crab-dancer scurries on.

PHILOKLEON

What's this creeping thing? A trivet? A spider?

PHOBOKLEON

That's the youngest—the shrimp of the family. They all act, but he writes. That makes it a real tragedy.

PHILOKLEON

O Karkinos, how you must jump for joy at your offspring!
And the whole bunch of little bounders has dropped on *us!*

To Phobokleon.

I must enter the lists. To celebrate my victory in the dance,
fix something for my opponents. A sauce. Use plenty of capers.
And now to see crabbed youth compete with age.

He moves to the center of the stage to begin the dance.

FIRST KORYPHAIOS

To the Chorus.

All right, men, let's pull back a little and give them room.
We don't want to be in the way when they try those whip-top spins.

The Chorus forms a large semicircle, in which the Sons of Karkinos begin their wild dance. Philokleon waits.

ENTIRE CHORUS

To the Sons of Karkinos.

Aloft! ye crustacean lords of gyration,
eccentrically tracing your dizzy descent from the
undulant loins of the God of the Ocean!
O Arthropod paladins, sires of Circuity!
Scuttle and pound on the sterile salt strand!
Scurry and stamp! O ye kinsmen to shrimp!

In wild revolution, in whirligig tension,
enjumble and fumble the force of a tragedy!
Mount to the climax with pouncing distortion,
then bound to the sky to confound the peripety!
Flick with your kick the shriek of a claque,
engulfing the plays in brainless applause.

To Philokleon as he spins into the dance.

In giddy glissade, let vertigo reign! Embellish the eddy
and spiral your shins to the stars!

To the Sons of Karkinos, as Philokleon spins among them.

Be bobbins, and reel to make ready
your master's turbinate triumph! Oh, wheel to the liege of the sea—
who scuds and unsettles those lords of the stage, his children three!

At this point the dancing contest turns into a rout. Philokleon, spinning and kicking, attacks in turn the three crabs and pursues them in a mad circle. The Chorus addresses the maelstrom plaintively.

Please lead us off. You can keep up the dance if you must, but *hurry!*
It's not that innovations annoy us, but we *do* have a worry:
We admit that many actors have had the chance to dismiss
the Chorus by using a final dance—
BUT NEVER A DANCE LIKE *THIS!*

Still gyrating and jumping, Philokleon pursues the three Sons of Karkinos off-stage; the Chorus and cast follow, dancing just as madly as their leaders.

Notes

page 9. *Korybants:* Priests of the goddess Kybele, whose rites were distinguished by wild dancing.

11. *that tanner Kleon:* The demagogue owned a leather factory, and Aristophanes never forgot it.

11. *Theoros was a sapsucker:* There is a play here in the Greek on Alkibiades' lisp, which substituted *l* for *r*, so that Theoros has the head of a *kolax* "flatterer" rather than a *korax* "raven." Rogers' *raven-cwaven* alternation is the nearest English. Better to forget the lisp.

13. *CROAK:* In the Greek, a play on the common billingsgate phrase *es korakas* "To the crows!"—i.e., "Go to hell!"

13. *thanks to luck:* By virtue of his victory over the Spartans at Sphakteria in the summer of 425.

14. *Not too refined and dainty for you, of course:* The first of a string of gibes at the intelligence of the audience. Also note that a good number of the points of the preceding program are contradicted in the course of the play. Thus slapstick abounds, Kleon is hit at every opportunity, and, if the scholiast is correct, Euripides appears, thoroughly worked over.

14. *SOSIAS:* As noted in the Introduction (p. 5), the texts of Coulon and Cantarella assign the entire address to the audience here to the slave whose name is Xanthias. I think this bad philology and bad dramaturgy, and have gone back to the texts of Rogers, Van Leeuwen, and Starkie, who break up the speech with Sosias' backchat.

15. *Long Line:* Athenian juries, in certain cases, established the penalty—or rather chose between one proposed by the defendant and one proposed by the plaintiff. The choice of the individual juror was indicated by a line drawn by a stylus on a wax tablet: short for minimum, long for maximum. The Stings which the Chorus wear would appear to be enlarged representations of this stylus.

16. *PHOBOKLEON:* The Greek name is Bdelykleon, "Loathe-Kleon," which is under two disadvantages for an English-speaking audience, i.e., it is at once meaningless and unpronounceable.

page 17. *peach-wood:* In Greek, *sykinou,* "fig-wood," with the consequent play on *sykophantēs,* "informer."

23. *Phrynichos:* The famous Athenian tragic poet of an earlier day. The allusion here may be specifically to his *Phoenician Women,* presented in 476.

25. *wasps' stings:* The location of these stings—front or back?—has occasioned some little discussion, and my solution may seem unattractive, particularly to those who deny the presence of the phallus in Aristophanes' plays. I only urge that objectors (1) look at a wasp, (2) consider that this sting, in the play, is (or was) not only the seat of the Chorus' might but of their manhood, (3) remember that "tail" is the whole lower end of the torso. (It is curious to conjecture what might have become of this play had Aristophanes known that the sting is borne only by the *female* wasp.)

26. *squeezed Sicily dry:* Laches' peculations are conjectural. He *did* lose a battle at Leontini in Sicily in 427 and undergo survey thereafter, but seems to have avoided conviction, since he fought at Delion in 424 and established a truce there in 423. Whether this refers to the former survey or a current one is unknown; it may only refer to a possible one, since the opposition between Laches, an oligarch, and Kleon, mainstay of "the people," would have been drawn on strictly party lines.

28. *Secret Agent in Samos:* A reference to the unsuccessful revolt of that island from enforced Athenian democracy in 440.

28. *a traitor from Thrace:* The Thracian cities Amphipolis and Eion were betrayed by their inhabitants to the Spartan general Brasidas in 424.

30. *Proxenides' bluster:* This man and Aischines were two well-known boasters, the Athenian equivalent for "hot air" being "smoke." (Which lies at the bottom of the translation "smudgepot" in line 151 above.)

31. *our Navy's going to pot:* Nothing has been—or will be—said about the Navy, or about Demeter's legislation in the parallel accusation in 379 below. The Chorus is pathologically suspicious, and can credit no one with good motives.

33. *Demeter's legislation:* One would expect the Chorus to say "Demeter's mysteries." The confusion is, of course, Aristophanes' way of indicating to what extent religion and politics have been confused by these litigious old men. At least, this is the usual explanation.

34. *Lykos my Master:* Son of the legendary King Pandion of Athens; his statue, in the form of a wolf (lykos) was set, we are told, before each court.

36. *and hold it high, Boys:* From this point until the Debate, the Chorus' actions proceed from an adolescent enthusiasm shakily reared on their senile decrepitude. To evoke this, I have translated here on the pattern of that archetypal fight song which daily greeted prepubescent Ameri-

cans from their radios in the late 1930's and early 1940's—the hymn to Hudson High School which prefaced the exploits of "Jack Armstrong, the All-American Boy."

page 43. *Brasidas:* Because of his recent and threatening victories in Thrace, the Spartan general was a name for the popular party to beat the conservatives with in 422.

43. *SUBVERSIVE:* A closer modern American equivalent for *synōmotēs* than the literal "conspirator," as "dictatorship" is nearer to *tyrannis* than "tyranny."

49. *his daughter:* The usual pun on *choiros* ("pig" and "female genitalia") that is so thoroughly employed in *Acharnians* 764 ff.

50. *Flee-onymos:* The Greek gives *Kolakonymos,* a punning compound of *kolax* (flatterer) and Kleonymos. Since Kleonymos was also a notorious coward (see, e.g., Xanthias' dream about the eagle, p. 10), Flee-onymos seemed a permissible liberty.

50. *silence from Phobokleon:* An attempt to supply some sort of a joke that seems to have been lost when knowledge of Euphemios (Euphemides?) disappeared. He was probably of the same moral stamp as Theoros—but this is obviously the scholiast's conjecture, based on this passage. Phobokleon, of course, *does* know Theoros.

56. *paying tribute to Athens:* One thousand tributaries seems a considerable overstatement, more than three times the actual figure. But Phobokleon, or Aristophanes, may have another method of counting than modern scholars.

56. *you can have Euboia:* Perikles, in 445, planted Athenian colonists on this grain-fertile island, and promise of the same became a pie-in-the-sky maneuver for the demagogues who came after him.

63. *chamber pot:* A false solution to the problem, but one with better comic sense than having the son produce a shrine. Philokleon's comparison between this and Kleonymos in the original—that Lykos has no shield either—helps the solution not at all. But it must have been pertinent, and I have tried to change it to something that might work.

65. *Chowhound:* In Greek, *Labēs* "Grab"—a pun on the general Laches, as the plaintiff (here "Fleahound") is *Kyōn* "Dog"—a pun on Kleon. The proper-name pun is not worth straining English, especially since Laches' trial is conjectural. Aristophanes' technique here is instructive of his whole approach. Most of the time, a delicate ambiguity is preserved: Chowhound, a dog, could equally well be a general. But at certain points, particularly at the testimony of the Cheese-Grater, the allegory breaks through, and the dogginess nearly disappears.

74. *to old Thoukydides once:* See *Acharnians,* 703 ff.

77. *Harden not your hearts, but melt it in mercy:* The syntactical apogee of Phobokleon's perplexity—is his father one man or a panel of jurors?

page 81. *into others' mouths:* Those of Philonides and Kallistratos, who produced Aristophanes' first plays. See *Clouds* 503 ff.

81. *who shall be nameless:* The rival comedian Eupolis.

82. *first performance:* Under his own name—*The Knights* of 424.

82. *informers:* Thus many critics identify the demons, presuming they were thus attacked in the *Barges* (*Holkades*), presented in 423. Others follow the scholiast and say the demons are the sophists lampooned in *The Clouds*. But the rather tortured Greek seems fairly clear in one thing: This is something which occurred *before* the production of *The Clouds*.

85. *the coming of the Persians:* The battles of Salamis and Marathon are mingled in the following account.

86. *the Archon's court, the Eleven's Court, the converted Odeion:* Three different tribunals: the court of the eponymous archon; the court of the Eleven (concerned with theft and police matters generally); and the Odeion, occasionally taken over to settle litigation arising from the grain-trade.

98. *Sybaris-story:* A conventionalized anecdote, purporting to have taken place in the city of Sybaris in southern Italy. These Sybaritic fables used human characters rather than animals, as in the fables of Aesop.

98. *FIRST SEMICHORUS:* This ode, a very crabbed bit of Greek on which no two commentators seem to agree, has been expanded to show how it may have meant *something*. The solution proposed, that Amynias is censured here for being a starveling, fits the Greek and the situation here, though it supplements rather than complements the information we have in *The Clouds* about this (or another?) Amynias. I have avoided conjecture about the politics involved, though firm theories abound. Here, as elsewhere in Aristophanes, precise hypotheses proliferate in direct proportion to the opacity of the passage.

99. *SECOND SEMICHORUS:* We have lost the antistrophe and the beginning of the speech here given to the Second Koryphaios.

99. *the author:* Probably. The allusion can hardly, considering *The Acharnians* and *The Knights,* be to the (probable) legal action taken by Kleon after *The Babylonians;* it may be some action or threat that followed those two plays, and led indirectly to Aristophanes' abandonment of political attacks in *The Clouds.*

100. *old or young:* A pun on *pais* "boy" and *paiein* "beat" underlies this Euripidean sententiousness.

100. *Phrynichos:* This reference to the other Phrynichos, the contemporary dancer, is clearly to set up the final scene.

103. *How's about it?:* I here abandon the hics! and thickening of sounds. Philokleon remains just as drunk.

106. *next time you get a black eye:* The manuscripts and scholia, as usual, furnish no information about the outcome of this skirmish. It is only fair

to note that editors and commentators, if they deign to discuss stage-action, are eager to balance the scales of morality—and accordingly award both victory and flute-girl to the virtuous son. I can only say that their choice deprives Philokleon's speech here of any motivation or meaning.

page 108. *A Man who looks like Euripides:* So a scholiast names him. Nearly every modern editor rejects this, though it is not the sort of thing that a scholiast would imagine on his own. The most telling argument against the tragedian's appearance is that he does not talk in the fustian that Aristophanes normally employs for him. I have changed his remarks into equivalent fustian, not to avoid the argument, but to supply a modern audience with something like the original effect—which, I think, was purely visual: an easily recognizable mask to identify the tragedian, here "worked over again" most violently.

109. *hedgehog:* In Greek, *echinos,* not only the animal, but a vase, and one associated with courtroom practice. But the straight translation seems to have the required degree of insanity, so I have let it stand.

110. *from the house:* The stage directions here are strictly *exempli causa,* the responsibility (or irresponsibility) of the translator. They have as their aim, however, something serious: To try to point out the comment that is here made by what is probably Aristophanes' most insipid stasimon, violently dislocated. It logically fits after the scene of preparation for the banquet, after line 1264—which is where Van Leeuwen, for one, "re-places" it. But had that been its original location, what ancient editor would have been such an idiot as to move it in the first place? No one but the author, I think, could have put it here—and he did it, not out of clumsiness, or a desire to insert another scene, but calculatingly. Coming as it does after the presentation of the reformed Philokleon, turned young, drunk, and disgusting, bait for the courtroom himself, it underlines, *per contra,* the utter defeat of Phobokleon's altruism. Further, its very flatness almost demands spectacle. Finally, though most commentators banish the flute-girl from the scene early, we know from the final scene that someone was playing the flute inside. Q. E. D.—quite shakily.

113. *at all their own steps:* The controversy over this last scene seems to have been settled by Roos's excellent work, *Die tragische Orchestik im Zerrbild der altattischen Komödie* (Stockholm, 1951). Simply, this is a satirical fling at the excesses of the "New School" of tragic dancing, which specialized in hyperathletic leaps and bounds to no apparent purpose—at least from Aristophanes' conservative viewpoint. The final song has been expanded in translation at the end of this scene to try to show the accomplishment: the gaudy wildness which obscures and ruins tragedy. I have not followed Roos' conclusions as to the nature of Philokleon's dance—a wild, drunkenly lascivious dance normally confined to the late hours of wild parties—but this is simply to let the pseudo-tragic state-

ment work. Anyone hardy enough to attempt this play is perfectly free to insert bumps and grinds at will, provided that the result is both funny and somewhat disgusting; Philokleon's victory is also his degradation.

113. *He runs off:* In most texts, Xanthias has most, if not all, of the lines here given to Phobokleon—a good way to send a scene teetering on the brink of meaninglessness right off the edge.

115. *Karkinos:* A tragic poet, upon the literal meaning of whose name ("the crab") the entire following dance scene is based.

Glossary

ADMETOS: Legendary king of Pherai in Thessaly befriended by the hero Herakles. He is a major figure in Euripides' *Alkestis* and the subject of an Attic drinking song.

AESOP, AISOPOS: Flourished ca. 570 B.C. The author of a famous collection of animal fables.

AGORA: The main marketplace of Athens, used for holding trials, public debates, and the transaction of business.

AISCHINES: A henchman of Kleon (q.v.) and a notorious braggart. His nickname was "Smoke."

AIXONE: A deme of Attika, birthplace of the general Laches (q.v.).

AJAX, AIAS: Son of Telamon and Greek hero of the Trojan War. In the contest for the armor of Achilles, he lost to Odysseus and went mad in consequence. Dishonored, he fell upon his sword and died.

ALKIBIADES: An Athenian politician (ca. 450-404) of great ability and brilliance. Of aristocratic Alkmaeonid descent, he was related to Perikles and was, for some time, a devoted disciple of Sokrates. Distinguished by wealth, birth, and spectacular personal beauty, he spent his youth in lavish display and debauchery (Pheidippides in *Clouds* has been thought to be a caricature of Alkibiades).

AMYNIAS: Son of Pronapes and one of Strepsiades' creditors in *Clouds*. He was not, however, a professional moneylender but a notorious effeminate and wastrel, probably addicted to gambling.

ANDROKLES: A homosexual.

ANTIPHON: A parasite and starveling.

APOLLO: God of prophecy, music, healing, and light; his two chief shrines were at Delphoi (q.v.) and the island of Delos (q.v.).

ARIGNOTOS: An excellent harper and a friend of Aristophanes.

ARIPHRADES: Son of Automenes and a notorious pervert. Indeed, his perversities (cunnilingual and perhaps worse still) seem to have struck Aristophanes as an altogether novel form of sexual self-expression.

ARTEMIS: Goddess of the hunt and the moon, sister of Apollo (q.v.).

ASKLEPIOS: Son of Apollo; god of medicine.

ASKONDAS: A contender against Ephoudion (q.v.) at the Olympic games; otherwise unknown.

ATHENA, ATHENE: Goddess of wisdom and war and patroness of Athens. On her breast she wore the *aegis,* a goatskin plated with scales and a Gorgon's head in the center.

BRASIDAS: Distinguished Spartan general of the Peloponnesian War, particularly famed for his victories in Thrace and his defeat of Kleon.

BYZANTION: A city on the Bosporus and a subject-city of the Athenian Empire. Its siege by the Athenians under Kimon in 469 was celebrated.

CHABES: An old juror, crony of Philokleon.

CHAIREPHON: A pupil and disciple of Sokrates; his scrawniness and emaciated pallor are constantly ridiculed by Aristophanes.

CHAIREAS: A man whose claim to fame was his son, a notorious pervert who was not even, according to the Scholiast, an Athenian citizen.

CHARINADES: An old juror, crony of Philokleon.

DELOS: Small Aegean island sacred to Apollo.

DELPHOI, DELPHI: A town in Phokis, celebrated for its great temple and oracle of Apollo.

DEMETER: The Earth-Mother; goddess of grain, agriculture, and the harvest, worshipped in her shrine at Eleusis in Attika.

DEMOS: In this play, not Demos, the personified populace of Athens, but Demos, the son of Pyrilampes, noted for stupidity and effeminacy, a victim of the pun in his name.

DERKYLOS: A drunkard.

DIONYSOS: God of vineyards, wine, and dramatic poetry; also called Bacchos, Evios, Bromios, etc.

DRAKONTIDES: His identity is uncertain, but he was probably a member of the oligarchical party and perhaps one of those who preferred charges against Perikles.

EKBATANA: A city in Media, once the capital of the Median Kingdom, and later the summer residence of the Persian kings. For the average Greek, Ekbatana was a kind of El Dorado, a distant city of fabulous wealth.

EPHOUDION: Victor in pankration (mixed wrestling and boxing) at Olympia in 464 B.C.

ERGASION: Evidently a farmer; otherwise unknown.

EUATHLOS: An orator and informer of no principles; it was he who brought charges against Perikles' rival, Thoukydides (q.v.), after his return from ostracism.

EUBOIA: A large and fertile island northeast of Attika. In 445 Perikles planted an Athenian colony on the island and otherwise exploited it. As a result the island revolted and had to be resubjugated. This time, however, Perikles' treatment of the island was so severe that it was commonly said (at least by his enemies) that he had "stretched Euboia on the rack of torture."

EUERGIDES: An old juror, otherwise unknown.

EUPHEMIOS: A boon-companion of Theoros (q.v.) and perhaps, like him, a demagogic orator. Nothing else is known about him, though given the context in which his name appears (*Wasps,* 599), it seems clear that nothing *good* could have been known.

EURIPIDES: Athenian tragedian (480-406 B.C.) whose character and plays were constantly ridiculed by Aristophanes. Euripides' mother may have been (though this is uncertain) a marketwoman who sold chervil, and Aristophanes never tires of twitting the tragedian about his mother's vegetables.

EURYKLES: A prophet who claimed to be possessed and thus to have the power to speak through the mouths of others.

HARMODIOS: Murderer of the tyrant Hippias (q.v.) and much honored in Athens; a famous drinking song records the tyrannicide.

HEKATE: Goddess of the moon, night, childbirth, and the underworld. At Athens a small shrine of Hekate was set up in the vestibule of every house.

HELLESPONT: Strait which divides Asia Minor from Thrace.

HERAKLES: Hero and demigod, son of Zeus and Alkmene; renowned for his great labors, his prodigious strength, and his gluttonous appetite.

HESTIA: Goddess of the hearth.

HIPPIAS: Athenian tyrant of the sixth century, murdered by Harmodios (q.v.) and Aristogeiton.

HIPPYLLOS: A debauchee; otherwise unknown.

INO: Euripidean heroine-in-tatters and wife of Athamas. She threw herself at her mad husband's feet, begging for mercy, but he refused to listen and threw her into the sea where she was transformed into the sea-goddess Leukothea.

KARDOPION: A semicomic name (it means "Little Kneading-Trough") used as a matter of convention in telling a certain kind of story (compare, for instance, "Little Audrey").

KARKINOS: An Athenian tragic poet whose poetry and three sons are all ridiculed by Aristophanes. Karkinos' name means "Crab."

KEKROPS, CECROPS: Legendary first king of Attika and reputed founder of Athens. Hence "country of Kekrops" is equivalent to "Athens," and "son of Kekrops" to "Athenian." He is usually represented as twi-form, i.e., with the head and upper trunk of a man, but serpent-shaped below (symbolizing his earthborn origin).

KLEISTHENES: A notorious homosexual, and one of Aristophanes' favorite targets.

KLEON: Son of Kleinetos; the most notorious and powerful of all Athenian demagogues. After the death of Perikles in 429 B.C., Kleon became, until his own death in 422, the leader of the radical democracy and the anti-Spartan extremists in Athens. An impressive speaker and a thoroughly unscrupulous and venal politician, he was bitterly loathed and attacked by Aristophanes. In 424 B.C., thanks to his coup in capturing the Spartan hoplites at Sphakteria, he reached the height of his power; so unchallengeable was his position that he was able to persuade the Athenians not to accept the handsome terms offered by Sparta in an attempt to recover her imprisoned hoplites. Filled with confidence in his military ability and tempted by the hope of further glory, Kleon took command of an Athenian army in Thrace, where, in 422, he was defeated and killed by the Spartan forces under Brasidas (q.v.).

In Aristophanes' *Knights,* Kleon is only slightly masked under the name of Paphlagon.

KLEONYMOS: A corpulent glutton and part-time informer; Aristophanes' commonest butt for cowardice (i.e., throwing one's shield away).

KORYBANTES: Frenzied priests of the goddess Kybele (the Phrygian Earth-mother whose worship was ecstatic and orgiastic).

KRONOS: Father of Zeus, Hera, and Poseidon. Deprived of his rule by Zeus. Synonymous with "old fogy."

KYDATHENEA: An Athenian deme; the birthplace of Kleon and Aristophanes.

LACHES: An Athenian general, defeated in Sicily in 427 B.C.; in 424 he besieged Delion, and may have been prosecuted by Kleon for peculation in Sicily.

LASOS: Of Hermione, a lyric poet.

LEOGORAS: A wealthy Athenian gourmet, addicted to horse-raising (or possibly to pheasant-breeding). Father of the orator Andokides.

LYDIA: A district of Asia Minor; under its greatest king, Kroisos (Croesus), it included almost all of Asia Minor from the river Halys to the Ionian coast. Its wealth and effeminacy were proverbial among Greeks.

LYKON: A debauchee; otherwise unknown.

LYKOS: Legendary son of Pandion and patron of jurors.

LYKINOS: A name; otherwise unknown.

LYSISTRATOS: An acid-tongued demagogue, evidently a starveling and a parasite.

MARATHON: The famous battle (490 B.C.) in which the Athenian forces under Miltiades crushingly defeated the first Persian invasion of Hellas.

MEGARA: The Greek state to the west of Attika. Subject first to the boycott imposed by Perikles' Megarian Decree (432 B.C.) and later to frequent Athenian incursions, plus the inroads of the Peloponnesian forces on their way to ravage Attika in the winters, it was reduced quite early in the war to extreme hunger and poverty.

MIDAS: A Phrygian slave.

MORYCHOS: A noted Athenian epicure and dandy.

NAXOS: An island in the Aegean, conquered by the Athenians under Kimon, probably about 468 B.C.

NIKOSTRATOS: A superstitious religious fanatic.

NIOBE: Mythical daughter of Tantalos, proud mother of six sons and six daughters, all slain by Artemis and Apollo because Niobe boasted herself to be better than Leto. The subject of tragedies by Aischylos and Sophokles.

ODEION: A covered theater in Athens which also did service as a lawcourt.

ODYSSEUS: King of Ithaka and hero of the Trojan War; renowned for his resourcefulness and cunning.

OIAGROS: An Athenian tragic actor.

OLYMPIA: A plain in Elis where the Olympic Games were celebrated.

PAIAN: Manifestation of Apollo as god of healing.

PARNASSOS: A high mountain to the north of Delphoi (q.v.); one of the chief haunts of Apollo and the Muses, but frequented also by Dionysos.

PAROS: An island in the Aegean, a site of a disastrous expedition under Miltiades in 489 B.C.

PHANOS: A henchman of Kleon, who seems to have lent his name to suits and investigations instigated by Kleon.

PHAYLLOS: A famous runner.

PHILIPPOS: An orator, amateur sophist, and informer.

PHILOKTEMON: According to the Scholiast, a glutton and drunkard, famous for keeping perpetual Open House.

PHILOXENOS: A pervert.

PHLYA: An Athenian deme.

PHRYGIA: A region of Asia Minor, once ruled by the Lydians and then incorporated into the Persian Empire. It was particularly prone to a kind of religion marked by frenzy and ecstatic excess, familiar to Greece in the worship of Kybele and the Phrygian Dionysos.

PHRYNICHOS: (1) An early Athenian tragedian, an older contemporary of Aischylos. (2) A tragic actor and dancer, contemporary with Aristophanes.

POSEIDON: Brother of Zeus and god of the sea. As god of the sea, he girdles the earth and has it in his power, as Poseidon the Earth-shaker, to cause earthquakes. In still another manifestation, he is Poseidon Hippios, patron god of horses and horsemen.

PROXENIDES: A notorious braggart and liar.

SAMOS: A large Aegean island lying off the coast of Ionia. It was a member state of the Athenian Confederacy until 440 B.C. when it revolted. The islanders resisted for a heroic nine months against the Athenians dispatched to reconquer it.

SARDIS: One-time capital of the kingdom of Lydia; under the Persians the residence of the satrap of Lydia. Ever since the time of Kroisos (Croesus), Greeks had regarded Sardis as a place of fabulous wealth and the frequent embassies sent there confirmed the reports.

SIMONIDES: Of Keos, the great sixth-century lyric poet.

SKIONE: A town situated on the peninsula of Pallene (cf. CHALKIDIKE). After it revolted from the Athenian Empire, the Athenians were forced to spend several months of extremely bitter winter weather in blockading it.

SOLON: Famous Athenian legislator (ca. 638-558 B.C.), whose achievement it was to have ended debt slavery in Athens.

SOSIAS: A common servile name.

STHENELOS: A vulgar, third-rate tragic poet.

STRYMODOROS: An old juror, crony of Philokleon.

SYBARIS: A famous and proverbially wealthy Greek city in Lucania, completely destroyed by the inhabitants of Kroton in 510 B.C. A Sybaris story was a fable which, unlike the fables of Aesop, used men rather than animals as characters.

THEOGENES: An Athenian braggart and beggar.

THEOPHRASTOS: A debauchee; otherwise unknown.

THEOROS: Flatterer, perjuror, sycophant of Kleon.

THESPIS: Poet, regarded by the ancients as the creator of tragedy (fl. 534 B.C.)

THESSALY: A large district in northern Greece.

THOUKYDIDES: Son of Melesias; not to be confused with the historian Thoukydides, son of Oloros. Leader of the conservative and anti-imperialistic party in opposition to Perikles. In 443 he was ostracized; when in 433 he returned to Athens, he was involved in a ruinous lawsuit on the charges of Euathlos (q.v.).

THRACE: The eastern half of the Balkan peninsula.

THRATTA: A Thracian woman; i.e., a common name for a female domestic slave of Thracian origins.

XANTHIAS: A common servile name.

ZEUS: Chief god of the Olympian pantheon; son of Kronos, brother of Poseidon, and father of Athena. As the supreme ruler of the world, he is armed with thunder and lightning and creates storms and tempests.

Ann Arbor Paperbacks

Waddell, *The Desert Fathers*
Chinard, *Thomas Jefferson*
Erasmus, *The Praise of Folly*
Donne, *Devotions*
Malthus, *Population: The First Essay*
Roland, *The Song of Roland*
Berdyaev, *The Origin of Russian Communism*
Einhard, *The Life of Charlemagne*
Edwards, *The Nature of True Virtue*
Gilson, *Héloïse and Abélard*
Taylor, *The Mind of Plato* (originally *Plato*)
Aristotle, *Metaphysics*
Kant, *Education*
Boulding, *The Image*
Duckett, *The Gateway to the Middle Ages: Italy*
Duckett, *The Gateway to the Middle Ages: France and Britain*
Duckett, *The Gateway to the Middle Ages: Monasticism*
Bowditch and Ramsland, *Voices of the Industrial Revolution*
Luxemburg, *The Russian Revolution and Leninism or Marxism?*
Rexroth, *Poems from the Greek Anthology*
Hook, *From Hegel to Marx*
Zoshchenko, *Scenes from the Bathhouse*
Hinks, *Carolingian Art*
Thrupp, *The Merchant Class of Medieval London*
Procopius, *Secret History*
Fine, *Laissez Faire and the General-Welfare State*
Adcock, *Roman Political Ideas and Practice*
Swanson, *The Birth of the Gods: The Origin of Primitive Beliefs*
Xenophon, *The March Up Country*
Trotsky, *The New Course*
Buchanan and Tullock, *The Calculus of Consent*
Hobson, *Imperialism*
Pobedonostsev, *Reflections of a Russian Statesman*
Kinietz, *The Indians of the Western Great Lakes 1615–1760*
Bromage, *Writing for Business*
Lurie, *Mountain Wolf Woman, Sister of Crashing Thunder: The Autobiography of a Winnebago Indian*
Leonard, *Baroque Times in Old Mexico: Seventeenth-Century Persons, Places, and Practices*
Bukharin and Preobrazhensky, *The ABC of Communism*
Meier, *Negro Thought in America, 1880–1915: Racial Ideologies in the Age of Booker T. Washington*
Burke, *The Philosophy of Edmund Burke: A Selection from His Writings*
Michelet, *Joan of Arc*
Conze, *Buddhist Thought in India*
Trotsky, *Problems of the Chinese Revolution*
Chesnutt, *The Wife of His Youth and Other Stories*
Gross, *Sound and Form in Modern Poetry*
Zola, *The Masterpiece*
Chesnutt, *The Marrow of Tradition*
Aristophanes, *Four Comedies*
Aristophanes, *Three Comedies*
Chesnutt, *The Conjure Woman*
Duckett, *Carolingian Portraits*
Rapoport and Chammah, *Prisoner's Dilemma*
Aristotle, *Poetics*
Boulding, *Beyond Economics*
Peattie, *The View from the Barrio*
U.S. Department of HEW, *Toward a Social Report*
Duckett, *Death and Life in the Tenth Century*
Langford, *Galileo, Science and the Church*
McNaughton, *The Taoist Vision*
Anderson, *Matthew Arnold and the Classical Tradition*
Cicero, *On Old Age and On Friendship*
Milo, *9226 Kercheval*
Weisheipl, *The Development of Physical Theory in the Middle Ages*
Breton, *Manifestoes of Surrealism*
Burt, *Mammals of the Great Lakes Region*
Lester, *Theravada Buddhism in Southeast Asia*
Scholz, *Carolingian Chronicles*
Ray and Farnsworth, *Richard Wright*
Marković, *From Affluence to Praxis*
Eden, *Crisis in Watertown*
Wik, *Henry Ford and Grass-roots America*
Sahlins and Service, *Evolution and Culture*
Wickham, *Early Medieval Italy*